MANAGING RETAIL PRODUCTIVITY AND PROFITABILITY

Also by David Walters

RETAILING MANAGEMENT
EFFECTIVE LOGISTICS MANAGEMENT
(*with John Gattorna*)

Managing Retail Productivity and Profitability

David Walters
and
Dominic Laffy

© David Walters and Dominic Laffy 1996

All rights reserved. No reproduction, copy or transmission of this publication may be made without written permission.

No paragraph of this publication may be reproduced, copied or transmitted save with written permission or in accordance with the provisions of the Copyright, Designs and Patents Act 1988, or under the terms of any licence permitting limited copying issued by the Copyright Licensing Agency, 90 Tottenham Court Road, London W1P 9HE.

Any person who does any unauthorised act in relation to this publication may be liable to criminal prosecution and civil claims for damages.

First published 1996 by
MACMILLAN PRESS LTD
Houndmills, Basingstoke, Hampshire RG21 6XS
and London
Companies and representatives
throughout the world

ISBN 0–333–64418–2

A catalogue record for this book is available from the British Library

10 9   8   7   6   5   4   3   2   1
05 04 03 02 01 00 99 98 97 96

Printed and bound in Great Britain by
Antony Rowe Ltd
Chippenham, Wiltshire

Contents

List of Tables ix

List of Figures xi

List of Abbreviations xv

Introduction xvii

Spreadsheet Model xix

PART I   EXPLORING CONCEPTS AND MODELS IN PRODUCTIVITY AND PROFITABILITY

1 Development in retailing and retail management   **3**
Introduction   3
Developments in retailing management   3
Towards a strategic view of retailing   7
Revisiting the 'strategy model'   11
A review of recent retailing decisions   21
Food retailing   21
Mixed and non-food retailing   27
Conclusions and implications for management   36

2 Productivity, profitability and performance: introduction to issues for cash flow and productivity   **41**
Introduction   41
Productivity and the planning gap   41
Broader issues   64
A range of performance measures   71
Corporate expectations   77
Summary   78

3 Profitability and productivity: decision areas   **79**
Introduction   79
Decision-making in retailing: a framework   80
The nature of retailing decision: facilitating decision areas   83
Performance facilitating factors   87

	The nature of retailing decisions: performance determination areas	92
	Operational and strategic decisions	98
	Summary	99
4	**Managing the margin spread**	**101**
	Introduction	101
	The margin spread	101
	Costs	104
	Improving margin spread performance	106
	Increase operational sales volume	108
	Improve productivity and profitability	113
	Summary	117
5	**Managing the asset base**	**120**
	Introduction	120
	Characteristics of asset productivity	120
	Fixed asset	123
	Net current assets	128
	Summary	132
6	**Modelling performance options**	**134**
	Introduction	134
	Customer expectations	134
	Corporate performance expectations and resource allocation	138
	Strategic performance	140
	Operational performance	144
	Time perspectives: operational and strategic trade-off choices	145
	Developing a performance measurement model	149
	Strategic decisions and actions	151
	Operational decisions and actions	153
	Managing cash flows	156
	Summary	159
7	**Productivity and profitability: planning and control**	**161**
	Introduction	161
	A visual approach	162
	An overall approach	167
	An illustrative example: Argos Plc	169
	Summary	171

PART II PRODUCTIVITY AND PROFITABILITY PLANNING AND CONTROL: DECISIONS AND INFORMATION

8 Productivity and profitability decision and information requirements — **177**
Introduction — 177
Establishing objectives — 179
Information for planning and control: a decision support approach — 182
Information content for productivity, profitability and planning and control — 188
Information presentation: a decision support system — 190
Summary — 195

9 Productivity and profitability planning and control: decision types — **198**
Introduction — 198
Planning and control for merchandise decisions — 201
Planning and control for customer service decisions — 217
Planning and control for store environment decisions — 231
Planning and control for communications decisions — 226
Summary — 237

PART III APPLYING THE PRODUCTIVITY/PROFITABILITY MODEL: THREE CASE STUDIES

Introduction — **242**
10 Doleys Plc — **243**
Introduction — 243
The need for changes — 243
Changes in the mid-1980s — 244
Planning for strategic repositioning — 244
Problems in the foreseeable future — 247
Some issues for concern — 249

11 Kookaburra Holdings Plc — **259**
Introduction — 259
A review of the component companies — 259
Comment: 1989–93 — 263
'Hypothesis 1994' — 264
Conclusions — 269

12 Floorwise Plc
Introduction 270
Floorwise merchandise strategy 273
The options 275
Conclusions 280

References 281

Index 282

List of Tables

9.1	Identifying a strategic response to changes in the competitive environment	206
9.2	Identifying an operational response to changes in the competitive environment: an operational merchandise decision	213
9.3	Strategic Repositioning: a response to a customer trend for 'service facilities'	219
9.4	Operational customer service decision to increase staff response to customer requests for in-store information concerning use of products	223
9.5	Strategic store environment decisions: a repositioning response (a ladieswear retailer)	228
9.6	Operational store environment decisions: responding to customers' preferences for merchandise co-ordination and ideas	232
9.7	Strategic communications decisions: developing customer loyalty and customer spend	236
9.8	Operation communications: a response to improve the perceptions of company prices	239
10.1	Customer preferences survey, 1988–93 comparisons (1988 = 100)	248
10.2	Tracking study: six-monthly reporting of customer perceptions of competitive performance, October 1993 and April 1994	250
10.3	Identifying operational response options to changes in the competitive environment	252
10.4	Performance review and revised objectives: current period + 2 years	255
10.5	Current and planned performance for key activities	258
11.1	Kookaburra Holdings: contribution to revenue and profit	260
11.2	Growth of revenues and profits	261
11.3	Calculation of Kookaburra maximum sustainable growth rates, 1990–3	266
11.4	Kookaburra Plc balance sheet 1993 and 1994 proforma (£m)	268

List of Tables

12.1	Floorwise Plc profit and loss account 1993/94	270
12.2	Floorwise Plc balance sheet data: 1989/90–1993/94	271
12.3	Floorwise Plc: primary performance characteristics	273
12.4	Branch assets: operation productivity and profitability for Floorwise Plc	274
12.5	Strategic productivity and profitability for Floorwise Plc (E000)	275
12.6	Product mix details, price levels, range profile, margins and sales	276
12.7	Floorwise Plc: concessions primary performance characteristics	277
12.8	Operational productivity and profitability (concessions only)	278
12.9	Strategic productivity and profitability industry concessions	279

List of Figures

1.1	A generic financial model of the firm	8
1.2	Alternative methods of filling the planning gap	12
1.3	Differentiation for competitive advantage	14
1.4	Strategic, operational and resource allocation activities	16
1.5	Examples of strategic decision making among major retailing businesses	37
2.1	Strategic and operational decisions	42
2.2	The BCG growth/share matrix	44
2.3	An ideal product life cycle	46
2.4	Merchandise format mix overtime for ladieswear retailer	47
2.5	Merchandise 'mix': cash generation characteristics and portfolio patterns	48
2.6	The importance of considering market segment characteristics	49
2.7	The growth/gain matrix showing the influence of the maximum sustainable growth rate on decision-making	50
2.8	A hypothetical assortment/business profile	54
2.9	Factors influencing the size of maximum sustainable growth rate	55
2.10	Using the planning gap for cash flow projection	57
2.11	Frontier curves: growth versus use of cash	59
2.12	Hypothetical assortment/format profile using frontier curve analysis	60
2.13	Target growth rates for the business (100 per cent cash retention)	61
2.14	Frontier curves when the debt to equity ratio is varied across a range of earnings retention rates	62
2.15	Identifying alternative methods for closing the planning gap	63
2.16	Components of business performance	70
2.17	Productivity/profitability performance measurement	73
2.18	Productivity/profitability performance measures	76
3.1	Performing-related decision-making to achieve productivity and profitability	82
3.2	A model of the business indicating decision influence areas	84
3.3	The role of innovation in determining performance	88

List of Figures

3.4	The components of service quality	90
3.5	The components of flexibility/customer satisfaction	91
3.6	The components of competitiveness: decision areas	94
3.7	Financial performance: decision areas	97
4.1	Components of the margin spread	102
4.2	The relationship between margin management and asset management	105
4.3	Improving the performance of the margin spread	107
4.4	The impact on gross margin of differentiation and competition	114
4.5	Components of the margin spread (and the asset base): managing productivity and profitability	117
4.6	Facilitating/determining factors and the margin spread	118
5.1	Influence on asset performance	121
5.2	Components of fixed and net current assets	124
5.3	Facilitating and determining performance factors and the asset base	132
6.1	Strategic and operational decisions using the strategic profit model	135
6.2	Corporate expectations and objectives	139
6.3	Overall implications and issues for strategic resources allocation	141
6.4	Strategic resource allocation: decisions and options	142
6.5	Overall implications and issues for operational resource allocation	144
6.6	Operational resource allocation: decisions and options	146
6.7	The effect of a volume increase in sales (25 per cent over two-year period) on profitability and operational cash flow	148
6.8	The SPM expanded (from Lusch)	149
6.9	An overall view of the productivity/profitability performance model	150
6.10	Strategic decisions and alternatives	152
6.11	Ratio analysis of strategic decisions and alternatives	154
6.12	Operational decisions and alternatives	155
6.13	Ratio analysis of operational decision and alternatives	157
6.14	Cashflow decision and options	158
6.15	Ratio analysis of cash flow issues – strategic and operational decisions	159
7.1	The GMROI model	162
7.2	Expanding the GMROI model to consider the resource/asset base at an operational level	164

List of Figures

7.3	The strategic performance model (SPM)	164
7.4	Graphical representation of strategic performance	165
7.5	Strategic and operational performance: an overall perspective	168
7.6	Strategic decision topics	169
7.7	Operational decision topics	170
7.8	Improving productivity and profitability: an example	172
7.9	Increasing margin spread performance; an example from Argos Plc (1993/94)	173
8.1	The overall productivity/profitability performance approach	178
8.2	Establishing overall objectives	180
8.3	A decision-making process	183
8.4	Strategic decisions for productivity and profitability performance	184
8.5	Operational decisions for productivity and profitability performance	185
8.6	Revisiting the margin spread and asset base	186
8.7	Strategic decision influence and the margin spread and asset base	186
8.8	Operational decision influences and the margin spread and asset base	187
8.9	'Auditing' customer' expectations and responses and corporate performance and response	188
8.10	Information content for strategic and operational decisions	189
8.11	Information for strategic productivity and profitability decisions	191
8.12	Information for operational productivity and profitability decisions	192
8.13	Structuring information: content and displays	193
8.14	Competitor performance measures	194
8.15	Strategic decision-making: funding options	196
8.16	Strategy decisions: alternative values	197
9.1	Positioning: A co-ordinatinated response to customer expectations	198
9.2	(a) Merchandising-led positioning,	199
	(b) Customer service-led positioning,	200
	(c) Customer communications are used to focus positioning,	201
	(d) store format and environment-led positioning	202
9.3	Strategic merchandise decisions	203
9.4	A strategic decision/performance trace: merchandise-led decisions	210

9.5	Decision options: strategic merchandise changes and the margin spread	211
9.6	Operational merchandise decisions	212
9.7	Strategic customer service decisions	218
9.8	Operational customer service decisions	222
9.9	Strategic store environment decisions	223
9.10	Operational store environment decisions	230
9.11	Strategic customer communications decisions	232
9.12	Operational customer communications decisions	238
10.1	Mapping the available options	256
10.2	Calculating the cost implications of proposed changes to positioning sales and operating profit	257
11.1	The components of the maximum sustainable growth rate	265

List of Abbreviations

AMS	Associated Marketing Services
BCG	Boston Consulting Group
CAD	computer-aided design
COGS	core product gross margin
CSFs	critical success factors
DCF	discounted cash flow
DPP	direct product productivity
EFTPOS	electronic funds transfer at point of sale
EPOS	electronic point of sale
ERA	European Retail Alliance
GATT	General Agreement on Tariffs and Trade
GM	gross margins
GMROI	gross margins return on investment
IT	information technology
MIS	management information service
NA	net assets
NCA	net current assets
NMROI	net margin return on investment
OMROI	operating margin return on investment
POS	point of sale
R&D	research and development
ROA	return on assets
ROCE	return on capital employed
ROE	return to shareholder
ROI	return on investment
SCP	structure–conduct–performance
SKU	stock-keeping units
SPM	structure–conduct–performance model

Introduction

Managing productivity and profitability in retailing has taken on a particular role since the onset of the recession of the late 1980s. Productivity can be improved simply by rationalising low-performing stores and merchandise ranges and by reducing the number of suppliers and employees. However, this is not necessarily a long-term solution. The purpose of this text is to propose a means by which a more proactive approach may be taken to improving both productivity and profitability.

We suggest that though productivity and profitability are clearly connected, it does not follow that by increasing productivity a proportional increase in profitability will also occur. Indeed, there may well be very good reasons for this not to happen.

The book also differentiates between strategic and operational productivity and profitability. At a strategic level the concern of the business is focused on productivity, profitability and issues which are financially orientated, such as asset circulation, capital structures which optimise productivity and, clearly, the profitability of the business. Operational issues are more concerned with 'micro-resource' issues such as space, stock, staff and branch (outlet) assets.

The central vehicle throughout the text is a model based upon the Du Pont model for planning and control of business activities. The Du Pont approach has been widely adopted and written about. It appeared in a modified form as the strategic profit model and it is this model version which we have modified. The advantages of this version are the strategic and operational perspectives that can be developed, enabling operational issues to be explored *within* the context of their impact on strategic factors and components. The model is also 'customer-driven', in that customer expectations may be used to establish specific characteristics or requirements. These requirements are translated into retail offer features: a merchandise profile, merchandise augmentation, visual merchandising (merchandise density), service augmentation (facilities and information), service density (merchandise sales area/customer services area) and service intensity (the number of employees per sales area measure). Each can be interpreted quantitatively and input into the model: the model can then be used to explore the productivity (cost) and profitability implications of meeting customers' expectations. Similarly the model may be used to explore potential positioning alternatives.

To facilitate the use of the concepts and the model a disk is available, containing the application of the model to the case studies in Chapters 10, 11 and 12, together with a facility for users to input their own data.

Spreadsheet Model

A spreadsheet is available containing the productivity and profitability model discussed in the book. It is designed in Excel 5.0, and is available in a variety of disk formats.

It allows the user to enter financial and managerial information for a retailer, then use the model to evaluate the strategic and operational impacts of various decisions. The model can handle both historic and projected information, and permits the user to choose from a variety of different graphical outputs.

The model is simple to use, and comes with its own short instruction booklet. The model has been designed such that minimal knowledge of spreadsheets is required. The majority of tasks are handled automatically when selected by the user.

To order your copy

Please include a cheque or postal order in pounds sterling to the value of £9.95 made payable to **Dominic Laffy** and send the package (i.e completed form overleaf and payment) to:

>Dominic Laffy
>(Ref: Ret/Prod)
>European Business School
>Inner Circle
>Regents Park
>London NW1 4NS

Goods will be despatched by first-class post within seven days of funds clearing.

Spreadsheet Model: Request Form
(Managing Retail Productivity and Profitability)

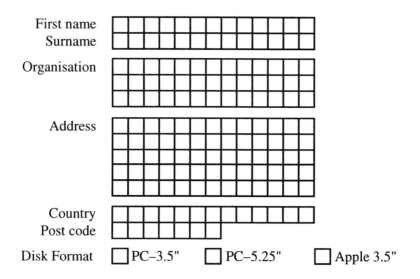

Please send this form along with appropriate payment to the address given overleaf

None of the information gathered from this form will be given or sold on to third parties

PART I

Exploring Concepts and Models in Productivity and Profitability

1 Developments in Retailing and Retail Management

INTRODUCTION

Retailing in most economies has experienced numerous and profound changes in its strategic and operational activities during recent years. Because (by definition) it is adjacent to the consumer it is not surprising that it responds rapidly to changes in consumer behaviour and response to economic, social and technological change. There have been many changes in the *retail business environment,* matched by as many responses from retailing companies.

Although there are many approaches to resolving the implications of change for the individual companies, it is the following three causes which are responsible for most of the change: they influence major consumer response.

- **Social change** – leads to consumer changes in expectations, behaviour and perceptions.
- **Economic change** – influences real disposable income levels, employment patterns and so on, in base markets and influences decisions to undertake market development and diversification opportunities elsewhere.
- **Technological change** – has resulted in changes in work patterns, in cost levels and profiles and in the way in which the retail offer may be delivered to the customer.

DEVELOPMENTS IN RETAILING MANAGEMENT

The changes that have occurred in recent years may be reviewed in time spans and are apparent in most industrial economies. The post-Second World War economic recovery resulted in the growth of consumer durables and apparel multiples as consumer spending and supply moved towards an unconstrained situation. As the growth continued into the late 1950s and early 1960s, the emphasis was placed on expansion and there were major multiple developments in both fast-moving and durable consumer goods markets. Initially focused on organic methods, retailers began to favour acquisition in an attempt to accelerate the rate of growth and to achieve volume dominance in retail markets.

The 1960s demonstrated the power of the retailer. By expanding rapidly not only did many retail markets become concentrated, with the largest companies exerting pressure on suppliers, but the use of retailer own brands and pricing became important traffic-building strategies around which customer loyalty was subsequently built.

Own brands developed during the late 1950s and early 1960s more as a means to 'beat the pricing regulations' set in place by the law concerning resale price maintenance. They were often priced 10–15 per cent below manufacturer brands and were of lower quality, their purpose being simply to offer lower-priced alternatives. Price competition came to be widely used, as retailers in almost all sectors sought growth. Retail advertising expenditure, which until this time was noticeable and significant – but nowhere near as much as it is at present – expanded, but did so primarily using price as a theme.

Retail own brands moved away from low price/low quality alternatives to become a means by which retail identity could be reinforced. Notable examples in the UK were Marks & Spencer (who had always used their own brand for merchandise) and Sainsbury, who pioneered own brands in food multiple retailing. As a result the quality differentials diminished as the multiple retailers began to use quality/price as opposed to quantity/price as major characteristics of their respective offers.

One major influence operating in the 1960s which was fuelled by both consumer change and economic change was the growth in apparel markets. The 1960s was certainly a period of affluence for almost all categories of consumer but particularly so for the younger age-groups. Concurrent with this expansion was an equally important growth in 'expressionism'. Young consumers (and some not so young) began to challenge dress codes more and used apparel purchasing to reflect their 'self' views. In North America companies such as The Gap and Limited presented examples for European multiples to modify the 'local' use. This resulted in a rapid growth of multiple apparel chains, with Burton, Hepworth and others moving into dominant mid-price positions. It also saw the beginning of the 'boutique', with Kings Road, Chelsea and Carnaby Street becoming recognised as 'trend-setters'. It is interesting to note that these events preceded the move towards using psychographic (or life style) techniques for segmentation and customer profiling. The technique was refined and became accepted on a very wide basis, such that by the 1980s it was standard practice for retailers and manufacturers alike. Conservative companies such as Laura Ashley and Dunn (menswear) could be seen to be implementing retail offers which clearly targeted a specific customer group.

The impact of technology on retailing has been considerable. The most cited examples are those relating to information technology and these have been very influential. However, we should not overlook technological developments in distribution, materials handling and packaging. These too have a considerable impact on retailing operations.

Returning to information technology: here we have seen both internal and external development benefits. The *internal* benefits that have accompanied EPOS (electronic point of sale) data collection and EFTPOS (electronic funds transfer at point of sale) are well documented. EPOS has enabled retailers to manage inventories much more effectively. Stock levels have generally been lowered for most companies and, at the same time, availability has increased. EPOS data has facilitated merchandise replenishment and reordering. The accuracy and immediacy of the data flows produced by EPOS systems also provides reliability, and as a consequence inventory planning and replenishment systems are able to operate on lower levels of stock and to shorter, more accurate, replenishment cycles.

Another feature available from EPOS data is the facility to schedule labour more effectively. It follows that by deploying labour at peak activity periods overall staff costs can be reduced significantly. EPOS also reduces operations costs such as price-marking. The benefit extends into the replenishment cycle: labour schedules in distribution centres may also be planned more cost-effectively.

The *external* benefits are equally important. The availability of EPOS data and the retailers' willingness to make the data output available to suppliers has brought about an entirely fresh approach to supplier–distributor relationships. Prior to the advent of EPOS systems, product movement data (not sales data as is recognised by EPOS) was available on subscription (through companies such as AC Nielsen) and only after a manual count and slow processing, which implies some delay. Its usefulness was limited. By contrast EPOS data is now linked with replenishment and production systems, thereby creating a supply chain. The benefits of lower costs and information currency are shared by members of the supply chain and, furthermore, the availability of the data has extended the supply chain such that packaging and raw materials suppliers can benefit.

It is interesting to contemplate the earlier channels theories, particularly that of postponement and speculation, in the context of developments in information technology. A current review would, we suggest, indicate not only that has the time span of the concept reduced considerably, but that the postponement and speculation relationships are very much closer than was suggested by the earlier theories.

Information techonology also has 'applied' examples. The use of catchment profiling software packages has increased the efficiency with which retail offers may be focused to meet specific customer requirements in an area.

Technological developments in other aspects of retailing are not as 'glamorous' as those of the information sciences fields. Nevertheless they have been notable in their impact. Most significant in terms of cost were developments in unitisation; ways and means by which the productivity of sales space and cube has been optimised to increase sales density and materials handling utilisation. Packaging and palletisation which have dual purpose offer large cost savings within the supply chain, as they eliminate handling and display costs (such as shelf filling and merchandising) often only requiring minimum attention throughout the distribution process. Developments in transportation have enabled both manufacturers and distributors to offer wider choice to customers – for example, the developments in chilled and frozen transportation have expanded food ranges considerably. Moreover, these developments have been made available at costs which are manageable, particularly when 'third-party' distribution service companies are involved in the supply chain.

One other notable aspect of distribution technology which is of interest in this discussion is the use of peripheral developments to extend the supply chain. An example of this can be seen with the use of vacuum packing applied to textile and apparel products. By using vacuum packaging the shipment of clothing and similar products from the Far East becomes viable. By reducing cube (by extracting the air and effectively shrink-wrapping a product) the cube–weight–cost equation becomes acceptable in the context of delivering products manufactured some 10 000 miles from markets to meet specific price targets.

During the 1980s the professional approach to retailing that had been apparent in the 1970s was increasingly dominant in the successful businesses. A sophisticated approach was very clearly seen as financial and marketing disciplines developed the strategic directions of the major retailers. Clear views were taken concerning the positioning of businesses within their target markets, with distinct differentiation of offers becoming visible: for example, there are obvious differences in the offers of major competitors in the DIY market – with appeals made to the 'maintainers', the 'repairers' and the 'home-improvers', and within the home-improver segment there can be seen differing approaches to fashion and style.

TOWARDS A STRATEGIC VIEW OF RETAILING

The move towards professional management of the retailing business required managers to consider the marketing, finance and operations interface areas of their businesses. From this view developed a view of strategy. This can best be explained by considering Figure 1.1, which illustrates a generic financial model of a retail business. The activities of significant importance are indicated in bold type. These are sales management, gross margin and operating margin management (which together comprise margin spread management), financial management, cashflow management, return on investment and asset management.

As we shall demonstrate, these activities are important components in the strategic management of the business. Without sales, the business is clearly not viable. However, even with a large sales volume, there will be insufficient cover for overhead charges (which includes depreciation), interest and a return for the shareholders unless marketing and buying, together with operations management, are managed effectively. Financial management has a particularly influential role because it determines the asset structure and funding base of the business and therefore the level of risk to which the business (and the shareholder base) is exposed. The decisions taken by the financial manager will influence both cashflow and, of course, the return on investment earned by the business.

The increasing professionalism of retailing was timely, because by the end of the 1980s it was clear that Western economies were entering recession. The boom of the mid-1980s, which saw almost explosive expansion by the durables and apparel retails, came quickly to a close. Large excesses of selling area existed and a number of major names moved very close to receivership; many medium and small companies were not to survive.

It is arguable that the recession which resulted brought with it fundamental changes to consumer attitudes. The 'aspirational eighties', a phenomenon of the Thatcher era, has been replaced by an overwhelming shift towards the '"value"-led nineties'. In this context value may be

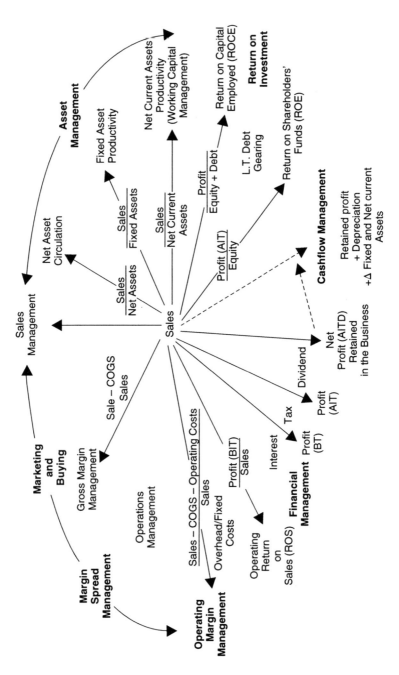

Figure 1.1 A Generic Financial Model of the Firm

based on quantity or quality whichever, it implies that consumer purchasing will be more functional or driven by utility rather than by fashion or fad. This suggests a 'return to basics' with quite different implications. Already the apparel industry (manufacturers and distributors) has adjusted its merchandise offers: the emphasis is now moving towards more classical styling and an increase in quality, the product features upon which companies such as Marks & Spencer and the John Lewis Partnership have built a strong customer franchise.

'Back to basics' has produced a clear view of management philosophy and style for the 1990s (and probably beyond) as the pursuit for increased profits focuses upon generating 'higher turnover with slimmer mark-ups'. Having pursued rationalisation and restructuring many businesses have emerged with much more favourable margins. The efficient companies have therefore positioned themselves so that they will be able to respond to growth opportunities with management and 'production' structures that will benefit from low operational gearing (fixed costs/total costs) and progressively increased net returns.

Restructuring has also taken in a view of 'what business are we really in?' which for many has resulted in major divestment of businesses or activities that have been identified as not being central to the profitability of the mainstream business. For example Storehouse divested Habitat and Richards. Habitat was acquired by IKEA and Richards by Sears. Both acquisitions have a more logical fit within the portfolios of their new owners. Sears, which has not performed at all well in recent years, has divested its menswear businesses, thereby enabling it to focus more clearly on its core business activity, ladieswear. The suggestion (discussed later) is that Sears may well be responsive to offers for British Shoe and/or the Selfridge department store.

This suggests that there is a move by large retailing (and manufacturing) businesses to review their activities and to redefine their core business.

The activities of some suggest a much more narrow definition of their businesses than the view given by market and customer focuses. Infrastructure service activities have been considered by some companies as *not* central to the purpose of profit generation. The philosophy that follows is that the core business is 'retailing' or 'manufacturing': consequently peripheral activities such as distribution have been 'divested' and a growth of service companies offering a full range of support activities has been seen. The logic is simple: managerial economies in non-competitive or sensitive support areas offers the distribution or manufacturing company two benefits. The major benefit is the release of capital which may then be invested in the more narrowly defined 'core business activity'. The second benefit follows: by divesting the support activities and using service support specialists, operating costs may be reduced and margins increased, even if volumes remain static. Thus the attraction to Mothercare of a management information service company is readily explained. By outsourcing their MIS needs they have released funds for investment in the core business and may have improved their information service to decision-makers.

For similar reasons strategic alliances and partnering have attraction. If investment requirements (and commitments) can be contained, together with a reduction in operating costs without a loss of competitiveness, the logical decision is to take advantage of the opportunity. The results for the successful company are:

- a reduction in overall investment and in fixed costs,

which offers:

- an increase in 'flexibility' – if we consider flexibility to comprise specification flexibility, volume flexibility, and delivery speed flexibility, we would argue that corporate response to customer satisfaction is enhanced;
- the opportunity to focus innovation by offering 'customised' R&D, which:
  — improves attributes of existing products/services
  — develops 'superior' attributes for existing products/services
  — facilitates the development of new formats or delivery systems, and
  — enables resources to be directed towards new products/services and the increase in their applications;
- an increase in service quality by focusing on relevant quality of the core business, such as: availability; communication/information; responsiveness; staff–customer relationships; access; and aesthetics.

The discussion thus far suggests questions that may be asked of the strategy models offered by the literature. An assumption that appears reasonable is that future opportunities for growth for many sectors are unlikely to reflect the rates of growth of the recent past. The slow, hesitant overall recovery of the UK economy (Autumn 1994) suggests support for this view. In the longer term the restructuring of international trade through the GATT negotiations and (perhaps more importantly) the development of more inwardly focused trading blocs such as the European Union (which is likely to be some 20 to 25 per cent larger in the very near future), NAFTA (also likely to expand to include South American countries) and two Far Eastern groups – Hong Kong, Malaysia, Singapore and China; and the Pacific Rim countries led by Japan. An interesting economic and political issue will be how the Far East develops: as one or a number of 'unions'. However, the issues remain much the same. What should be the focus of corporate strategy? And how should the changing business environment be accommodated?

REVISITING THE 'STRATEGY MODEL'

One of the authors (together with co-author Derek Knee, see Knee and Walters, 1985) offered a modified version of Ansoff's original product-market strategy matrix (see Figure 1.2). It suggested a model suitable for retailing businesses, which should consider:

- **Consolidation and productivity improvements** – which would include:
  — rationalisation of under-performing formats, outlets and merchandise ranges;
  — rationalisation or increased utilisation of support infrastructure, such as distribution facilities;
  — price adjustments: price increases for merchandise items and merchandise groups for which there is evidence that customers are insensitive to price changes (that is, the elasticity is one or more) and price decreases in competitive areas of the assortment for which there occurs compensatory volume increase.
- **Repositioning** the retail offer (or elements of it, such as merchandise or customer service) to meet the changed needs of existing customers. For example:
  — adjustments to merchandise characteristics such as 'width', to offer choice; or perhaps to depth to provide a greater 'service' by offering a range of sizes, colours, and so on, which provides increased product-service.
- **Growth** – which would involve 'product development' or 'market development' (in the context of Ansoff). Examples of growth were given as:

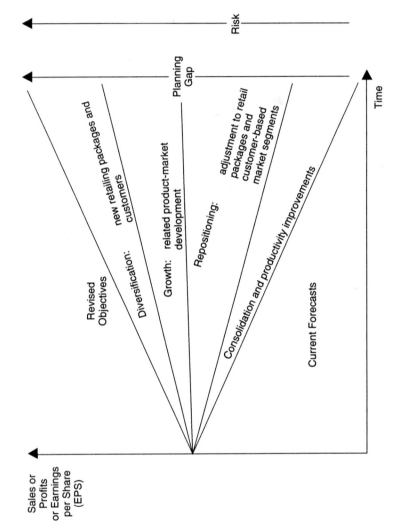

Figure 1.2 Alternative methods of filling the planning gap

- — the development of specialist merchandise and/or outlets in response to customer demand for wider ranges of merchandise and support service products;
- — the expansion of an existing format into areas (territorial locations) in which the company has no presence and which offers economies of replication.
- **Diversification** – the move by a retailer into product-markets that have no link with the business but which, none the less, have attraction. Examples were suggested:
  - — food multiples developing joint-venture activities in DIY, or fast food outlets;
  - — companies with specific expertise in, say, multiple apparel retailing acquiring department store groups.

In a subsequent text (*Strategic Retailing Management,* 1988), the author suggested that:

- **Differentiation** based upon either productivity or marketing-led features was increasingly important. Figure 1.3 illustrates this concept. The basis of the choice for differentiation made by a company depends very much upon customer expectations and perceptions, together with the company's perceptions of its needs. Davidson and Doody (1966) suggested that: 'Differentiation is an attempt on the part of the retailer to adapt his offer to the differences that exist in the needs and wants of consumers.'

Customer-led (marketing-led) differentiation results from a situation whereby the company can, through positioning, influence customer perceptions. This is achieved by identifying customer expectations and developing a response such that:

$$\text{customer perceptions} > \text{customer expectations}$$

which implies that not only has the business achieved an acceptable level of customer satisfaction but it has identified specific characteristics of competitive advantage (which may be developed) that are adding value for customers, hence the perceived benefits. By contrast productivity-led differentiation enables the company to utilise managerial economies (such as scale, replication, procurement, promotion) in order to achieve greater productivity from resources and thereby greater profitability from the business. Figure 1.4 describes the differentiation model.

14   *Exploring Concepts and Models*

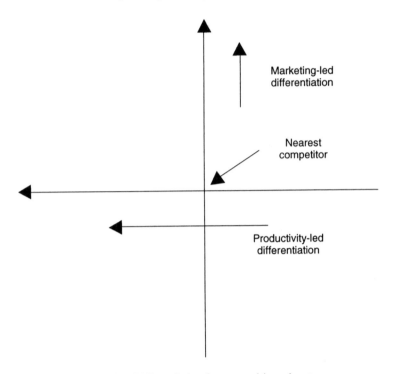

Figure 1.3   Differentiation for competitive advantage

Michael Porter's industry structure model (1980) places considerable emphasis on a firm's relative positioning (or differentiation) within its industry and on the relative strength of its competitive advantage. One must conclude that the competitive thrust of the firm, therefore, depends upon:

- achieving the differentiation which is necessary in order to ensure that a situation in which customer perceptions exceed customer expectations results and thereby establishes competitive advantage;
- distinctive competence(s) of the company on which competitive advantages might be based (that is, a balance of strengths and weaknesses mapped on to marketing or productivity-led opportunities through cross impact analysis);
- a managerial view of the relative risk profiles of each strategic option matched against their own attitudes towards risk.

There is thus much in common between Ansoff's early model and Porter's approach. It has to be said that Porter benefited from developments in strategic thinking resulting in much clearer definitions and refinements of such concepts as market segmentation, target marketing, market positioning and so on.

The concept of differentiation, and in particular the notion that it has two components, is of particular interest and relevance for our present analysis. The focus by many companies on a narrower definition of their core business – largely as a result of a difficult trading environment brought about by the recession, but clearly also within the context of increasing productivity and profitability – suggests that perhaps the approaches of the 1970s and 1980s may well benefit from some revised thinking.

The model described by Figure 1.4 assumes that most businesses are managing their activities at operational and strategic levels. In the revised model there are five operational direction decision options and four strategic options. Additionally, there are operational and strategic resource allocation and rationalisation activities which reflect the earlier examples given, in which companies appear to be focusing on a narrower definition of what their business is and what it is attempting to achieve.

- **Consolidation and productivity** – essentially a decision-making area concerning the productivity of resources. Topics would include outlet and assortment adjustments whereby under-performing resources would be modified, or perhaps withdrawn from service, in order that the overall performance of operational objectives be improved. Such rationalisation would need to be considered within the context of longer-term issues. For example, the closure of an under-used distribution facility, or perhaps a retail outlet should be undertaken after the strategic implications have been considered and the resource is not considered to have a long-term application. Adjustments to pricing may be considered within this option. Adjustments to price which take advantage of low price-sensitivity or 'monopoly' situations and price reductions to benefit from price elasticity situations are considered within this category. Pricing to achieve volume increases, such as 'multi-buys', may also be considered in this category.
- **Operational repositioning** – occurs in the short term as and when management considers it necessary to respond to changes in customer characteristics and/or expectations. This can be achieved by making small adjustments to the 'offer' attributes: a reformulation of merchandise characteristics which reflects incremental responses to

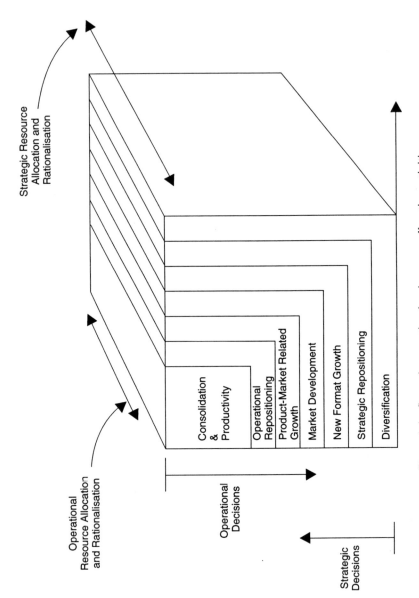

Figure 1.4 Strategic, operational and resource allocation activities

customer changes but which does not result in very different overall offer attributes. The purpose of operational repositioning is to maintain their loyalty. It is not aimed at creating a new customer base or at penetrating new market segments; that is much more the role of strategic repositioning.

- **Product-market related growth** this is the development of the business within its areas of expertise. It is aimed at extending, widening or deepening the existing merchandise assortment so that customer transactions may be increased. Merchandise/service augmentation (adding accessories or peripherals to the existing offer either as merchandise items or, indeed, as related merchandise groups) is aimed at increasing both average transaction value per customer and gross margins. Growth related to product-market occupies a position overlapping both operational and strategic direction, together with market development.
- **Market development** – concerns the existing business. It occurs as geographical expansion of a successful existing format. Market development relies largely upon economies of replication for effectiveness. By expanding the number of outlets offering the same merchandise, service and store environment, numerous benefits accrue. The increased sales volume has an impact on buying terms, thereby improving gross margins. The risk is low and the benefits can be quite large because the resultant sales volume is not required to cover those fixed costs already met. Hence the gross profit is largely undiluted and this is an attractive option. (Risk may increase if saturation is approached, as margins can be eroded either by the need for competitive pricing or perhaps by sales lost through intra-company competition.) Add to this the benefits of promotional economies together with the improved overhead recovery rate, and the incremental profitability created by market development may be quite large.

The options for strategic decisions require resource allocations for *new* directions rather than the expansion of existing (and successful) activities. They include the following options.

- **Strategic repositioning** – whereas operational repositioning results in small adjustments to the offer attributes, strategic repositioning is a response to the requirements of a new or additional segment. It may not require a complete shift by the business but rather an overt statement by the business that it has recognised the customer opportunity and the response is an offer which meets the customer needs identified. For example, recent development of limited range food outlets by two of the major food multiples could be seen as strategic repositioning. The restructuring of merchandise and service offer attributes by furniture and footwear retailers, often using separate fascia brands, is another example of strategic repositioning which involves changes to the 'offer' that direct its appeal towards an opportunity offering expanded growth. This may be customer or competitor-determined.

- **New format growth** – the development of new offers which may, but not necessarily, be based upon activities that have proven to be successful in a limited capacity. Thus the development of specialist offers which have been prompted by the prior success of a merchandise or service group may result in successful new format directions. It is possible that the activity was minor within an overall offer but, perhaps due to external environmental shifts, becomes self-supporting. An example is the growth of prepared food items in food outlets. For some such retailers their city centre locations were no longer viable for conventional food retailing. However, by shifting the focus of the offer on to high margin, high added-value take-away ranges, they have developed successful new formats.
- **Diversification** – these activities include both acquisition and organic expansion of the business into unrelated areas. The growth through acquisition, prominent in the latter half of the 1980s, is an example of this form of strategic direction. It was largely achieved by increasing corporate gearing, but rights issues were also favoured. For many it was followed by retrenchment as diversification resulted in less than ideal 'fits'. Consequently, having experienced serious operating losses they subsequently disposed of some part or all of the acquired businesses at substantially lower prices. Financial services companies have been significant in this respect. Diversification has also been built around joint-venture activities whereby strengths from two or more companies may be developed. More recently strategic alliances have been created among a number of companies in related product-market activities. The purposes of a strategic alliance are numerous. Recent activities have been based upon exploiting marketing and procurement opportunities in the expanded European Single Market.

Clearly there is an overlap between strategic and operational decisions. Figure 1.4 suggests that the implications of strategic decisions may extend well into the operational decision-making area. The longer-term issues of competitive reaction to branch closures and range rationalisation have been raised and situations can be thought of where operational repositioning decisions may well have long-term implications.

Resource allocation and rationalisation for operational and strategic effectiveness

Implicit in the management process is the fact that resource allocation and rationalisation is undertaken in order that both productivity and profitability objectives are met in the short and long term. Figure 1.5 illustrates the suggestion that there are two dimensions to be considered if a company is to focus on its core business.

(i) Operational resource allocation and rationalisation

It does not follow that the productivity requirements of the business will lead to the constant search for cost savings. It is obvious that many consolidation and productivity decisions do result in a reduction of space, stock and staff. However, productivity is measured by comparing outputs and inputs; thus it follows that if outputs (sales) can be increased by applying resources such that the incremental increase in sales exceeds that of the costs, productivity may be increased. For example, an increase in sales may follow if a retailer uses an EPOS system to improve the merchandise offer and stockholding profile. Clearly this implies an investment in resources rather than a reduction.

Similar arguments may be made for investment in supply chain activities. A number of retailers, concerned with quality control, have 'invested' in quality control management and are resident in supply markets throughout the world. The costs of supervision are clearly outweighed by the benefits of consistent standards.

Another example of operational resource allocation and rationalisation may occur as a business vertically integrates backwards into either production or distribution in order to improve the overall productivity of its operations. Rationalisation occurs when the retailer decides to focus on the core activity (retailing) and uses 'service companies' to provide infrastructure services.

(ii) Strategic resource allocation and rationalisation

In a similar manner the argument concerning strategic productivity and profitability can be seen to consider both the application and rationalisation of resources. Often following an acquisition management may consider the business to have assumed a quite different common denominator. There are a number of examples of adjustments (disposals and acquisitions) to 'fit' following a major acquisition of one business by another as time has shown the new management that it does not have the relevant skills to manage all of its new components effectively.

A number of the acquisitions of the late 1980s have subsequently resulted in divestment of components of the amalgamation which have not 'fitted' the overall structure of the new business. The Asda/MFI merger which took place in the early 1980s was clearly a mistake (as may have been the group's proposed venture into car sales) and is an example of how difficulties accrue when a business loses sight of its core business and its common denominator. A similar view may be taken of the disposal by Burton of Harvey Nichols.

But expenditure may be increased. For example, there have been a number of acquisitions in which part of the motivation for the action has been the opportunity to expand buying volumes and to develop expertise in customer service and similar functional activities. The Kingfisher acquisition of Darty may be seen as having these motives.

Another dimension of strategic resource allocation and rationalisation has been the use of strategic alliances to achieve buying and marketing economies (and additional expertise). The large UK food multiples have met the opportunities and threats of the Single Market by creating strategic alliances with similarly large Continental food operations. Safeway's activities in the European Retail Alliance are notable in this context.

Resource allocation and rationalisation adds a further two dimensions to the original model. It is arguable whether the recession was the primary reason for the decisions taken by Burton, Sears and Storehouse for rationalisation, or whether they would have occurred as the management groups in these companies eventually refined their strategic direction.

This discussion has not attempted critically to review the literature in the area. Rather it attempts to modify previous work and to identify changes that should be made to reflect the changes in the environment within which businesses have operated during a difficult period of recession.

The likelihood is that though the recession will eventually end, many companies will consider the problems it brought as significant lessons for the future. The model proposed here is an attempt at identifying trends in management practice and exploring the extent of the practice on a small sample of companies.

A REVIEW OF RECENT RETAILING DECISIONS

The remainder of this chapter considers the decisions made by a number of major retailing companies during the 1990–4 period. The decisions are compared with the model developed in Figure 1.4 (repeated in a simpler form as Figure 1.5). The decisions are commented upon and referred to in Figure 1.5 by the numbers 1 to 9 . For example, a decision involving consolidation and productivity activity would be shown as 2. Multiple activities are reported by indicating in parentheses the number of times the company is reported – for example, market development, Storehouse (2). The research comprised an on-going review and monitoring of company reports and comments from the financial press.

FOOD RETAILING

Asda Stores

During recent years Asda has been under considerable competitive pressures and, at the same time, was experiencing funding difficulties. Their new chief executive implemented some major policy changes in both the strategy and operations of the business.

A substantial reduction in overhead structure and costs was implemented together with a decrease in operating costs through a wage freeze (2). New formats have been introduced (6). Dales is a discount-based offer, aimed at competing for an expanding segment of the food market, while Renewal was seen as a repositioning exercise to reinforce a move back towards the price-led offer upon which the company once relied. This action was accompanied by focusing on assortment variety while maintaining price competitiveness (3). Produce ranges have been expanded to compete with high street specialists (4); non-food participation was also a concern, with notable expansion taking place in recorded music, specifically CD products. The company, clearly concerned with space productivity and utilisation, undertook a number of range rationalisation activities (2); for example, a review of the pack varieties of brown sauce revealed nineteen different bottles. This number was considerably reduced.

For the year 1992/93 the return to the 'Asda value' strategy of the 1980s, together with a greater emphasis on fresh foods (where it has lagged behind Tesco, Sainsbury and Safeway) and the implementation of the cost reduction programme, resulted in a 13 per cent improvement in profitability (2).

Tesco Plc

An extensive store opening programme, together with a strong merchandise development programme were major features of the Tesco activity. The financial press did comment on the extent of the capital programme and pointed to the fact that the new store openings accounted for a large proportion of sales growth (5). A general view was that this contribution was perhaps too large. It was also noticed that sales productivity was continuing to increase, but doing so at a decreased rate. By September 1993 the gross margin (after store and distribution costs) decreased from 8.97 per cent (1992/93) to 8.91 per cent (1993/94), these being first-half year comparisons. Price promotions have been a response to decreasing average transaction; and joint promotions with Acorn (computer vouchers for schools on purchase values of £25). Local pricing has been implemented as a means by which local price competitive situations may be resolved. 'Multibuys' have also been a response to decreasing transaction values (2).

The store opening programme included large superstores and an expansion of the smaller 'Metro' format stores in the busy urban/commercial areas. New Metro stores are imminent in Aberdeen and Liverpool (6). The large stores were significant in the company's move towards generating larger operating economies, and the resulting increase in operating margins. The smaller stores increased market penetration in urban areas and could be seen as an element in the customer service programme by providing seven-day extended hours service to residents of inner city areas.

Organisational changes were made, in which branch management structures were revised: functional management replaced product management and considerable savings in costs were the result (2).

The acquisition of Catteau, a French food retailer with a diverse range of outlet types, will provide Tesco with a number of benefits. For example there will be expertise gained in operating both a subsidiary at some distance from the main centre of the business and a more diverse range of stores; the facility of an added dimension to merchandise development and, of course, the potential to improve upon buying margins through the effect of increased volumes (8) (9).

A number of significant points were made concerning performance after the publication of the 1993/94 half-year figures. It was noted that this was the first time in ten years that margins had not risen: while gross margin has decreased, operating margin is unchanged. A view has been expressed that the company has felt the impact of the discounters' competitive activities more than its competitors have done. The Tesco response (a range of low-price 'Tesco Value' own label products) indicates the company's concern (3). It is also suggested that the Tesco move towards the relatively more upmarket positioning occupied by Sainsbury and Safeway is so recent that its customers' loyalty is more fragile. This would follow as Tesco customers are younger and more C2/D and B/C1, and have been more vulnerable to the effects of the recession. The impact of the repositioned Asda may well have attracted Tesco customers, as may the discounters and, of course, an expanding KwikSave.

Comment has also been made concerning the lack of store presence in North London, where a large and profitable market exists. It has been noted that the existing store format does not have the appropriate 'fit'.

Current developments have not been totally focused on price: initiatives have been outlined which will improve customer service and store ambience. Checkout operators are likely to be more than 'checkout operators', additional services are to be introduced and store ambience will be improved (3).

KwikSave

KwikSave has enjoyed relatively uninterrupted growth for a number of years as it expanded in areas typically 'under-shopped' for food outlets. We have seen the competition within the discount sector of the food market intensify and KwikSave has not been slow to respond. An own-brand programme has been launched across the range, clearly with the intention of enhancing gross margins (2). A large expansion programme, 100 additional outlets throughout Scotland, is planned for 1994 (5).

Increases in gross margins, sales volume and customer satisfaction are in mind, with the use of concessions for produce sales in the stores. Clearly the company is also conscious of the impact these will have on transaction values. It is also very likely that the produce concessions will enhance operating margins: KwikSave have the sales benefits (albeit at a discount) but not the costs of preparation, storage and distribution, and waste (4) (1).

The use of information technology to manage stock levels and space allocation has been accompanied by range extensions (1) (4). This will provide KwikSave with a dual benefit: they will be able to increase average customer transaction values (and customer satisfaction) and they will also increase gross margin yield. It could also be added that their operating margins should benefit through improved stock and space management and, by inference, labour productivity. The company can be seen to be using information to ensure that cash generation as well as profit is achieved (1). An expansion of the distribution infrastructure has improved both customer service and corporate service and efficiency (1).

Sainsbury

The strong growth and profit record of Sainsbury is due to the resolute focus on its main core business. The company has avoided high risk diversification opportunities by joint-venture programmes with partners who provide the expertise Sainsbury lacks. The focus of the company's development has been on investment in existing stores to improve operating efficiency (1). The increased expansion would appear to be planned to optimise economies of scale in operations, distribution and promotion (5). Sales growth and gross margin management have been reinforced by investment in product development (4): during 1992/93 the company introduced 1400 new items and 1000 were reformulated.

An awareness of the business environment, its changes and its opportunities, through a marketing research programme ensures that Sainsbury can respond with appropriate location and merchandise decisions (3). An example of the co-ordinated marketing research/marketing decision process working well for the company is the success achieved by exploiting the own-brand detergent, Novon (4), a decision resulting in a doubling of Sainsbury's market share in that sector.

The effective implementation of the corporate financial structure is reflected in the way in which the proven format is maintained and is managed to promote profitability and cash generation through high sales intensity, lower costs and smaller price increases (2).

For the half-year 1993/94 Sainsbury had achieved sales of £5532 m, an increase of 11 per cent over the same period for 1992/93. The company had responded to difficult trading by increasing its promotional emphasis on own label products, with price reductions on some 300 of these items. It anticipated gross margins would be reduced by 1 per cent, but this was expected to be recovered by increased volumes, suppliers' increased efficiencies and company efficiency improvements (1) and (2).

Gross margins have also decreased as more customers opted for the basic versions of produce products: the convenience of pre-washed and prepared vegetables has less appeal during a recession. This factor, together with the decline in sales of high-margin produce items (exotic fruits), has halted the growth of gross margins, save for the increases that may be available from the actions described in the previous paragraph.

Operating margins were increased. In the first half of 1993/94 distribution efficiency improvements resulted in cost savings of 0.1 per cent of sales which, on the reported sales volume of over £5500 m, was a contribution of £5 m. Similar small increases in operating efficiencies help to convert a sales increase of 9 per cent into a 13 per cent rise in operating profits for the food operation of the company (3).

The expansion of sales outlets continues (5). An increase in sales volume through the additional outlets amortises fixed costs over the higher sales revenues: the result is higher net profits as less of the gross margin is required to support overheads. This allows the company to offer more competitive pricing without diluting profitability.

Gateway

Gateway is a store group that has experienced financial problems. With the company generally being thought to be over-geared, its senior management has spent much of its time with its financiers restructuring its debt. Burdened with this debt Gateway has struggled to meet interest payments, most of which (if not all) have absorbed the profit that has been generated. Following the apparent lack of any significant success with Somerfield, Gateway turned to Food Giant (6) a price-led offer to promote the sales volume clearly needed if it was to generate a contribution to profit, overhead and the interest payments. Food Giant was based upon a format which comprised 10 000 to 12 000 sq. ft selling areas, a 'basic' store environment in off-centre locations. Prices were some 10–15 per cent below average prices set by competitors across volume selling manufacturers' brands. The concept is to be expanded to 100 stores. Once this is achieved, the benefit of volume on cashflow and profit will be realised.

Debt restructuring continues to be a problem for Gateway and its parent Isosoles and it has been suggested that further disposals of selected stores to raise cash are a possibility (9).

Budgen

Budgen has also had its problems. Essentially a small but specialist retailer, it has focused on a specific segment of the food market. It lacks the benefit of volume to generate acceptable margins, and profitability performance has been disappointing. The involvement of the company in a buying consortium with Londis and Circle K (9) will go some way towards rectifying the gross margin problem, while the introduction of IT-based merchandise systems should contribute to improved buying and operating margins. These are likely to be further enhanced by the improved operating efficiencies developed in distribution (1).

Local pricing (2) is an important feature of the Budgen offer. By pursuing a specialist format, price flexibility improves buying margin management. The Budgen offer relies heavily on exclusivity and choice, together with a visual merchandising treatment that reinforces a 'quality' positioning. One of the problems of such an offer is that merchandise density is typically low and may result in low customer transaction values; values which are much lower than the superstore competitors operating large stores, out-of-town, with considerable car parking facilities. The company announced an experimental format in July 1993. Penny Market is a low-priced offer competing in an expanding segment of the food sector (6).

The Penny Market decision was influenced by large shareholder REWE (who purchased a 29.5 per cent stake in Budgen in the early months of 1993). This influenced is also responsible for price reductions in the Budgen stores. The Penny Market operation is set for rapid expansion during 1994/95 and some 36 stores are planned for the south of England, where margins are higher and the competition from Aldi and Netto is less intense. REWE has a £16 m turnover from 1800 stores in Germany. It has considerable experience in discount operations and this, combined with the established distribution infrastructure of Budgen (which has excess capacity), should make Penny Market a formidable operation.

Argyll/Safeway

The Argyll Group has been very active in building responses to both the recession and the European opportunity. By following an aggressive store opening programme for Safeway the company has built volume and hence margins approaching those of its competitors, Sainsbury and Tesco. This has also enabled it to develop cost-effective operations and to maintain operating margins at an optimum level. As a major partner in the European Retail Alliance, Argyll has taken a long-term view concerning its operations (9). Buying and marketing benefits are available to members: their joint purchasing volume is estimated to be £30 b.

By maintaining its Lo Cost and Presto brands Argyll remains competitive in the expanding discount sector (5). Expansion of the

Safeway format continues, typically in areas where competitive presence is low, and where the existing support services may be more fully utilised (5).

MIXED AND NON-FOOD RETAILING

Marks & Spencer

Marks & Spencer have been aware of the problems caused by the recession. A pricing strategy was introduced to shift the product mix towards the lower price points popular with customers. Prices of the more staple clothing and food items were also reduced, to achieve volume objectives (for example, the popular ranges of jeans were reduced from £22.50 to £19.50), in an 'outstanding value' campaign. Furniture prices have also been adjusted (3).

However, conscious of sales volume, transaction size value and gross margin achievement, the company has introduced merchandise augmentation characteristics where possible. The availability of wedding list services, self-service produce, butchery, and store-to-car service are a few of the examples of merchandise augmentation and customer service introductions made recently. The wedding list service is all-embracing: it offers a catalogue selection, a store-wide computer listing of wedding gifts already purchased in each of the thirty-five participating stores. These moves could be seen as an attempt to reposition the company to meet changes in customer expectations (3).

Merchandise development has continued to expand both the departments and the ranges within departments (4). Planned store development emphasises expansion of the existing format in the UK and on the Continent, with concentration on large stores and food-only satellites. The company reports numerous requests from overseas for Marks & Spencer involvement (5). Although the company suggests that it may expand the format internationally, the Far East being one possible area, it does not foresee any further acquisitions. Indeed there is an intention to undertake expansion into Japan on a joint-venture basis: the Japanese partner will provide local knowledge while Marks & Spencer manages the retail operations. In its 1992/93 report the acquisitions, which were performing at a disappointingly low level, were now beginning to contribute. By September 1993 overseas profits had improved by 42 per cent to £18.6 m. However, this was not large in the context of the £307.8 m for the first six months of 1993/94. Real growth in sales and market share in food and clothing had occurred during this period. Price increases were reported to be around 2 per cent while general merchandise grew by 7.3 per cent and food sales by 6.4 per cent.

Expansion of UK outlets is planned to continue. Four locations are planned, ranging from 40 000 to 70 000 sq. ft. Clearly Marks & Spencer share the philosophy of Sainsbury and others, whereby net profits are enhanced by increasing volume over a steady fixed-cost base (1) (4) (5).

Storehouse

During the Spring/Summer of 1992 Storehouse rationalised the business by disposing of (or announcing the intention to dispose of) those components it saw as lacking 'fit' (compatibility) with the core business (9). At the same time four layers of management were dismantled and there was a significant reduction in store employees. Some 800-full time staff were replaced by 2000 'key timers' who work between 12 and 20 hours per week (2). Service departments, such as architecture, were closed and quite radical developments, such as Mothercare eventually 'putting out' its IT and information management activities to a service company, were encouraged (1).

Within the rationalised business (BhS and Mothercare), strong and purposeful visual merchandising has been introduced with the objectives of advising customers of project co-ordination possibilities and to build transaction values (4). A store loyalty card has been introduced with the object of encouraging repeat visits (BhS and Mothercare become destination purchase stores) thus increasing both gross margins and average transactions from price-insensitive customers (5).

Supplier rationalisation has been implemented, with improved gross margins and more flexibility as the objectives (2). Space productivity will be improved due to the 'increase' of space by some 30 per cent by replacing floor standing wardrobes with wall fixtures (2). As space increases, visual merchandising and merchandise density are likely to be used more effectively in the drive to increase sales volume.

Once Blazer has been sold, the BhS/Mothercare business will be expanded by replication (5). Further acquisitions are not seen as a profitable method of growth.

It would appear that Storehouse has reviewed its strategic direction. The rationalisation of the business into the two major activities suggests a core business which may be defined as essentially an apparel-led business with middle-market appeal to the C1/C2 consumer (9). This will improve the return on assets and net margins.

Kingfisher

Kingfisher, by contrast to Storehouse, has expanded its conglomerate activities with considerable success. A joint venture with Staples has established the company in additional product-market (8) and the Darty acquisition has expanded sales and profits. Darty enables the company to improve buying margins in Comet. One commentator suggested 'It (Darty) earns some of the best margins in the world'. Furthermore, Darty's expertise in manufacturer branded product sales will benefit cash margins through higher selling prices (9). In addition to the impact on earnings Kingfisher will gain from the expertise Darty has developed over recent years in customer service. It is in areas of merchandise and service augmentation that competitive advantage can be built. If this can be done cost-effectively (in other words, with the benefit of very large international volumes) the impact on gross margin (through cost additions) can be minimised. Darty provides Kingfisher with this opportunity.

Future growth of the business is seen to lie in 'growing markets'. Kingfisher describes these as markets which 'mirror demographic and lifestyle changes of the times ... an older and better off consumer, at ease with technology and may be working from home. Someone with active brain-working pastimes' (7).

The Darty acquisition also suggests that the company is cognisant of the important of purchasing volumes in a European context. Large retailing businesses will be 'indispensable to any manufacturer supplying the European market'. Clearly by expanding the reformatted Comet and Darty (planned to expand from 130 stores to between 180 and 200 by the end of the decade) Kingfisher will be a significant retailer in the consumer durables product-market (4). Such expansion would appear to be more effective than that achieved by a domestic acquisition (such as Dixons). Growth can be managed and to a degree is accompanied by relatively less risk.

Sears

Sears is also one of the UK's largest retailing conglomerates, comprising Selfridges, British Shoe, Miss Selfridge, Wallis, Warehouse, Richards, Adams, Millets, Olympus Sports and Freeman.

In recent years it has struggled to return British Shoe to profit, which occurred in 1993 when the 1992 loss of £34.7 m became a £9 m profit. The importance of this to Sears can be seen when it is considered that footwear accounts for £253 m of the total turnover of £1734 m. This has occurred after an extensive period of rationalisation (in the mid-1980s the company operated some 2500 outlets, by mid 1993 this was 1150 stores and 552 concession operations) (2). Freemans also underwent a cost-reduction exercise, losing some 300 staff. Profitability has also returned because of sourcing improvements: buying is now from both China and Brazil (2). A new format, Shoe Express, based upon self-service, is being expanded after a successful introduction. Outlets are appearing in former Curtess locations (6).

The ladieswear activities were less profitable – the recent acquisition, Richards Shops, continued to make a loss – while in children's wear, Adams reported having a 'tough time'. The same comments were reported for Olympus Sports, where there was strong competition from Reebok.

Commentators point to medium and long-term issues concerning growth. The comments of Liam Strong, Sears' chief executive, comments suggest possible strategic rationalisation: 'we are a retailer or clothing and shoes in mass markets'. Hornes and Foster were disposed of and Richards acquired, and the debate concerning Selfridges' 'fit' in the Sears' portfolio continues. Taken together with Liam Strong's comments, this suggests a review and re-evaluation of the core business direction (9).

Dixons

Despite the impact of the recession Dixons has managed to maintain creditable sales volume and profit margins. Some rationalisation of its business has contributed towards this. In the UK it is rebuilding management, procedures, systems and service. Curry's is being repositioned into an off-centre superstore centre (7). Silo has run up losses of £58.6 m and closures will leave 185 stores. Two new formats were tested: they specialised in brown goods (emphasising computers and home office equipment) and did not stock white goods. However, losses continued to cause concern and in the Autumn of 1993 Silo has sold (9).

The company, due to its extensive overseas sourcing, expects an adverse effect from the 1992 devaluation of sterling, forecasting possible price increases in the region of 5-20 per cent. In a price-competitive market (one which forced the electricity boards' retailing activities to consider their future seriously and from which London Electricity retreated) this could cause Dixons some problems.

Operating profits for 1992/93 increased. This comprised a £200 000 contribution from PC World, an increase in market share and the increased number of Curry's out-of-town superstores (18 were opened) brings the total to 133, all of which operate at lower costs and higher margins.

Littlewoods

A somewhat secretive company. However, the move out of food and the concession agreement with Iceland (9) suggests that volumes were insufficient to earn satisfactory margins from their high street locations and that resources were likely to be more productive if focused on the core business. A reduction of staff in the mail order operation suggests further problems (2).

Tie Rack

Tie Rack can be seen as the most successful of the specialist retailing formats. Having experienced some difficulties, the company has begun to make profits. It has developed a merchandise strategy which is based on a focused range of ties and scarves with some related products such as waistcoats and shirts. The strategy requires frequent design changes, thereby maintaining a fashion interest in the range and maintaining customer awareness and a high visit frequency. This strategy is likely to establish Tie Rack as a destination purchase shopping mission (4). A competitive view of pricing (2) is another component of the merchandise strategy, together with product development activity looking at own brands and corporate neckwear – both of which will offer the opportunity to improve the gross margins of the merchandise assortment.

A concurrent rationalisation programme has been implemented. The relationship with suppliers has been improved, resulting in better buying terms through bulk purchasing discounts (2). The UK operations' costs have been reduced by closing a warehouse (2). The introduction of an EPOS system at a cost of £3 m is aimed at improving cost control and operating margins (1). Further rationalisation has been achieved by closing loss-making stores (2).

Though the company has reduced its number of outlets and reduced its franchised operations, it has improved overall performance. Further expansion will be sought in the UK and on the Continent. (8).

Burton

Burton has felt the impact of the 1989/92 recession. Like many other apparel retailers it has experienced the sharp reduction in consumer spending.

In responding Burton undertook action both to reduce costs and, at the same time, to increase the sales productivity of its outlets. A number of staff restructuring activities aimed at decreasing full-time staff and replacing them with flexible part-time employees (2). A standardisation of employment terms, equal pay, and the reduction or removal of 'benefits' was implemented with the objective of simplifying management and administration.

Merchandise ranges were reviewed. Low-volume ranges (and those lacking 'fit') were rationalised, resulting in (on average) 30 per cent fewer items per branch. This has released more selling space for the remaining ranges and enabling the availability of sizes and styles to be increased (2). An increase in selling area was also achieved by revising layout and replacing fixtures (2). As a result a more effective visual merchandising programme has been possible. It has more impact at a lower cost. The company has also implemented a programme in which fascia brands are being focused on their customer segments – for example, Top Shop is being returned to an offer characterised by low prices and Dorothy Perkins and Principles have received similar operational repositioning (3).

For the financial year 1992/93 sales were reported at £1893 m, an increase on 1991/92 of 7.3 per cent: pretax profit was £18.5 m, a reversal of the 1991/92 loss. However, it would appear that the company still has problems. The 1992/93 report identifies the fact that Debenham (subjected to considerable efforts to rationalise the merchandise offer and staffing levels earlier in 1993) is the mainstay. Debenham, contributing some £60 m in operating profits, offset the poor performance of the multiples (Burton, Top Man, Top Shop, Dorothy Perkins and Principles) whose first half-year performance was considerably better than that for 1991/92, but which slumped in the second half of 1992/93 to a loss of some £12 m. It has been suggested that this may be due to the rationalisation, which reduced sales area by 90 000 sq. ft, and to the intensification of price competition. The company has appeared to move away from volume to margin objectives.

It is also suggested that the company's review of fascia brands and catchment potential has resulted in a short-term decline in profitability (2) (3). The review of fascia brands and catchment suitability is currently continuing. At the same time there has been range rationalisation in the chain: Champion Sport and products with a 'young man's appeal have been removed from Burton stores. The rationalisation has been extensive but thus far has only affected some 25 per cent of locations (2) (3).

A long-term problem for Burton, as it is for many other high street-based retailing companies, is the legacy of high-cost expansion. Burton, like BSC, Next and others, expanded their property/outlet bases in the mid-1980s, accepting very high-cost leases. The subsequent collapse of consumer spending left Burton and the others with a large cost burden on current and future profitability. As *The Guardian* (12 November 1993) suggests, this compensates for lower rates in the early years after the sale and lease back deals were struck, low costs which also helped to inflate reported profits in those years.

MFI

Furniture retailing has had similar difficulties. Many of MFI's management decisions have been directed towards increasing operating efficiencies and sales productivity. An investment in systems has resulted in improved operations with lower staff numbers in stores. Stock control systems and distribution efficiencies have reduced warehouse space requirements (1). Improved store layouts and visual merchandising has increased sales by approximately 6.5 per cent (2) and Sunday opening has also helped improve sales volumes (3). An optimum store size has been developed, which has also contributed towards improved warehouse productivity (2).

Further economies have been achieved by implementing a programme of backward vertical integration. This has considerable impact: a 1 per cent increase in sales results in the addition of £2 m to profit (9).

Next

Next faced serious problems at the end of the 1980s and early 1990s. Having expanded by increasing selling area and increasing the fascia brands, it found a confused and disenchanted customer who, because of restricted disposable incomes, high levels of personal debt, redundancy and an increasing lack of confidence, no longer gave Next the support it enjoyed in the early and mid-1980s.

The company's response has been effective. It rationalised the fascia brands (2) and returned the business to the format that had accounted for its huge success. The merchandise strategy focused on style and finish, offering the style/quality/price combination successful in the early 1980s. Ranges are now restructured to appeal to the same target market. Choice has increased and development of the merchandise offer is based upon the existing assortment (3).

A store rationalisation programme has reduced the number of stores (from 361 to just under 300). Sales in 1992 increased by 20 per cent, while space decreased by 13 per cent (2). The resulting productivity has been apparent in the improved performance. Productivity improvements continue, enhanced by improved information management which ensures replenishment of fast-selling items – a problem in the past (1).

Visual merchandising has been made more effective. Both instore displays and window displays are changed more frequently: the co-ordinated merchandise displays once again improving transaction values and providing customers with co-ordination advice (service augmentation). Next is returning to its 'destination purchase' shopping mission status. For the 1993/94 interim, sales increased by 16.2 per cent and operating profits increased from £4.1 m to £11.8 m. There are 298 stores, but it is envisaged that eight will be added during the next year. Sales per square foot reached £198. Sales and profits from the Next Directory have increased by 8.4 per cent to £54.3 m and profits from £2.7 m to £3.5 m. The Next Directory sells the same merchandise as the stores, which has reduced costs and enabled it to offer a better quality product (2). Club 24, the credit operation, contributed £5.9 m. Profits for the first six months of 1993/94 rose from £8.3 m to £23 m and EPS more than doubled to 5.5p.

Boots

Boots have made some major changes to their retail organisation which have resulted in significant increases in performance. Buying and merchandising have been reorganised into business centres based upon product groups, and this has enabled buyers/merchandisers to develop greater knowledge and expertise within merchandise groups rather than across a number of unrelated areas (2). Store operations have also undergone changes. Operations management has been reorganised into large and small stores groups; it was found that the problems were quite different and more effective management was possible by this change (2). Space productivity has been improved by the effective use of Spaceman for merchandise ranging and space allocation (1).

Operating efficiency has also been improved through EPOS installations, completed throughout the chain of 1100 stores (1). This was expected to result in stock reductions of some 20 per cent over 1993–94, some £50/£60 m less in working capital. The EPOS facility is also expected to improve staff scheduling such that it will be easier to meet the pattern of demand in the stores. A change in the balance between full-time/part-time staff is envisaged. A 1 per cent reduction in staff costs results in a saving of £270 m.

Improved gross margin performance has resulted from a revised product mix (2). Direct product productivity (DPP) control of 42 000 lines has also increased gross margins (2). DPP has facilitated range decisions by store location and store size. The sophistication of the information system provides information on price sensitivity, particularly important for own label products. Sales of seasonal lines are tracked and prices adjusted to ensure the 'sell through' at optimal margins through price adjustments. The information system provides for rapid replacement of fast-moving items (1). Customer transactions are increased by cross-promotions (e.g. films and sun tan oil), another feature of the information system. The development of a loyalty scheme, based upon 5 m customer medical records, is also a service provided by the information system.

Developments in the merchandise areas have paralleled store operations changes and these have supported the development of specialist retailing activities such as Health and Beauty, Opticians and Photographic Processing (6). An expansion of the Health and Beauty Store portfolio has been extended by an agreement with Sainsbury to open concessions in Sainsbury superstores offering the Health and Beauty format from 100–200 sq. m instore outlets (9). The company has been innovative and ready to experiment: a sandwich outlet was experimented with in London in 1992 (6).

Benetton

Benetton is a company that has caused comment for a number of reasons. Well known for its vertical integration, it has focused on manufacturing costs and improved its contribution margins by some 38.1 per cent to 39.2 per cent. (This, in the context of a vertically integrated business, has significant implications for overall profitability.) A new production facility has reduced the number of employees from 800 to 280, energy costs have been reduced by some 30 per cent and packaging costs have been reduced by 40 per cent by the introduction of a new packaging system (1).

Sales are expected to rise following list price reductions of 4.8 per cent for 1994, reinforced by the lira's devaluation (2). In some markets this will mean a 20 per cent price reduction.

Despite the recession, Benetton forecasts a 10 per cent increase in profits and sales in 1993/94 (3). Corporate diversification (sports equipment) is planned to continue and Benetton aim to develop ten world leading brands! (8). In this way the management overhead may be used more productively.

Argos

Argos announced 1993/94 results showing a sales increase of 10.6 per cent (£10 b to £11.1 b) and a profit increase, pre-tax, of 57.8 per cent (£52.9 m to £83.5 m).

Sales increases were achieved by identifying opportunities to increase volumes by price reductions (2) (the gross margin fell by 0.1 per cent for the year). This is an interesting achievement, since its suggests that (unlike many retailers) sales were increased through competitive activity, not simply by opening sales outlets.

Cost savings were achieved by closing a warehouse facility (2) and a reduction of stockholding and storage costs by increasing the number of merchandise items delivered directly to customers (1). Efficiency has also been increased (gross margins improved) by expanding the number of products which are imported directly by the business (rather than through an import intermediary): this has the effect of increasing gross margin and through this operating profits (which showed an increase of 21.4 per cent for 1993/94 (2).

CONCLUSIONS AND IMPLICATIONS FOR MANAGEMENT

The five-year period which this study covers has given the subject companies adequate time to respond to the trading conditions imposed by the recession. Figure 1.5 summarises the activities of some of the major retailing companies in the UK.

It is immediately apparent that the focus of decision-making has occurred in areas of the business where risk is low and where the impact of the decisions has an immediate effect on profitability. From Figure 1.6 we can see that 'operational efficiency' decisions accounted for almost 50 per cent of the decisions recorded. Decisions directed towards long-term profitability accounted for 14 per cent of the total. It follows

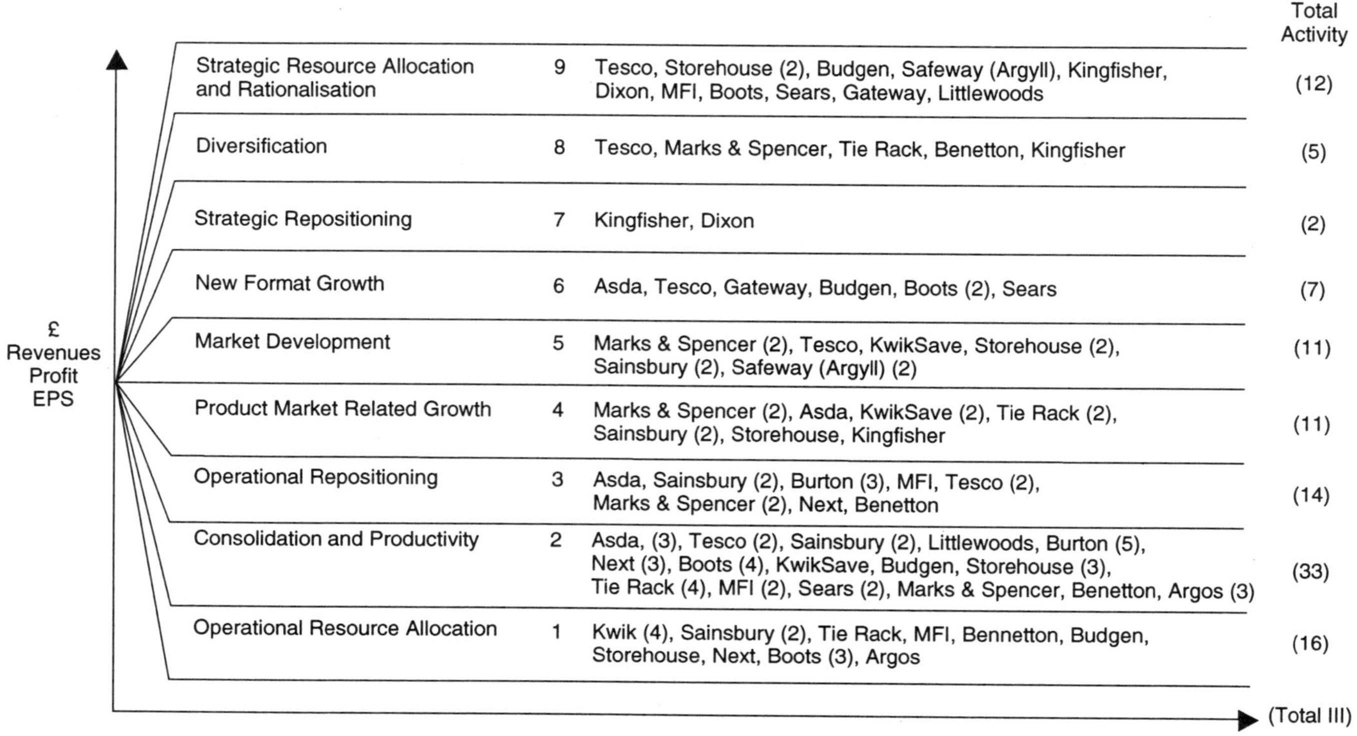

			Total Activity
Strategic Resource Allocation and Rationalisation	9	Tesco, Storehouse (2), Budgen, Safeway (Argyll), Kingfisher, Dixon, MFI, Boots, Sears, Gateway, Littlewoods	(12)
Diversification	8	Tesco, Marks & Spencer, Tie Rack, Benetton, Kingfisher	(5)
Strategic Repositioning	7	Kingfisher, Dixon	(2)
New Format Growth	6	Asda, Tesco, Gateway, Budgen, Boots (2), Sears	(7)
Market Development	5	Marks & Spencer (2), Tesco, KwikSave, Storehouse (2), Sainsbury (2), Safeway (Argyll) (2)	(11)
Product Market Related Growth	4	Marks & Spencer (2), Asda, KwikSave (2), Tie Rack (2), Sainsbury (2), Storehouse, Kingfisher	(11)
Operational Repositioning	3	Asda, Sainsbury (2), Burton (3), MFI, Tesco (2), Marks & Spencer (2), Next, Benetton	(14)
Consolidation and Productivity	2	Asda, (3), Tesco (2), Sainsbury (2), Littlewoods, Burton (5), Next (3), Boots (4), KwikSave, Budgen, Storehouse (3), Tie Rack (4), MFI (2), Sears (2), Marks & Spencer, Benetton, Argos (3)	(33)
Operational Resource Allocation	1	Kwik (4), Sainsbury (2), Tie Rack, MFI, Bennetton, Budgen, Storehouse, Next, Boots (3), Argos	(16)
			(Total 111)

£ Revenues Profit EPS

Figure 1.5 Examples of strategic decision making among major retailing businesses. (Figures in brackets indicate number of multiple mentions of the company's activities.)

that productivity-led differentiation would seem to offer higher operating and net profitability (examples being Boots, Sainsbury, Argos, Tie Rack and KwikSave).

However, customer-led (marketing-led) differentiation through strategies which pursued; new format growth, strategic repositioning and diversification were not ignored. Altogether this accounted for over 10 per cent of activity, suggesting that the companies involved were monitoring opportunities and have perhaps developed a more risk-averse attitude to diversification than that prevailing in the mid-1980s.

Two options that accounted for a significant amount of management attention were growth related to product-market and market development (17 per cent of the total). The interesting features of this type of expansion are that it is low risk (neither options take the business far from its core activity) and that in terms of costs it is a relatively attractive option. Because both options are essentially extensions of activities in which the businesses are well established and successful, not only is the risk low but the benefits can be quite large – because the resultant sales volume is not required to cover the fixed costs already met. This 'gross to net margin' effect has been common strategy among food multiples and the DIY operators, who have expanded the number of outlets operated. These activities have prompted suggestions from a number of commentators that a risk of store saturation exists (particularly in the South East of England). However, while the rate of expansion has probably declined it certainly can be seen to be continuing.

Operational repositioning for most large companies appears to have been ongoing. In some situations the repositioning has been a competitive response. The entry into the UK food market by Aldi and Netto have influenced consumer expectations and attitudes towards prices of 'commodity' food products. Responses by established UK companies varied. Tesco and Sainsbury introduced a price offer across the relevant products in their assortments, while Asda and Budgen have developed new formats similar to those of Aldi and Netto.

The long-term issues, particularly those concerning European opportunities and threats, have shown interesting responses. Safeway has been active in creating a strategic alliance with Ahold (Holland) and Casino (France). The ERA (European Retail Alliance) has a sister organisation AMS (Associated Marketing Services), and this includes Migross (Switzerland), ICA (Sweden), Mercandona (Spain), Kesko (Finland), Dansk Supermarketed (Denmark) and All Kauf (Germany). The combined purchasing total is estimated at £30 billion. Strategic alliances offer considerable benefits to their membership. From being a 20 per cent stakeholder in the national manufacturer's business the national retailer becomes a 5 per cent (or even smaller) business with the expanded 'European' manufacturer. The relationship changes and the influence that having 20 per cent of a manufacturer's business infers is no longer there. The strategic alliance re-adjusts the balance.

There appear a number of implications for future decision-making.

First there is a clear requirement for management to identify its core business activity and to evaluate its profitability. Concurrently it should evaluate the return on investment of its infrastructure or support activities. By doing so the profitability of incremental investment alternatives may be evaluated. It may be that such an approach could result in a shift in emphasis of the business within its value-added chain; for example, a consumer durable retailer considering the divestment of its service activity may find that an attractive profit opportunity exists by expanding the activity and offering the capacity to other durable retailers.

Productivity-led differentiation based upon consolidation and rationalisation offers a business clear advantages. The resulting higher operating and net profitability places the company in a stronger financial position from which it has flexibility to expand existing sales (by reducing prices, and margins, in product groups which are price elastic) or it can respond quickly to acquisition opportunities with a cash-based offer rather than attempting to make a 'leveraged' acquisition.

Customer (market)-led differentiation remains an attractive option for companies. The important consideration to be made concerns the 'distance' from the core business of the opportunity. The further the distance, the greater the risk. The attraction of home shopping offers retailers an opportunity to extend their activities into new formats: Marks & Spencer, Next and Mothercare have been successful in this direction. The reverse direction has recently been announced and implemented by Racing Green (a successful catalogue-based business) which has opened a store in Regent Street. The history/nostalgia-based Past Times has been similarly successful. In each of these examples risk has been contained by relating growth directions to the core business.

Strategic repositioning (decisions requiring investment) have much the same requirement. Tesco and Safeway's small 'city'-based developments do not take either company far from the core activities. They are food-related and have similar operating functions: thus the risk is contained and additional productivity and profitability from the existing fixed cost structures is obtained.

The diversification option has clearly been reviewed. Overseas expansion occurs only when the 'fit' is close to the existing business. Furthermore, recent examples (Kingfisher/Darty) suggest that not only should risk be contained but that opportunities for synergy should be sought.

One other conclusion can be reached: there is evidence of a clear awareness of the need to monitor resource productivity and profitability. The emphasis on 'consolidation and productivity' decisions (almost 50 per cent of the decisions recorded) suggests that retailing management is very conscious of the resource allocation decision. To this end, the thrust of this book is towards developing an approach that can be used across a range of both operational *and* strategic resource allocation decisions. We shall demonstrate that effective resource allocation does not necessarily restrict growth. The model developed in the subsequent chapters enables managers to evaluate alternatives and to explore change without taking the risks involved in investment.

Bibliography

The research for this chapter has been undertaken over an extended period. It was a process by which the companies identified were 'tracked' by monitoring published sources of information. The publications used were: company reports; *Mintel* (various reports); *Verdict* (various reports); *Marketing Week*; *Financial Times*; *Guardian*; *Independent*; *Sunday Times*; *Independent on Sunday*; *Evening Standard*; *Retail Week*.

2 Productivity, Profitability and Performance: Introduction to Issues for Cash Flow and Productivity

INTRODUCTION

This chapter explores the concepts of productivity, profitability and performance. It initially examines the need to *manage* productivity and profitability if the means by which growth is to be achieved are realised cost-effectively. To do this we review the basic requirements for cash and profit generation and consider how the retail business might best be managed to provide the necessary resources.

We commence by suggesting that it is the role of senior management to establish a policy that ensure that the cash for growth is, ideally, generated internally. The reason for this is quite obvious: if the business has insufficient internally generated funds, it follows that it will require external funds. If this involves the business in assuming debt, it also involves the company in meeting a tax burden. Provided that growth of resources follows at an acceptable (and planned) rate, profit will be enhanced. However, if planned growth fails to materialise, then the burden of the debt continues and profitability declines.

In the discussion that follows we consider a number of concepts that will explain the relationship linking productivity with cash and profit generation.

PRODUCTIVITY AND THE PLANNING GAP

The concept of the planning gap was developed by Ansoff (1965) whose model of strategic analysis and the classification of strategic options has formed the basis of numerous subsequent contributions to the strategy literature. Figure 1.2 (p. 12) illustrates the planning gap which results when management evaluates the performance required if growth objectives are to be achieved.

Filling the planning gap is the result of a methodical process by which low-risk options such as consolidation and productivity improvements and repositioning are initially pursued, which typically require the business to become more efficient at its current activities. Figure 2.1 illustrates a modification to the planning gap for retail management purposes. Both consolidation and productivity and repositioning requires effective use of existing resources: a focus on productivity. The result of planned productivity improvements will be to generate more cash (as stock levels are lowered and thus cash released) and profit increases (due to improved gross and operating margins). The overall effect will be to provide internally generated resources which may be used to pursue growth and diversification.

More recently there has been a clear intention by retailing management to focus upon its 'core business', the view being that it is the core

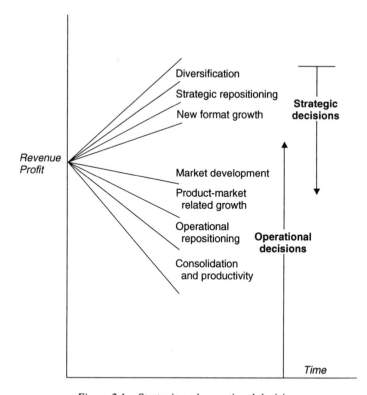

Figure 2.1 Strategic and operational decisions

Cash Flow and Productivity Issues

business that should generate the greater return on investment (ROI) and that resources should be directed towards developing the profit (and cash) generation capabilities of the core business assets. By contrast support functions and activities have often been divested: for example, Mothercare 'divested' its information generation function during 1993. Other companies have been more extensive: Sears have divested their menswear businesses (Foster and Hornes) and have acquired a ladieswear business (Richards) and have invested in their existing ladieswear businesses. Burtons have disposed of their property portfolio. This 'strategic' and 'operational' resource allocation and rationalisation process has been described by one of the authors elsewhere (see Walters, 1994).

Returning to the planning gap, development work by the Boston Consulting Group (BCG) between 1970 and 1975 offers a very useful point of departure. The BCG growth/share matrix is probably the group's best-known contribution. The thesis of the growth/share matrix is that a well-managed portfolio of products (or businesses) will provide the cash required for developing other products (businesses) and thus will avoid the need to resort to external sources of funds. The growth/share matrix together with the product life cycle provide a useful introduction to a discussion on productivity (see Figure 2.2). Although it may be argued that the BCG approach is dated, it remains a powerful analytical tool; particularly when both cash and profit generation are essential to the success of the business.

The portfolio approach suggests to management that they should review the cash generation capabilities (and requirements) of products (or individual businesses) and manage the 'mix' of products so that the characteristics of the products are identified and used in such a way that the overall portfolio contributes a planned cash flow contribution. There are a number of issues to be considered. The first is volume: it is obvious that as volume sales increase so too should sales revenue. However, revenue does not mean cash and the Boston Group's work on cost behaviour (the experience effect) resulted in the suggestion that as market share increases many of the costs of production and the distribution process decrease at a constant (and predictable) rate. It follows that as volume increases, market share also increases and average costs decrease. The result is that large market share implies low costs *and* relatively large cash generation. From this the emphasis on growth rate and market share in the growth/share matrix follows logically. There are some conditions. It is assumed that a large degree of standardisation exists in both the production and distribution processes: if this is absent

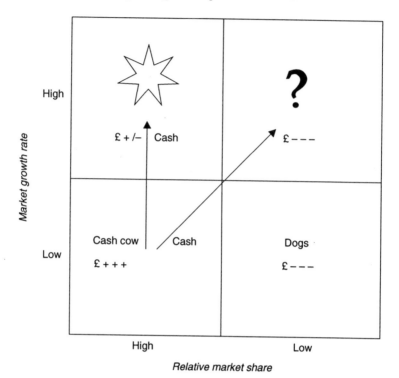

Figure 2.2 The BCG growth/share matrix

it presents problems, particularly for the production process, because low-cost volume processing becomes difficult and cost reductions do not occur.

There is also an implied assumption concerning product/business management activities. The cash generators are likely to be *low* risk and have 'ideal' life cycle profiles. These two aspects are connected. Kotler Ras suggested the ideal product life cycle to have:

- low risk;
- low R&D market development costs;
- rapid introduction and growth readily accepted by distributors and consumers;
- a prolonged maturity period of decline during which both customer acceptance and technology exhibit stability;
- a relatively long period of decline during which both customer acceptance and technology change over a period of time sufficiently long for the product/business to be withdrawn gradually, to ensure

that remaining cash and profit residuals may be maximised and that a minimum disruption of customer satisfaction occurs.

It follows that such products (see Figure 2.3) should form the basis of a merchandise assortment, and typically these are the characteristics of core merchandise groups (core items within the groups). They can, and do, change over time but this can be easily accommodated by monitoring consumer expectations (and perceptions) through tracking studies and similar research methods.

If core merchandise products form the basis of the merchandise offer, then the customer groups that look for fashion, style and other variations may not be attracted to the offer unless these requirements are met. Clearly these demand attributes are likely to change more rapidly and have, from the retailer's point of view, a much higher risk profile. Although the precise timing of fashion (and fad) life cycles is difficult to predict, their shapes follow predictable patterns.

Often core merchandise products develop into specialist areas (for example, recent developments by Boots – opticians, photographic services, and so on – and Marks & Spencer – menswear and food 'stand alone' outlets). The slow but steady growth during the 'maturity' stage of the cycle reflects the increasing consumer recognition and awareness of the specialism such that the offer becomes a destination purchase shopping mission.

Clearly the merchandise offer comprises a 'range' which is planned to appeal to a target customer group and which should appeal to both their basic and varying needs. Hence we expect the assortment to be planned around core ranges and items supported by merchandise which reflects the fashion changes acceptable to the target customer group. Figure 2.4 suggests a 'mix' of life cycles that results from this requirement. It should be noted that these comments also obtain for 'retail offer' formats (that is, combinations of merchandise, customer service and store environment). Performance at any particular time, for example, will comprise contributions from each assortment category.

Returning to the earlier discussion on portfolio issues, it follows that there is a strong relationship between life cycles and the BCG growth/share matrix. In Figure 2.5 we consider the merchandise 'mix' characteristics expressed as life cycles in Figure 2.3, within the context of the BCG growth/share matrix. It should be noted that segment share has replaced the 'market share' measure (horizontal axis); typically most retailing businesses are more interested in segment performance than overall market share performance. Many retail markets (for

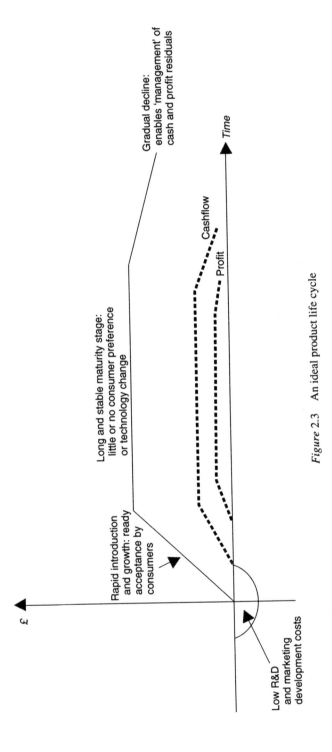

Figure 2.3 An ideal product life cycle

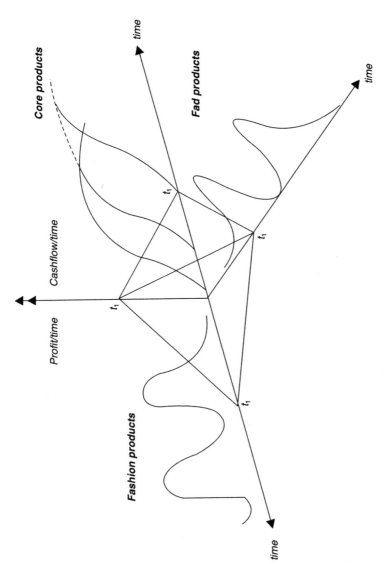

Figure 2.4 Merchandise (format) mix over time for ladieswear retailer

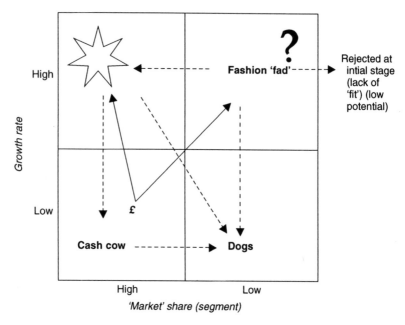

Figure 2.5 Merchandise 'mix': cash generation characteristics and portfolio patterns

instance, ladieswear) are very large and very clearly segmented: it follows that companies such as Laura Ashley and Country Casuals are therefore close competitors who are targeting similar customer groups. It often happens that performance variations across segments is quite different and concern with overall trends may be quite misleading. In Figure 2.5 the 'pathways' of merchandise categories may be plotted. It is suggested that 'cash cows' are derived from assortment categories for which demand becomes well established and for which the business builds a strong (destination purchase) reputation: these products may, over time, become core products. Examples of these merchandise items and groups may be observed with Marks & Spencer knitwear, underwear and recipe meals. Woolworth has built similar core merchandise groups in confectionery and music while the John Lewis Partnership has a reputation for furnishing and tailoring fabrics. The impact of this view on the growth/share matrix is shown in Figure 2.6.

Performance characteristics may also be examined using another BCG tool: the growth/gain matrix. See Figure 2.7(a) and (b). This approach is a helpful analytical method because it indicates two useful additional aspects. The first is the comparison between business growth rate and

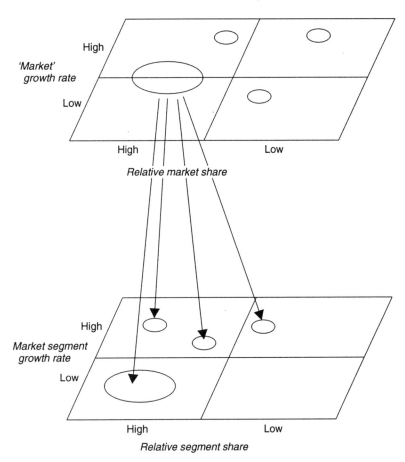

Figure 2.6 The importance of considering market segment characteristics

market growth rate (or product group growth rate). The second aspect concerns the 'maximum sustainable growth rate,' the rate of growth the business is able to maintain within specified growth/risk parameters'. Though we may have what we consider to be an assortment currently producing satisfactory levels of both profit and cashflow, it is possible that in 'market' or 'market segment' terms it does not share the same rate of growth. (Rates of growth may be compared by the position of a product or business relative to the 45° diagonal in Figure 2.7(a): any product/business growing at the same rate as the market will be *on* the diagonal; if the growth rate is less than that of the market, the product will be positioned above the diagonal; and if it is greater, then it will appear in a position below the line.)

50

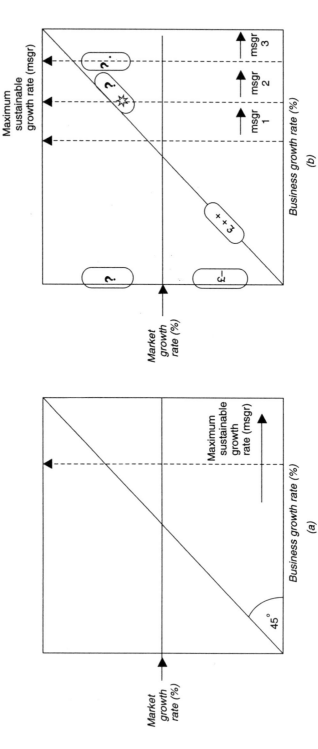

Figure 2.7 The growth/gain matrix showing the influence of the maximum sustainable growth rate on decision-making

The maximum sustainable growth rate is of particular interest for productivity and profitability performance planning and control. The determinants of corporate growth are:

- the rate of return of the business
- the use of debt
- the dividend/retentions policy pursued
- recourse to external equity funds.

Dividend payout and capital requirements determine the availability of funds generated by the return on the assets employed in the business. It is essential that management understands the implications of the use of each source of funds.

The rate of return

The *rate of return* a business generates is usually a reflection of the 'going rate' for the industry. It is influenced by size, the competitiveness of the industry and environmental influences. It is argued (Robinson, 1986) that it is difficult to exceed the 'industry norm' by very much, because if the firm generates too high a margin (for a sustained period) it will: attract competitive entry; lose market share; forgo turnover (a function of elasticity); and will grow more slowly than the market average. From this we conclude that returns are limited unless asset productivity or perhaps margins is increased. The extent to which the improvement in the resultant rate of return will result in competitive entry depends very much on factors such as industry structure, barriers to entry and overall market/segment growth rate.

The use of debt

This can increase the return on shareholders' equity (the realistic measurement of management's success). The use of high levels of debt permits the firm to 'gear' up (use leverage on) the returns on investment into a higher return on equity. The use of high levels of debt enables the firm to: accept lower profit margins and overcome short-term cost disadvantages by making rapid progress down the experience curve, thereby developing a larger market share than it might otherwise have achieved; pay more for assets (particularly those with 'productive' or 'distributive' capacity capable of generating higher productivity); and maintain a higher growth rate than the market norm. However, the impact of increasing financial gearing on risk should not be overlooked.

Dividend policy

This influences growth rate simply because there exists a trade-off between current and future dividends. Clearly current high levels of dividend *and* growth can only be maintained if the rate of return on investment is high or if debt is used. The alternatives are either to change the dividend policy or to increase the equity funding.

External equity funding

The use of external equity funding is not necessarily an easy solution. Two major problems obtain.

- The additional equity may have the effect of diluting control and may also generate conflicts of interest between established and new equity holders – particularly large, institutional shareholders.
- The cost of servicing new equity can be very high when equity financing is substituted for debt, particularly with a high dividend payout policy.

Let us return to the growth/gain matrix and the notion that growth activities may be funded from a well-structured and managed product/business portfolio. Zakon (1971) derived a relationship to express the factors influencing the maximum sustainable rate of growth of a firm by using internal sources and the use of debt:

Profit = f (return on investment, gearing and interest rate)

$$P = r(D + E) - iD$$

where:

P = profit
r = return on investment
D = debt
E = equity
i = interest rate

Collecting the terms and dividing by equity (E):

$$\frac{P}{E} = \frac{D}{E}(r-i) + r$$

Dividend payments reduce the rate of growth. The effect of dividend payments can be modelled by multiplying by the proportion of retained earnings. This gives:

$$g = \frac{D}{E}(r-i)p + rp$$

where:

g = the sustainable growth rate
D = debt
E = equity
r = return on investment
i = interest rate
p = the proportion of earnings retained

This relationship may be used to calculate the maximum sustainable rate of growth, under given debt, equity and dividend policy, which can be funded from internal sources.

Returning to Figure 2.7, we can see how the maximum sustainable growth rate (msgr) may influence the shape of the merchandise portfolio. In Figure 2.7(b) three possible positions of the msgr are shown. At msgr 1 there is limited growth potential within the firm's capabilities as there are no cash generation candidates (cows). However, an expansion of the msgr to msgr 2 would improve the company's prospects significantly, because at msgr 2 it has growth 'star' products and potential products (?) for future growth. At msgr 3 the stars are increased and further growth product capacity can be funded. Figure 2.8 provides a hypothetical example of a firm which has determined its msgr.

Zakon's relationship suggests an msgr that considers internal funding as its only option. Clearly this constraint may be relaxed. For example, if there was a change in dividend policy whereby a larger proportion of the residual profit was retained for investment or perhaps if debt was to be increased or lower rates of interest funds became available, the msgr could be increased. The msgr could also be increased by increasing the return on investment and this may be achieved by improved productivity performance.

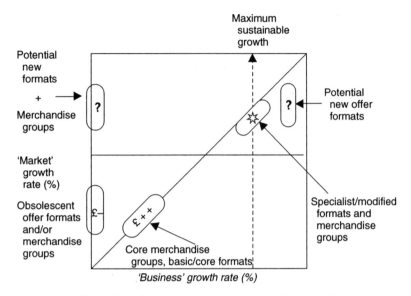

Figure 2.8   A hypothetical assortment/business profile

In Figure 2.9 we illustrate a situation whereby it is desirable to increase the msgr. To do so would effectively move 'question mark' products into 'star' category by enabling investment to be directed into expansion of the business. Two components of msgr are identified: asset management and margin management.

- **Asset management** comprises:

    Fixed capital intensity = $\dfrac{\text{Gross book value of fixed assets (\%)}}{\text{Sales}}$

    Fixed capital utilisation = $\dfrac{\text{Actual sales throughput (\%)}}{\text{Standard (maximum sustainable) sales throughput}}$

    Working capital intensity = $\dfrac{\text{Net current assets (\%)}}{\text{Sales}}$

    = $\dfrac{(\text{Stocks} + \text{Debtors} + \text{Cash} - (\text{Creditors} + \text{short term debt}))\ (\%)}{\text{Sales}}$

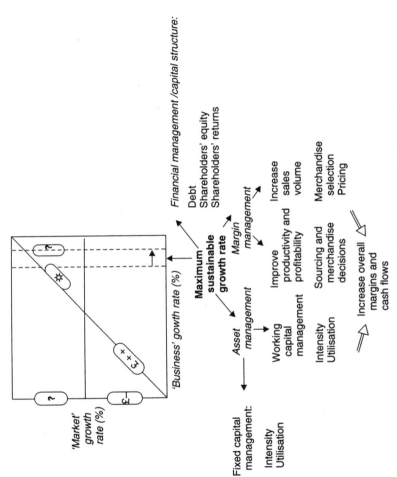

Figure 2.9 Factors influencing the size of maximum sustainable growth rate

Working capital utilisation = $\dfrac{\text{Sales} \quad (\times)}{\text{Net current assets}}$

Additional ratios that are useful in this context are:

$\dfrac{\text{Sales (stockturn)}}{\text{Stocks}}$ $\qquad$ $\dfrac{\text{Trade creditors}}{\text{Sales}}$

or: $\qquad\qquad\qquad\qquad$ *or:*

$\dfrac{\text{Purchases (COGS)}}{\text{Stocks}}$ $\qquad$ $\dfrac{\text{Trade creditors}}{\text{Stocks}}$

- **Margin management** has two components. First, an *increase in operating sales volume* (that is, sales from the *existing* business), through increased market penetration; merchandise development programmes; market development; operational repositioning; specialisation and possibly strategic repositioning. Effective margin management will result in increased cash flow as well as profitability improvements. Secondly, an *improvement in operational productivity and profitability*. To achieve this, attention must be given to making changes which will improve both buying and merchandising effectiveness, and operations effectiveness. Again the impact will be seen on both profit margins and cashflow.

Both asset management and margin management will be discussed in detail in subsequent chapters. Figure 2.9 also shows that there is a *financial management/capital structure* influence which is exercised through the nature of the funding of the assets.

Traditionally discussions concerning business growth have considered the notion of a planning gap. The planning gap is concerned with both revenues and profits; it has also used earnings per share as the 'objective' datum. In Figure 2.10 we use the planning gap concept to illustrate the dynamic requirements of cash flow. The diagram demonstrates the importance of thinking through the cash needs of the business as individual life cycles are pursed. It suggests that at any time in the future estimates may be made of cash generation and cash uses. From these estimates, cashflow shortfalls may be identified ahead of their occurring and action may be taken accordingly. This may involve a review of internal operations with a view to asset or margin management

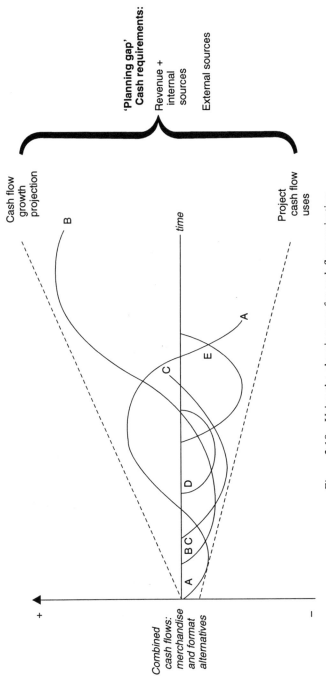

Figure 2.10 Using the planning gap for cash flow projection

improvements to alleviate the problem, or enabling management to negotiate overdraft facilities (or alternatively to revise future planned activities).

Another contribution by BCG is helpful. *Frontier curve analysis* is a seldom-used but helpful technique which portrays the growth rate of the business in a portfolio compared with the cash used (Moose and Zakon, 1972). Figure 2.11 illustrates the technique. The annual growth rate of profits is shown on the vertical axis and the cash used (as a percentage of earnings) is plotted on the horizontal axis. The company's identified profit centres are plotted on the resulting matrix according to their growth and reinvestment characteristics over a selected period of time. The location of the profit centres (and these may be merchandise groups, format types, and so on) indicates the 'value' of the profit centre to the business. For example, a merchandise group showing a 15 per cent growth in profits and a 100 per cent use of cash generated is using all of its resources to grow at 15 per cent. Such a situation, which has high growth and is self-financing, suggests a 'star'. By contrast a merchandise group which is not increasing its annual growth rate in profits, but only using 60 per cent of its generated cash to maintain a competitive position (thereby making the remainder available for redeployment), may be described as a cash cow. The authors suggest that in general

> 'cash cows would be expected to have profit growth rates of less than 5 percent and cash usage rates of 70 percent or less. Stars would be expected to be roughly in cash balance with growth rates in excess of 10 percent. Wildcats (question marks) would be expected to have similar growth rates of profits to stars, but higher cash usage rates. Dogs, if properly managed should have low growth rates and be cash generators, albeit small' (Moose and Zakon, 1972).

The theoretical positioning of the portfolio is shown in Figure 2.11(b) and a detailed classification appears as Figure 2.12. The authors suggest that 'businesses' not conforming to these guidelines are problem areas and may represent cash traps.

Robinson (1986) suggests that corporate cash needs in the form of dividends, interest and overheads are to be covered and that often the analysis overlooks this requirement. The BCG suggestion is that each business should be assessed on the percentage of net assets employed and that the given percentage of corporate dividends, interest and overhead should be deducted from profits before the percentage reinvested is calculated. Clearly the result will be to reduce the number of cash gener-

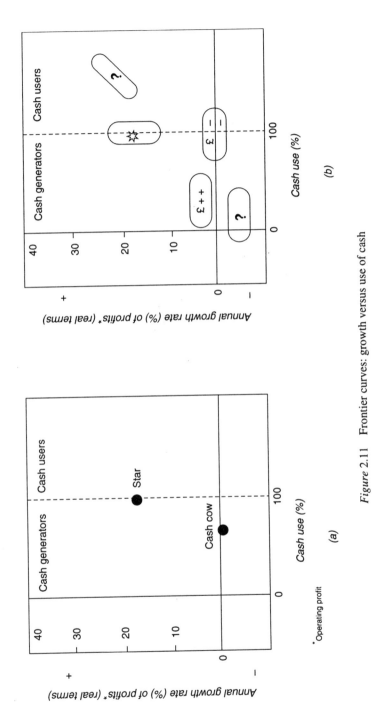

Figure 2.11 Frontier curves: growth versus use of cash

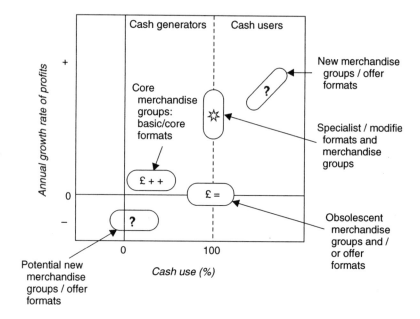

Figure 2.12 Hypothetical assortment/format profile using frontier curve analysis

ators and/or the amount of cash generated. Robinson also directs attention to the fact that care should be exercised concerning cash use and cash generation: proportions of both can be represented by the 'area' (or 'size') of the merchandise group/format used in the plot.

The formula quoted earlier (p. 53) can be modified and restated to consider overhead and dividends:

$$g = \frac{D}{E}(r-i)p + (r-e)p$$

where 'e' is an after-tax charge on assets to cover corporate overhead and dividends. Robinson suggests that for given, constant values of D, E, r, i and e, the equation reduces to:

$$g = Ap$$

where 'A' is a constant. If p (proportion of earnings retained) equals 1.0 (100 per cent cash retention) then g is equal to the msgr for the corporation and the result is a series of straight lines for various targeted rates. (see Figure 2.13). Opportunities along the line are equally attractive, those below the line are less so and those above the line are more attrac-

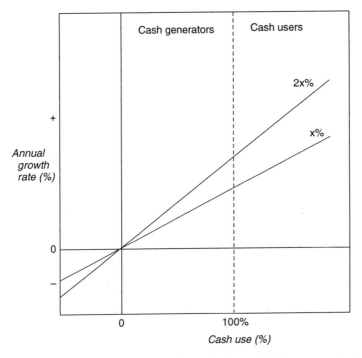

Figure 2.13 Target growth rates for the business (100% cash retention)

tive because of their *potential* for higher growth with the same cash use. The areas of the circles representing the chosen portfolio above and below the line can be compared to assess the cash flow characteristics of the desired portfolio.

The straight lines in Figure 2.13 assume that the debt: equity ratio is constant. Frontier curves can be generated for different debt: equity ratios as a function of cash usage. These curves may be plotted by taking g (the msgr) various return on investment rates (r) and interest rates (i) and varying the debt: equity ratio across the range of p, the proportion of earnings retained. This results in the curves generated in Figure 2.14.

This discussion suggests that productivity of resources and corporate profitability are critical if growth objectives are to be met. At an operational level management activity to improve both the margin spread and the utilisation of operational assets can increase the return on assets (profitability) and improve cash flow. In the long term the use of financial gearing can be supported by low-growth, cash-generating businesses. High-growth businesses should be less highly leveraged. The decision as to the level of gearing can only be reached after an analysis

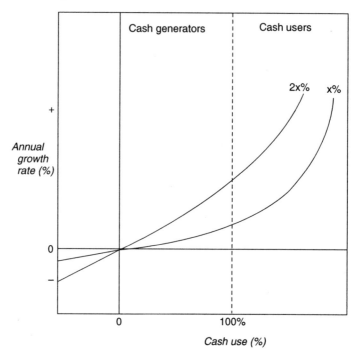

Figure 2.14 Frontier curves when the debt/equity ratio is varied across a range of earnings retention rates

of the cash generation/cash use situation of the portfolio. An important conclusion that may be reached is that effective productivity planning of the merchandise assortment performance may reduce the requirement for external funding to finance growth.

We can summarise the discussion thus far by referring to Figure 2.15. It is suggested that a continuous review of customer expectations results in identifying the level of success of the current offer and the developments and trends that are occurring. Additionally growth options are identified, evaluated and reviewed for investment requirements. Accepting the notion of a self-financing business portfolio, a review of the productivity and profitability performance of key profit centre areas (merchandise groups or perhaps delivery formats) identifies both their capabilities and capacities to produce the profitability required to meet stakeholder requirements and the cashflow necessary to fund growth candidates: the planning gap. This will enable the exercise to move on to identify the cash needs of the key resource areas if growth activities are to be pursued – the options for closing the planning gap. By closing the planning gap (or identifying the

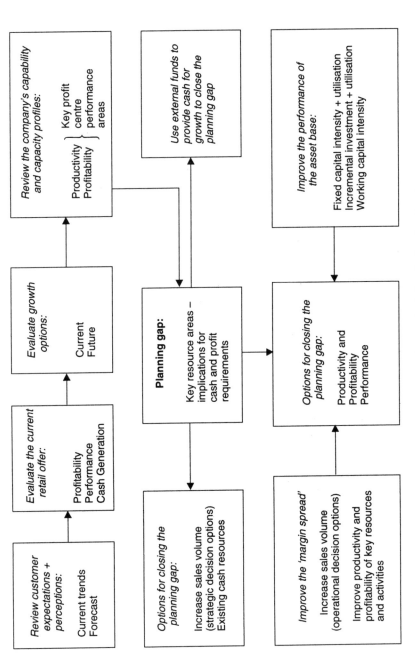

Figure 2.15 Identifying alternative methods for closing the planning gap

extent to which it can be closed using cash from current activities and establishing the extent of external funding needs) we are determining the maximum sustainable growth rate achievable by using internal funds and the ideal sustainable growth rate necessary (or required) if the growth options are to be pursued. This would consider varying levels of debt funding. Comparison of the internal maximum sustainable growth, the ideal sustainable growth rate and the market and financial risk will lead to a decision on growth direction and funding.

The interests of this work are focused on the management of productivity and profitability necessary to meet the profit requirements of stockholders and the cash flow needs for maintaining liquidity in the existing business *and* the cash flow required for growth. With these requirements in mind we shall discuss the issues and the alternatives involved in managing the margin spread (Chapter 3) and the asset base (Chapter 4) if profit and cash flow generated by the business is to be optimised. We suggest that optimisation rather than maximisation is a necessary approach if current customer satisfaction is to be maintained.

BROADER ISSUES

Eilon and Gold (1976) made a significant contribution to the issues concerning the study in this area. Their interests

> 'arose as a result of studies in the analysis of performance within decentralised organisations, where the performance of cost or profit centres needs to be measured in order to facilitate the control of planning of future operations and in order to provide a means of both motivating and judging the performance of the managers concerned'.

They suggest that widely-used concepts of productivity have serious shortcomings and that these concern their failure to focus on specific measures to achieve indicated overall productive efficiency (for example, the output per man-hour). Furthermore, any increases that are indicated are often achieved by a combination or resources, such as labour and capital.

Their conclusion is that:

> 'the analysis of productivity must be embedded in the cost and profitability structures [of the firm]: The appropriateness of a particular measure reflects the objectives and managerial goals of the unit

concerned, which in turn are derived from those of the firm. And it follows therefore, ... that guidelines as to *how* to measure productivity may be gained from an analysis of why we should wish to measure it.'

There are four reasons suggested:

- **for strategic purposes** – to compare the performance of the firm with that of competitors, both in terms of aggregate performance and in terms of major components of the business.
- **for operational (tactical) purposes** – to enable management to control the performance of the firm by identifying the comparative performance of individual functions within the business;
- **for other managerial purposes** – such as collective bargaining, the assessment of the impact of government restrictions, and so on;
- **for planning purposes;** to compare the relative benefits accruing from the use of different inputs or by varying the proportions of those inputs, in the short and/or long run, as a basis fo considering alternatives for future periods.

Our focus will be on the first three reasons. In recent years the influence of unions and collective bargaining has declined significantly. In any event the model proposed in subsequent chapters has the facility to consider changes in labour rates. Our concern is with the need to adjust the various resource inputs to achieve a customer-determined level of output.

This objective raises an interesting issue, one identified by Eilon, and this is that inputs are heterogeneous and often difficult to measure. This results in four major problems:

- **measuring output** – particularly when the 'products' differ markedly;
- **measuring inputs** – because of the range of types of resources and their combinations;
- **determining the particular input–output comparison that is most relevant** – because of the range of alternatives available;
- **interpreting findings** – because of the need to differentiate between the influence of internally controllable and externally imposed factors.

A review of the literature identifies a number of approaches to measuring productivity. A brief review helps to put the issues involved in context.

Financial ratios

These use revenues and costs as a means by which the heterogeneity of physical inputs and outputs may be considered as homogeneous. Risk (1965) uses the return on investment as a starting point and then by dividing assets between departments the respective ratios of outputs to assets managed are used to measure the performance of departments. We shall return to this approach in detail.

Productivity costing approach

This emphasises the contributions made by individual products rather than operating units. The 'productivity' of a product is measured by its 'efficiency' in making a profit. Bahivi and Martin (1970) measure only work that is productive. It is assumed that costs remain stable over the whole normal range of variation of output and that once the production facilities have been identified, productivity can be measured by total earnings of the productive facilities and the rate at which cash product generates profit. They constrict various productivity indices based on optimal facilities usage. The approach is focused entirely on costs and revenues and ignores the physical resource flows and input factor prices.

Transfer pricing

This has been suggested by Horngren (1965) who recommends that transfer prices be used as a measure of efficiency. If supplying divisions meet external price competition and orders are retained in the company, it suggests that market prices are no less than manufacturing variable costs.

Value-added

This forms the basis of a number of approaches. Here the measures used are wages, salaries and gross profit (with possibly the addition of depreciation). Eilon suggests that this calculation does not make much of a statement concerning productivity.

Gold (Eilon *et al.*, 1976) argues that there are five essential features for productivity analysis. It is necessary to:

- clarify the **nature** of productivity adjustments;
- develop more effective **measures** of changes in productivity;

Cash Flow and Productivity Issues

- explore **sources** of significant changes of productivity;
- trace the successive linkages whereby productivity adjustments **affect** costs, prices and profitability; and
- **integrate** all of the foregoing into a **managerial control system** designed to enable management to:
  — appraise alternative means of changing productivity;
  — appraise managerial alternatives on the application of such innovations; and
  — determine the effects of past as well as of prospective innovations.

A basic limitation of productivity analysis is grounded in its early development in agriculture and manufacturing. And, as Gold suggests,

> 'The shifting of such efforts from relatively primitive production operations to highly complex activity systems and from the context of engineering measurements of physical relationships to that of managerial appraisals of economic relationships, requires far-reaching re-adjustments in purposes, concepts and methods ...'

And further:

> 'To analyse the complex domain of input-output relationships in modern industry ... it is necessary to broaden the concept of the nature of productivity adjustments to include the effects of changes: in the quality and degree of utilisation of any or all inputs, as well as in the quantitative proportions of various inputs; and in the qualitative characteristics of each product as well as in the quantitative proportions of different products. As a result, three new problems of measurement must be dealt with: how to combine different product (or input) flows into meaningful aggregates; how to deal with qualitative changes in particular inputs or outputs through time[;] and ... how to keep input and output measures independent of one another.'

It follows that there are a number of issues to be considered in the management of productivity and profitability. Distribution business activities add some complexity, in that there are some essential differences in the way productivity is measured, compared to its measurement in a manufacturing context. Gold suggested some of these. For example, there is the qualitative nature of the inputs: though merchandise may be similar, the ambience of the store environment and the extent to which customer service may differ will result in very different 'products.' It follows that the total costs of inputs will differ markedly. Clearly, these are issues which we must address.

Gold also discusses the varying needs of management for information for productivity analysis. At a strategic level (top management) broad financial management measures are often sufficient (together with a facility to obtain detailed data when required). At an operational level the focus is more on physical inputs and outputs. But again we have some differences with distribution, in that some physical counting may be very difficult and, furthermore, too detailed to be of significance.

Another issue to be discussed concerns the precise use of the terms employed when measuring organisational achievements. Performance is an all-embracing term. It can be used when describing the effectiveness or efficiency of the assets producing a return to the shareholders. We do not aim to be unnecessarily pedantic, but it is important to ensure that any confusion that might enter the discussion is identified and dealt with. In support of this approach we would argue that productivity, profitability and performance are central to planning and control decisions in any business organisation. We would argue further that the decisions made by the business are influenced by the structure, conduct and performance of the industry within which it operates. There is here an interesting overlap between the interests of the industrial and the managerial economist. Davies (1991) suggests that managerial economics considers the performance of the firm: in industrial economics the emphasis is upon the behaviour of entire industries. He reminds us that the typical approach of the industrial economist is the STRUCTURE–CONDUCT–PERFORMANCE (SPM) approach, in which the structure of the industry is seen as an important determinant of its conduct and performance. We would argue that these issues are also very relevant to the decision-making process of the individual organisations within the industry. This becomes apparent when we consider the dimensions of structure–conduct–performance.

- **Structure** has a number of dimensions:
    - the level of concentration
    - barriers to entry
    - the degree of product differentiation
    - the extent of vertical integration.
- The **conduct** of an industry refers to the behaviour engaged in by component organisations:
    - company objectives

Cash Flow and Productivity Issues 69

- — the extent of the competitiveness of their activities
- — pricing policies
- — advertising policies
- — strategic directions.
- The **performance** of an industry concerns results; among the measures commonly being used are:
  - — profitability
  - — growth
  - — resource productivity
  - — export performance/international competitiveness.

The industrial economist would suggest that the structure of an industry should be treated as exogenous and that structure should be seen as the cause of conduct and subsequent performance. Though their interests are 'macro', in that they study links between the level of concentration across industries and their profitability performance, the point should be made that individual (or 'micro' level) decisions are also made taking industry structure into account and developing a conduct format based upon this and a number of assumptions concerning the changes that may occur in competitor responses.

The likelihood is that planned performance is a result of the trends in the structure as identified in an analysis of the environment and the opportunities that are apparent to the individual organisation, rather than the structure of the industry having a conditioning effect. This is even more likely to result in organisations expanding capacity and adopting growth strategies which will be expansive in the use of resources. The reaction of indigenous companies towards new entrants is less likely to be as conservative particularly if they are confronting the reverse situation: zero growth or a decline.

In these situations not only may conduct and profitability differ markedly, but so may productivity. This suggests that profitability and productivity are likely to benefit from a strategic or operational view based upon an ongoing review of the structure–conduct–performance trends. The strategic planning model (McCammon, 1970) is one approach which offers a facility to consider the issues: see Figure 2.16. This is the approach suggested by Risk (1965) and discussed earlier by Eilon et al. McCammon's application is one of many. Although very basic, this model has considerable potential for expansion and can be used to consider the profitability and productivity issues of planning within a dynamic business environment. It enables management to identify the factors that influence the company's return to the shareholders'

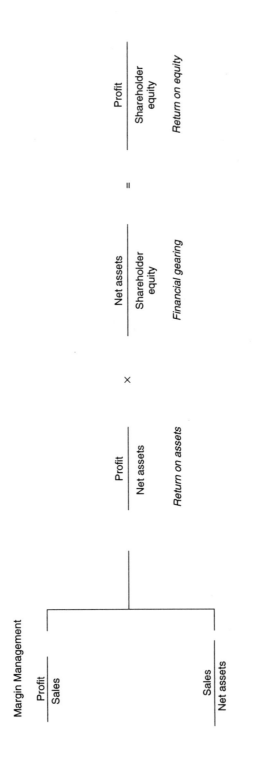

Figure 2.16 Components of business performance

equity investment. In doing so it examines the value of the company's return on assets (asset utilisation or productivity) and the margins generated from sales. Another feature of the model is its ability to consider the impact of corporate debt (financial gearing) on the return to the shareholders. We shall return to this application in subsequent chapters.

A RANGE OF PERFORMANCE MEASURES

Thus we can see the need to consider alternative potential performance outcomes based upon judgements derived from an interpretation of the structure–conduct–performance trends within the business environment. It would be more useful if we examined the concepts and consider how views might change depending upon structure–conduct–performance trends. Organisational success occurs when a planned response to environment opportunities is implemented. To do this effectively requires resource allocation decisions and performance measures that reflect organisational objectives. The selection of performance measures is based upon strategic and operational intentions. From the foregoing discussion it follows that these should consider both the nature of the objectives to be achieved (management's interpretation of the opportunities available) and the time horizon over which the planning is to take place and be effective. This gives the facility for strategic and operational decision-making.

The basic SPM model described above suggests that performance is measured in two components: margin management and asset management. It also suggests that performance should be measured by considering financial decisions (the management of resource allocation). Clearly the process of management, in its hierarchical approach, will consider the financial implications of decisions at all levels and, as suggested by the SPM, is ultimately concerned with the financial return to the shareholders.

However, it has been suggested that, from a control point of view, managers control activities more effectively than they do costs (Cooper, 1989). Cooper suggests that this is a worthwhile relationship to consider. We suggest that there is a link between productivity and profitability. For example, the chief executive is interested in the return on capital employed (ROCE) and associated ratios, which would include gross, operating and net margins, asset circulation and cash flow. At a more specialist level other directors will focus upon less-aggregated performance measures; for example, merchandise and buying directors are interested in overall and merchandise group margins and stock/sales performances: they will also be concerned with in-store merchandise availability, sell-through rates and local or regional performance differences.

Management is a planning and control process. The implementation of corporate strategic decisions is manifested in a hierarchy of plans which, when they are interpreted at store level, are more related to the physical performance requirements of resources than they are to financial performance. Typically a store manager is expected to achieve a desired level of performance by ensuring that physical stock and space deployment plans are adhered to and that staff levels are maintained within the labour scheduling plan derived by operations management. This suggests two dimensions of performance measurements:

- strategic/operational; and
- financial/physical.

These two dimensions can be represented in the form of a matrix (see Figure 2.17). In broad terms the matrix represents the type of performance measures which are to be expected. The remainder of this chapter will discuss measures that may appear in each cell. Two comments should be made at this point. The first concerns the overlap that will occur between both categories. The greatest overlap is likely to occur between financial and physical performance measurement at the operational level and to a lesser degree at the strategic level. Overlap between strategic and operational levels is less likely: strategic performance is about aggregate resources and consequently the data will reflect this and is more likely to be represented as financial data.

The second comment concerns the units of measurement to be supplied at the strategic and operational levels. At the strategic level, profitability should be a measure that reflects the earning activities of the business. There are numerous views on which items should be included (and which omitted) to ascertain a value profit calculation. Holmes and Sugden (1993) suggest *trading profit* as a primary measure: trading profit being turnover less cost of sales (materials, labour, production costs and depreciation), distribution costs and administrative expenses (which include a number of head office expense items). It does not include income from other sources, or interest received, nor does it include amounts written off previous investments or interest payable.

We would prefer to use the following description of operating profit and of strategic profit.

Cash Flow and Productivity Issues

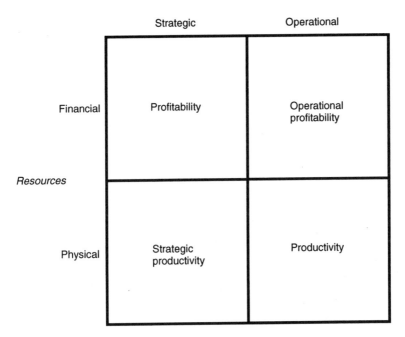

Figure 2.17   Productivity/Profitability performance measurement

Operating profit

	Sales
less	Costs of goods sold (purchases)
equals	Gross profit
less	Store operations staff costs and associated expenses
	Store occupancy costs; rental charges, utilities, etc.
	Distribution costs
	Direct services (e.g. systems)
	Depreciation (applicable to operations, e.g. stores and distribution)
equals	Operating profit

Strategic profit

Operating profit

plus   income from undertakings associated with the business (for example, from manufacturing and processing)

less	Interest payable
less	Depreciation (outstanding)
equals	Strategic profit.

Some explanations are required. The first point to be made concerns the availability of data. It should be remembered that we are concerned with the individual company's performance, not (at this stage) with a sector comparison. It follows that our concern is directly with the performance of the business at operational and strategic levels of accountability and responsibility; hence our interest is in the performance achievements at those management/internal accounting sources.

A second point concerns the charging process for distribution, direct services and depreciation. Here we would argue that where we are concerned with measuring operating performance only those costs directly involved in managing operations should be included. Clearly the methods by which these charges may be applied are important, and will be discussed in a subsequent chapter.

In reaching a measure of strategic profit we are suggesting that at this level of decision-making we are concerned that the financial implications of such decisions are included. It follows, for example, that the decisions to introduce debt into the capital structure, and the resulting interest charges this will involve, should be included in the calculation of strategic performance. A similar argument is made when income from undertakings associated with the business is considered. For example, revenue and profit earned from a food production/processing activity which is considered as a separate activity (and has not previously been included, that is, creating double counting) should also be included.

Having proposed suitable measures for both strategic and operational profitability, we are now concerned with productivity measures – dealing first with operational productivity. Figure 2.17 suggests that operational productivity should be measured by using physical resources as a base. Thus we are looking for measurements that will indicate the productive use of space (square or linear feet), employees (to be expressed as full-time equivalents) and stockholding (the sterling value). It is common practice to measure productivity within retailing by measuring sales generated by units of physical resource. For this reason we shall consider operational productivity to be a measure of the sales produced by unit values of physical resources.

Cash Flow and Productivity Issues

There is another reason for using sales in the measurement of operational performance, and this is customer productivity. Customer productivity is not easily measured. However, the increasing sophistication of information technology, together with its decreasing costs, is now making this possible for many retailers. Among the performance measures to be included are:

- purchasing visits/ browsing visits
- average transaction per visit
- items purchased
- range of purchases
- customer loyalty (repeat buying visits).

Productivity and profitability should be measured throughout the business. This concerns both activities and levels. Figure 2.18 suggests how interest in operational and strategic performance may be viewed. At an operational level the focus is primarily on physical resource efficiency. At this level of management (branch and field management) the performance emphasis is on the effective use of resources: resource input prices (labour rates, rents, and so on) are typically negotiated centrally and not by local managers, hence the focus is on the productive use of space, employees and stockholding. The interest of senior managers in operational productivity can be monitored by measuring operating profit (branch contribution) and expressing this across the resources used.

Strategic performance concerns the productivity of financial components (that is, net assets: fixed assets and components of working capital) expressed as physical resource efficiency using sales as the output measure. Financial resource efficiency is the measure of profitability that interests the board. The measures used would be both operating and net profit performances compared with net assets and the components of capital employed (equity and debt).

The differences in the perspectives reflected by measuring sales and profit (productivity and profitability) is also based on the varying needs of management for information for productivity analysis. Earlier we suggested (from Gold) that at a strategic level (top management) broad financial management measures are often sufficient but at an operational level the focus is more on physical inputs and outputs: whereas the operational manager is concerned with obtaining a maximum level of responsibility, the perspective of top management differs. Here the concern is with effective combinations of resources as well as with specific unit productivity.

Performance measures

	Strategic			Operational	
Financial	$\dfrac{\text{Sales}}{\text{Net assets}}$	$\dfrac{\text{Net profit}}{\text{Net assets}}$	$\dfrac{\text{Operating profit}}{\text{Net assets}}$	$\dfrac{\text{Operating profit}}{\text{Sales}}$	(Return on sales: ROS)
	$\dfrac{\text{Sales}}{\text{Capital employed}}$	$\dfrac{\text{Net profit}}{\text{Capital employed}}$	$\dfrac{\text{Operating profit}}{\text{Capital employed}}$	$\dfrac{\text{Operating profit}}{\text{Branch Assets}}$	
	$\dfrac{\text{Sales}}{\text{Equity}}$	$\dfrac{\text{Net profit}}{\text{Equity}}$	$\dfrac{\text{Operating profit}}{\text{Equity}}$	$\dfrac{\text{Operating profit}}{\text{Space}}$	
	Financial + Operational gearing Liquidity + Cashflow Dividend payout/retentions Net asset value Market capitalisation			$\dfrac{\text{Operating profit}}{\text{Staff}}$ $\dfrac{\text{Operating profit}}{\text{Stockholding}}$	
Resources / Physical	$\dfrac{\text{Sales}}{\text{Net trading assets}}$		$\dfrac{\text{Net/operating profit}}{\text{Core business assets}}$	$\dfrac{\text{Sales}}{\text{Branch assets}}$ $\dfrac{\text{Sales}}{\text{Space}}$ and	$\dfrac{\text{Occupancy costs}}{\text{Space}}$ (%)
				$\dfrac{\text{Sales}}{\text{Staff}}$ and	$\dfrac{\text{Staff costs}}{\text{Sales}}$ (%)
	$\dfrac{\text{Sales}}{\text{Region/format type, merchandise groups}}$		$\dfrac{\text{Net/operating profit}}{\text{Region/format type, merchandise groups}}$	$\dfrac{\text{Sales}}{\text{Stockholding}}$ and	$\dfrac{\text{Stockholding costs}}{\text{Sales}}$ (%)
				Activity costs (e.g. distribution) $\dfrac{\text{Costs}}{\text{Sales}}$ (%)	

Figure 2.18   Productivity/Profitability performance measures

Hence we might expect senior management to be concerned with alternatives. For example, their concern should be with alternative formats and the sales and profit performance potential of other means by which the business might deliver its offer. Concern at this level also focuses upon behavioural issues: so management and employee motivation and incentives are often based on sales performance levels. Furthermore, the confidential nature of profit performance is often a reason for not making it widely available. Finally the nature of its calculation may also be 'at contention' through: market-based rents, distribution and overhead charges. Thus, for a number of reasons, sales/productivity measures may be preferable to profitability/input measures at an operational level.

For planning purposes, however, profitability at a unit level clearly is essential. The model which will be discussed in a later chapter demonstrates how format and environment decisions may be considered using variations of inputs. Thus it is important to be able to view the sales and profit outputs of alternative input configurations, such as different merchandise, service and store environment components. There is also the overriding issue concerning customer expectations: it is essential that the impact of changes in customer expectations on input costs be explored. Similarly changes in input structures, aimed at increasing productivity and profitability, should only be considered after having first examined the qualitative marketing issues and implications.

CORPORATE EXPECTATIONS

The purpose of this text is to explore productivity and profitability in treating businesses and our focus will be on corporate performance measures in the context of these two topics. We suggest that *productivity is measured by the sales produced by resource inputs*. This is a useful measure and is often used by retailers as a means of identifying basic performance data, for example, physical sales per employee or per square foot of selling area; stock turns (sales/inventory holding). We also suggest that *profitability* is in fact *operating* profit – that is, profit generated by retailing activities, by the business and *not* including profit contributed by sources or activities external to the business, such as returns from interests in non-related businesses.

Another aspect of performance measurement (identified earlier) concerns the management level at which decisions are taken and therefore the perspective (and responsibility) of the decision-makers. It follows that performance measurement should consider the level of the activity (that is, is it strategic and/or operational), the resources (physical and/or financial) and the nature of the decisions (controlling performance at unit or outlet level or planning future development – sales or operating profit).

The difference between operational and strategic measurements reflects a number of issues. First, the level of aggregation is important: senior management requires a company and regional view against which individual stores may be compared. Secondly the two levels reflect accountability and responsibility: the difference should reflect the levels of managerial responsibility – operational levels may be set for regional and store level reporting. Thirdly, for the reasons suggested by Eilon, management at a senior level is concerned with competitive comparison and planning decisions as well as tactical control purposes.

SUMMARY

This chapter has reviewed issues concerning cashflow and profitability and the importance of managing the activities of the business to ensure that opportunities to optimise both are an integral part of management's tasks. The work of the Boston consulting group (in the 1970s) was reviewed and the growth/share, growth/gain matrices, together with frontier curves, were used to demonstrate how cashflow and profit generation might be linked with productivity and profitability management.

Other concepts introduced included the structure–conduct–performance (SCP) approach favoured by industrial economists. It is interesting to find that their approach does make a distinction between productivity and profitability. We shall return to this model in the next chapter.

The extensive work of Eilon *et al.* was considered briefly, and of particular use to us was the discussion concerning managerial issues and methods used to measure productivity and profitability. Through Eilon we introduced the strategic profit model, which we plan to use as the basis for a detailed model capable of measuring productivity and profitability (and for identifying options) at operational and strategic levels of decision-making.

3 Profitability and Productivity: Decision Areas

INTRODUCTION

Before we consider decision-making in detail we do need to consider a framework within which we can assess the effectiveness of the decisions made within the business. Fitzgerald *et al.* (1991) made a major contribution to the area of performance measurement in service businesses. They offered a controlling framework for service businesses which includes both quantitative and qualitative measures. They argue that many businesses offer a product which is

> intangible ... it is difficult to measure performance: 'hard' measures such as profitability tend to drive out 'soft' measures like customer satisfaction, even though the intangible aspects of services may be important sources of competitive advantage. Monitoring the amount spent on them and their efficiency and effectiveness may be vital to competitive success.

It is for this very reason that we included 'customer productivity'. The authors make the point, as have many other authors from a range of management disciplines, that performance measurement often focuses on narrowly or easily quantifiable aspects such as costs and productivity, profitability and cash flow. While these topics have obvious importance, other quantitative criteria which have equal or possibly greater impact upon competitive advantage and success are ignored or perhaps they are omitted because of perceived difficulty in their measurement.

Fitzgerald *et al.* suggest what they describe as six generic performance dimensions:

- competitive performance (market share, segment share, growth);
- financial performance (profitability, liquidity, capital structure, market ratios);

- quality of service (reliability, response, availability, access, and so on);
- flexibility (volume flexibility, delivery, flexibility, variable specifications);
- resource utilisation (productivity, efficiency);
- innovation (performance of the innovation process and its outputs).

These are classified into two categories. Competitive and financial performance are measures of the *success* of the factors that *determine* competitive success: 'means' or 'determinants'. This structure they suggest, may be able to 'make visible the "trade-offs" between short-term financial return and long-term competitive position, or between resource utilisation and service quality'. It is a very useful approach and will be used in the development of our own.

DECISION-MAKING IN RETAILING: A FRAMEWORK

The decision-making process clearly varies from company to company. There are differences in sourcing, distribution and operational, retailing (delivery) processes. This is understood and our discussion shall consider these issues: we shall identify common factors and discuss differences in other areas.

Decisions are likely to be either strategic or operational – consequently there are issues to be considered concerning the interpretation of performance intentions at both levels.

This chapter establishes a framework within which the areas that have an influence on organisational performance are identified and described. In addition the chapter will consider the range of operational and strategic decisions typically made by retailing organisations.

If we accept that operational decisions occur during the implementation of strategic decisions, the need for an information link which communicates and instructs is clearly necessary. Also necessary is the facility to consider alternatives, Fitzgerald *et al.* offer this in their range of performance measures. We suggest that some formal method of doing this should be built into the productivity–performance–profitability model. A possible approach is to consider the process of analysis used by the industrial economist, *Structure–Conduct–Performance* (see Figure 3.1). If we add to this process some assumptions concerning the influence of structure on conduct together with an explicit input from consumer expectations, the model offers a useful format. One further addition is necessary to compete effectively in the market place and this concerns the *critical success factors* (CSFs).

In very brief terms critical success factors are those characteristics with which consumers identify. For example, in the personal computer segment of the data management market there are a number of critical success factors. These include:

- a rapid response service organisation;
- a 'user-help/advice' service, free and easily accessed;
- 'interchangeability' with leading formats.

Without such features it is hardly likely that a PC manufacturer will be able to penetrate distribution or user markets; hence they become critical success factors! Figure 3.1 offers a framework against which decisions may be made.

In Figure 3.1 competitive activities and consumer expectations result in the industry's decisions (not necessary collectively) which result in the characteristics identified. Each of these can be attributed to a view of the opportunities (and threats) confronting the industry as a group of companies. Consumer expectations are likely to lead to *decisions* concerning the degree of differentiation and extent of diversification that the sector settles upon. Typically it results in segmentation and invariably there emerge major companies with offers based upon price, quality and service. In addition there are likely to be a number of niche operators offering product, market or customised specialisms. This activity results in a definable market which develops clear critical success factors for each discernible segment.

Sector conduct is the resulting corporate responses to the alternatives that have been derived. The individual companies match their strengths and weaknesses with the critical success factors as well as with the opportunities and threats. The result for each competitor is a statement of both objectives and strategic direction aimed at addressing the selected alternative.

The resulting performance of sector profitability, growth and productivity is an aggregation of the individual performance achievements. To the list that was proposed by Davies we should add *positioning*. Positioning is a consumer perception based upon the marketing activities of a business. If the positioning is strong, it suggests success on the part of the company in persuading the consumer to visualise the company and its 'offer' precisely (or as clearly) as was intended. In this context positioning is clearly an activity to be measured. Within the coverage of

82 *Exploring Concepts and Models*

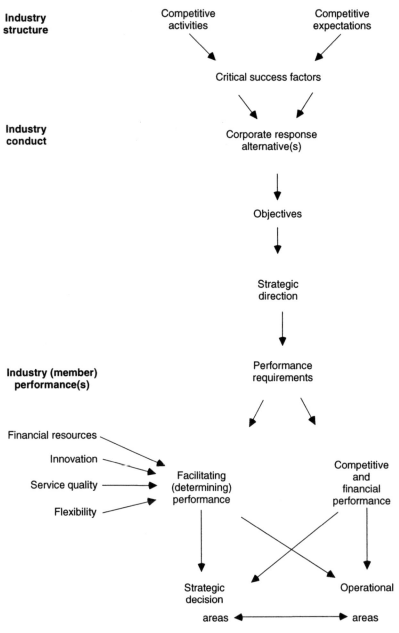

Figure 3.1 Performance-related decision-making to achieve productivity and profitability

performance, profitability and productivity should be measured to ensure that the resources consumed have resulted in levels of performance that were planned and furthermore that the long-term (strategic) and short-term uses of resources have resulted in performance outcomes that reflect the company's intentions. Similarly the intended levels of customer performance should be monitored.

THE NATURE OF RETAILING DECISION: FACILITATING DECISION AREAS

Retailing, just like any other business organisation, operates with specific objectives which relate to the need to generate satisfactory returns to its stakeholders. Therefore as well as earning satisfactory returns for the shareholders the activities must also provide a satisfactory performance to ensure customer satisfaction, adequate remuneration for management, continuity of employment for staff, continuity of business with suppliers and profit and revenue increases which encourage favourable reporting from investment analysts.

Financial resources and structure

A starting point for analysing the range of decisions made by retailing is a basic financial model of the business. Figure 3.2 represents a number of decision that retailing businesses are required to make. The model shows the primary requirement of the business: to achieve a determined 'return on investment' (as Figure 3.2 suggests, this may be measured in a number of ways). There are a number of points at which decision-making is important in the model.

- **Marketing and buying decisions**: here the interest is on sales generation activities and buying and merchandising, both of which are of primary importance to the success of the business. Successful sales and gross margin management occur as a result of effective marketing research and subsequent implementation of findings based upon the research. Thus we are looking at accurate forecasting of segment potential and accurate positioning, such that the customer identifies with the positioning statement and responds in terms of sales (and repeat sales) behaviour.
- **Operating decisions** areas are also significant for decision-makers. Store operations management is responsible for implementing mer-

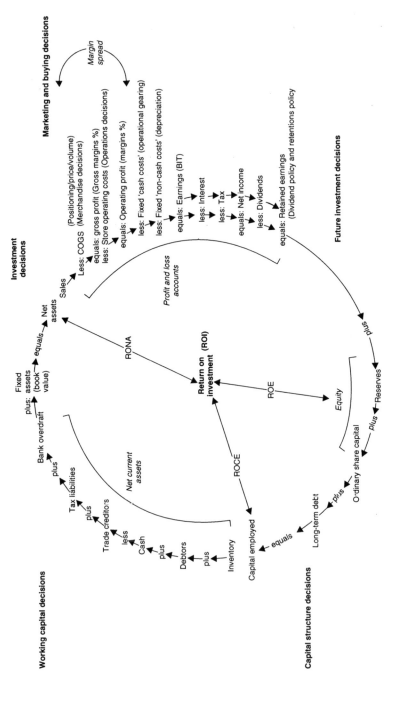

Figure 3.2 A model of the business indicating decision influence areas

chandise, customer service and store environment strategy decisions. It does so by the effective management of space, staff and inventory. This task requires store operations to manage a budgeted level of resources (inputs) in order that the 'offer' (outputs) made to the customers (availability, choice, waiting-time, effective and informative displays, and so on) achieve planned levels.
- **Margin spread** the effectiveness of both marketing and buying efficiency and of operating efficiency is reflected in the size of the margin spread.

These three measures are fundamental to the success of the business because they must be sufficiently large to be able to cover the expenses of running the business and providing a satisfactory level of profitability to the shareholders.

- **Operational gearing** is a measure of the effectiveness of the flexibility of the business. Operational gearing measures the relationship of fixed costs to the total costs of the business. The higher the fixed costs of a business the greater its vulnerability to changes in levels of turnover:

$$\frac{\text{Fixed costs}}{\text{Total costs}} \text{ or } \frac{\text{Profit (BIT)}}{\text{Profit (BIT)} + \text{Fixed costs}} = \text{Operational gearing}$$

Clearly the higher the proportion of fixed costs, the greater is the impact of fluctuations in profit. Although this is an advantage as sales increase, it is not so when revenue decreases. As sales decline the rate of decrease in profitability is much greater for companies with high operational gearing than for competitors with lower levels: thus it follows that the highly geared company has less flexibility for competitive response by lowering prices or increasing promotional expenditure.

Thus far we have discussed operational decisions – however, it could be argued that the structure of the operating costs is in essence a strategic decision. Clearly, there is an overlap in the decision-making process and this is likely (if not almost certainly) to differ across a range of companies, reflecting the nature of the individual businesses and their managements' perceptions (and acceptance) of risk. We move on to consider decisions in a *strategic* context.

- **The retention of profit decision** is one indication of the board's view of investment potential and how it considers investment should be funded. It is also important from the shareholders' viewpoint, as the dividends policy is closely related to this decision. By using retained earnings for expansion the business is usually doing so, at the lowest cost of capital. Clearly if it could obtain funds at a lower rate of interest elsewhere it should do so, having first considered the impact of debt upon the business. This leads us into:

- **Capital structure decisions**, a strategic decision area. Financial management will decide, having considered the proposed strategic direction, how best to fund the programme in order that the resulting capital structure will maximise performance. For example, it must be decided whether the level of financial gearing (the relationship between debt and equity funding) could (and should) be increased. The implications of increasing the debt content are that, because the interest payments are deducted before tax is paid, the profitability of the business will be increased. Clearly this can be considered to be an efficiency issue.
- **Working capital decisions** can be considered as an efficiency issue. For retailers the impact of inventory holding costs is a significant issue. For many, such as food multiples, there is the opportunity to use suppliers' working capital in the business: many of the product categories incorporated in merchandise assortments have a very high rate of sale ('perishables', such as bread and milk) such that any one order batch from a supplier will have been sold (and indeed replenished) well before payment to the supplier is due. It follows that the retailer may well be able to fund many of its business activities on lower levels of working capital. The opportunity for this is greater for organisations with assortments that are predominantly convenience goods rather than durables. The point is that efficient planning and operations can lower the overall level of working capital in the business, some of which may be funded by overdraft.
- Finally, we consider **investment decisions**. There are two basic issues: one concerns the efficiency of the investment, the other concerns how funds may be acquired. The efficiency of the investment considers the deployment of resource into long-term applications. It follows that the company should investigate returns and risks associated with the intended investment. Many retailing organisations continue to invest in off-centre superstore facilities in areas in which the coverage by such outlets is becoming critical in terms of saturation. In such situations, the risk levels are important. However, the decision is influenced by other factors, such as the incremental increases

in volume and gross margin (and hence on the margin spread) as often the expansion is not accompanied by a proportional increase in fixed costs. The method of acquisition is important (and overlaps with capital structure decisions). Often, leasing is popular, as this not only lowers long-term risks but also releases capital for use elsewhere in the business. It is becoming common practice for retailing organisation to restrict investment to core areas of their business, often leasing assets for other activities or even 'buying-in' non-core functions (such as distribution and, more recently, information management).

PERFORMANCE FACILITATING FACTORS

There are other facilitating considerations to be made. Fitzgerald *et al.* (1991) suggest *innovation* to be one of these factors. They also suggest other areas: *quality of service*, *flexibility* and *resource allocation*. We would prefer to consider resource allocation as part of the productivity–profitability performance model: resources are considered to be primary inputs, basic issues in decision. Here we consider innovation, quality of service and flexibility.

Innovation

Innovation, clearly, can be seen as a facilitating or determining influence. In this context we are considering decisions to develop and introduce either new product or new services; develop new applications; to improve the attributes of existing product services (so that they are clearly superior to those of competitive offers); or to develop new 'format' or delivery systems. Figure 3.3 displays these factors.

- **New 'format' or delivery systems** are important if changes in customer life styles and expectations are to be recognised. The growth of companies such as Racing Green, Landsend and the catalogue offers of 'institutions' such as the Victoria and Albert Museum are examples of recognition of the shifts in consumer time budgeting.
- **New product or service** offers reflect similar concerns but do so by positioning adjustments to the product or service applications. The recognition of increasing interest in outdoor and activity-based leisure has led to changes to apparel ranges by both manufacturers

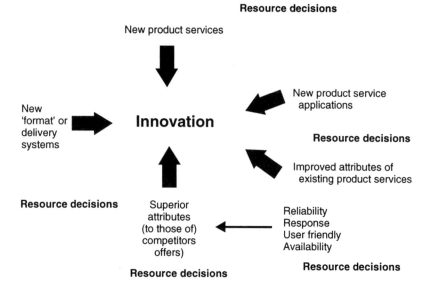

Figure 3.3   The role of innovation in determining performance

and retailers; for example, the Marks & Spencer's clothing offer has expanded its activity leisure content significantly.

- **Improving the attributes of the existing product or service offer** is possibly considered to be a competitive necessity. However, it may be argued that proactive changes that are reflections of researched changes in consumer behaviour and which are *likely to result* in changes in expectations may be seen as innovatory. For example, the notion of user-friendly products was not generally applied until the computer manufacturers developed the personal computer market, where upon 'user friendliness' became a product-market critical success factor. The concept is now widely applied to a much wider range of products and services and has influenced consumer expectations in this respect.
- The development of competitive advantage through focusing upon overall **superiority of product or service attributes** has been a policy of a number of retailing companies for some time. The impact, in terms of success in customer response, is very clear: companies such as Marks & Spencer, Sainsbury, the John Lewis Partnership, Country Casuals, have demonstrated that 'selective superiority', such as quality, style, exclusivity, built into the product-service offer has clear benefits to both company and customer.

Quality of service

Fitzgerald *et al.* (1990) deal with both the product–service and service–product aspects of service quality. They comment on the difficulties inherent in measuring service quality, but comment on the necessity to do so in a competitive market.
They define service quality as

> the quality of the entire service package: the goods – the tangible, physical objects that are used within the service system or removed from it by the customer; the environment where the service takes place; the service provided, that is the treatment of the customer or the 'things' belonging to the customer.

The quality issues or decision areas for retailing companies are discussed within the framework offered by Figure 3.4.

- **Ambience/aesthetics decisions** contribute towards perceptions of the company that may be created and communicated to customers to support other elements of the 'offer'.
- The level of **availability** of staff and facilities can have a major influence on quality delivery. High levels of availability of both aspects are expected in service-led businesses.
- **Communication/information** quality is reflected in the effectiveness of the information transmitted to customers; persuasion and information are both possible in well-designed programmes. The speed and detail of response to customer queries and complaints is typically used by customers as a measure of both the sincerity and the quality of the activity.
- **Responsiveness** may be seen as an all-embracing characteristic. However, for retailing the issue is speed of response to orders, deliveries and enquiries (order progressing). Speed of transactions (waiting time at transactions points) is a very important feature.
- **Staff–customer relationships** is an issue requiring decisions concerning staff recruitment and training; customers have been found to be very sensitive in this area and there is a specific need for management to be aware of how vital it can be for overall business. The well-documented SAS case study demonstrates how important the role of staff–customer contact can be in service-based businesses.
- **Access**, through effective store signs and layout designs which direct customers towards merchandise regularly purchased, but which still

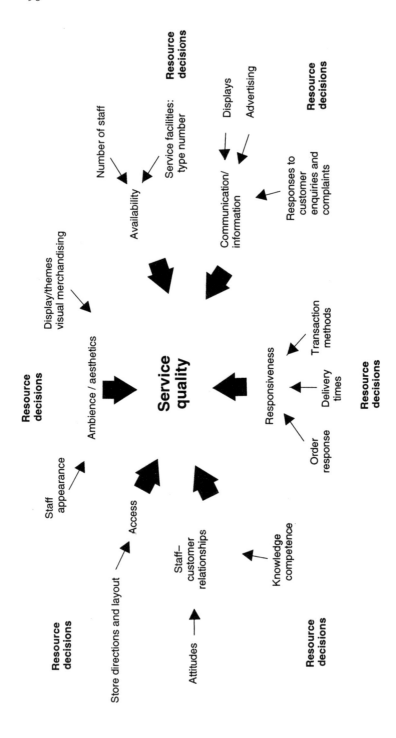

Figure 3.4 The components of service quality

expose not necessarily the entire assortment but relevant merchandise, should be the aim of management. The use of effective price ticketing together with information helpful to customer selection emphasises the quality of an offer.

Flexibility

There are three aspects of flexibility suggested to be important determinants of customer satisfaction. It will be seen from Figure 3.5 that overlap does exist in some areas. Furthermore, it is clear that some of the elements are difficult to implement for retailing businesses.

Retailing, unlike many other service activities, is very visible, thus part of its offer is not easily differentiated: to do so would cause difficulties in self-service stores together with (probably) disproportionate levels of cost increases.

- **Specification flexibility** is often only feasible for stores with a very large service content which may be adjusted, based upon customer expenditure and loyalty factors. Typically a merchandise offer is

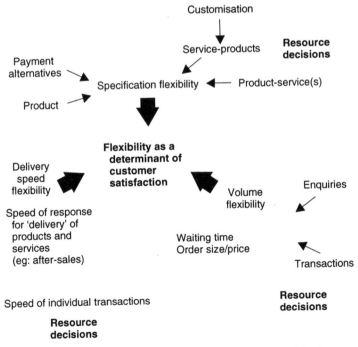

Figure 3.5 The components of flexibility/customer satisfaction

standard – unless of course the product may be offered either made to order (customised) or perhaps, as with flat pack furniture, across a range of options: such as cash and carry, delivered or delivered and assembled. Payment options may be considered here: store groups such as John Lewis Partnership offer customers a range of optional payment methods.

- **Volume flexibility** relates to an organisation's ability to respond to variations in the volume of customer transactions and enquiries. The willingness to relate price to volumes purchased by constructing a price schedule readily available for customers is another aspect of volume flexibility. Often, apparel retailers relate time and price, by setting 'sell-through' targets for merchandise which will predetermine discount/time structures to ensure that sales volume targets are reached at optimum margins.
- **Delivery speed flexibility** concerns the effectiveness of the delivery process of both products and services (particularly after-sales service). Effective flexibility may reflect customer segmentation, based upon volume, loyalty (frequency or size of period spend) or some other criteria. This feature may also be a measure of the speed with which transactions are effected (not waiting time) and is a function of capital investment, that is EPOS systems.

The factors discussed so far are decisions which contribute **towards** the competitive success of the organisation. We shall return to these topics in some detail in subsequent chapters. When issues concerning resource allocation and resource performance expectations are considered.

THE NATURE OF RETAILING DECISIONS: PERFORMANCE DETERMINATION AREAS

Fitzgerald *et al.* suggested that competitive (and financial) performance 'reflect the success of the chosen strategy: "ends" or "results"'. They suggest that competitive performance is reflected by market share and position, sales growth and measures of the customer base. Their proposals for measurements and mechanisms for measuring competitiveness reflect the difficulties in this area for retailing businesses.

Their study proposals for 'mass service' companies (a newsagent chain) were:

- **Measures**

Customer-focused	Number of customers
Competitor-focused	Competitors' prices and product ranges

- **Mechanisms**

Customer-focused	Customer survey
Competitor-focused	Competitor surveys

Although this is a useful initial approach, it is not sufficiently detailed. We would suggest that a more detailed approach would consider macro and micro measurements. The decisions required in the context of performance determination concern market issues but can only be set in the reality of the collection of appropriate data.

The estimate of retail market dimensions is notoriously difficult, such that the value of size and share estimates is doubtful, particularly when considering their use for planning and control purposes. An example of the difficulties posed can be seen in the apparel market, which is very large and within which there are numerous segments: this characteristic is a problem for quite large companies who, if their market share could be measured accurately, would find it to be very small in an overall context. Furthermore, they would have additional difficulties in attempting to measure segment shares because, while these maybe clearly definable, the competitors within them may have offers in other sectors of the market; unless there is access to disaggregated data it follows that accurate estimates of directly competitive sales volumes is not possible.

These problems suggest that alternatives should be sought, and these are proposed to be:

- customer-based measures;
- sales responses perceptions;
- catchment-based measures (profit);
- overall sales (profit)/increases;
- merchandise group sales (profit)/increases.

If performance measures such as these are to be adopted, a number of decision areas should be considered; these are identified for *competitiveness* in Figure 3.6. If a retail business is to be effective in competing with other major organisations within a market segment or sector, there are a number of decision areas to be considered. Essentially, we are

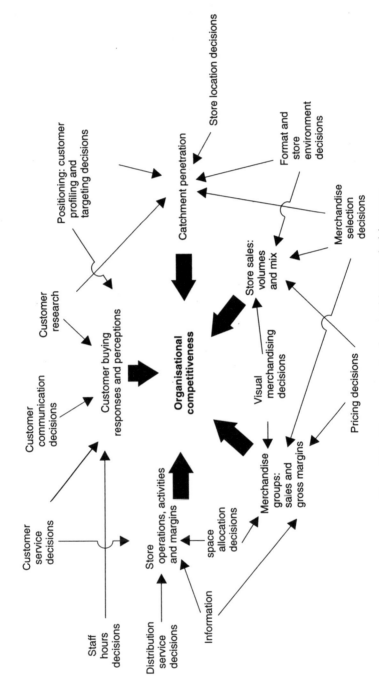

Figure 3.6 The components of competitiveness: decision areas

concerned with customer response, effective market penetration and growth of sales and profits. These are achieved by accurate customer identification followed by a clear offer or positioning (merchandise, store environment, customer service and communications), which is implemented efficiently (the store operations activity). These topics are featured in Figure 3.6.

- If the firm has achieved a high level of **buyers' response and positive customer perceptions** the first requirement is comprehensive customer research which identifies both current and future needs and measures the effectiveness of its response (the 'offer' made to the target customer). An important decision is the nature and level of customer communications which will initially identify for the customer the offer being made.
- **Catchment penetration** will be an extremely important component for success. Customer research, the positioning/targeting decisions and effective store location decisions will play a major role, as will relevant format and store environment decisions (which are an integral component in the positioning activity).
- Store format and environment will also have an important influence on achieving **store sales volumes and sales mix objectives**, but there are other important features, such as decisions on merchandise selection, pricing and visual merchandising and these can be seen to have an important influence on:
- **Merchandise group sales and gross margins**.
- **Store operations activities and operating margins** are influenced by space allocation and information usage decisions. In addition successful performance by the store operations function will be very largely influenced by distribution service decisions, staff scheduling and the extent and intensity of customer service decisions. The importance of operating margins and gross margins (margin spread) was discussed earlier and we shall focus upon both in detail in later chapters.

Financial performance

Accounting ratios have been used for analysing company performance for some time. The work by DuPont establishing ratios for planning and control purposes is well documented, as are their imitations. However, provided care is taken to ensure consistency (that is, standardised policies) and 'real' values and that the comparisons are relevant to the levels of accountability and responsibility at the point of performance review, the use of ratios is very helpful. It is usual to compare a series of ratios such as profitability, liquidity, capital structure and investment ratios. However, not only will the information value of ratios vary by type of retailing organisation but the types of ratios themselves may vary; much depends upon the characteristics of the business under review.

We suggest six areas of financial performance analysis – again, the point is made that these are likely to vary across a sample of companies. It is also worth reminding the reader that the method of comparison requires careful consideration. Two types of analysis may be used. Horizontal analysis identifies year-on-year changes over time of key, specific, strategic, and operating factors. Vertical analysis, the comparison of similarly important factors with total revenue, monitors topics that have major influence because of their size in comparison with other account items. Trends should be monitored for both horizontal and vertical analyses. Figure 3.7 identifies the seven decision areas for which performance monitors are usually established.

- **Financial productivity** decisions determine the performance requirements for space, employees, stock, fixed over working capital. It will be shown later that the decisions should reflect the performance necessary by these resources if both marketing and financial objectives are to be met.
- **Liquidity** decisions set parameters for stockholding (and thereby inventory policy), cash holding and payment policies (for example, suppliers terms and settlement discounts).
- **Profitability** measures indicate both financial and marketing performance expectations: the importance of both gross and operating margins (through the margin spread) has been discussed earlier. The marketing implications are expressed through the influence of the positioning decisions that determine margin expectations. The returns for capital employed and equity are determined by shareholder expectations and the requirements for development funds.
- **Gearing** decisions will be influenced by management's view of both risk and return: it is necessary to balance both items when developing an expansion plan. Gearing also affects the cost of capital to the organisation and this is influenced by a view of the returns to the business from its activities and the risk involved.
- **Growth** decisions involve board directives for capital intensity, earnings retention rate and the rate or levels of re-investment of profit, generated by the activities of the business.

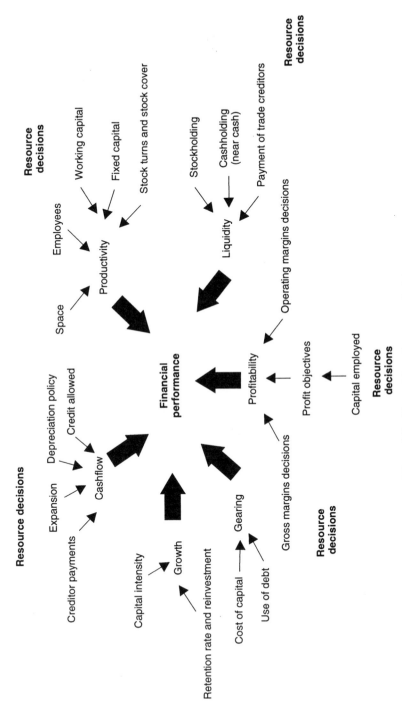

Figure 3.7 Financial performance: decision areas

- **Cash flow** is essential if the business is to pay short-term liabilities and for longer-term activities such as the purchase of fixed assets and acquisitions. Asset renewal, payments policies and credit policies are features of these decisions. Depreciation policy is an important input, as it is in the determination of profitability, and is included in the calculation of cashflow.

The ratios used in developing planning and control decisions will be discussed in the following Chapter 4.

OPERATIONAL AND STRATEGIC DECISIONS

Having reviewed the areas in which decisions are taken concerning performance, this final section identifies the operational and strategic decisions typically made by retailing organisations.

It is unlikely that operational decisions will be clearly separated from each other. Furthermore short-term and long-term trade-off situations often occupy much of the decision-making activity. Having identified the decision-making areas and activities which influence performance, the process itself can identify the issues confronting an organisation. For example, a simple situation may require a company's management to consider the short-term impact on profitability of committing additional resources to resolve a delivery speed flexibility problem such as 'increasing the speed of transactions at the point of sale'. The long-term (but intangible) benefits that may accrue from store loyalty encouraged by faster service may be an increase in customer transaction values and customer loyalty.

The other dimension of decision-making that is very important is the determination and subsequent implementation of strategic direction. As we identified in Figure 3.1, this is the major activity for any organisation and it is here that significant amounts of resources *are* committed to achieving objectives. This section identifies the major decision areas involved in this process.

There is a spectrum of decisions that are typically made by retailing managers. These will include operational and strategic decisions, as described by Figure 1.5 earlier. The structure of Figure 1.5 might suggest an incremental approach to decision-making. Clearly this is not likely for most businesses. More likely is the need for decision-making which responds to opportunities: these may be operational or strategic responses and are taken at all times within the planning cycle. Business

Profitability and Productivity: Decision Areas

dynamics do not occur at convenient times; rather they have a somewhat haphazard behaviour.

At this point we should revisit some of the topics covered in Chapter 1, specifically the sorts of decisions typically made in the context of productivity and profitability. Figure 1.5 suggests a three-dimensional approach to decisions. The reason for this is influenced by current management trends which favour the deployment of resources into core activities, be they operational or strategic in their influence on the business. There has been an increasing movement towards divesting activities, even subsidiary businesses, which consume resources that might otherwise be allocated to mainstream business activities – for example, Mothercare's recent (1993) decision to use an outside facility to manage information processing; for some time distribution has been outside company structures (but clearly controlled by agreed performance criteria). At a more strategic level of decision-making we have seen businesses divest subsidiary companies (for example, Sears moving out of menswear) to release capital and management resources for a more specialist focus on core activities (for example, Sears acquiring Richards). Similarly Storehouse has divested Habitat (now part of IKEA) to focus its resources on BhS and Mothercare. Figure 1.5 describes such approaches as *operational resource allocation and rationalisation* for decisions which result in a narrowing of the service/functional structure of the business. *Strategic resource allocation and rationalisation* describes decisions with longer-term implications.

The purpose of this section has been to identify and to introduce broad areas of operational and strategic decision-making. Subsequent chapters will extend the discussion into the process of the decision-making but will emphasise the performance criteria required for effective planning and control.

SUMMARY

This chapter has been concerned with the process by which decisions concerning resource allocation are approached and the nature of the decisions that are required. Two previous models were examined and modified during the early part of the chapter. The approach of the industrial economist on *structure–conduct–performance* was combined with that of Fitzgerald *et al.* and resulted in the model depicted by Figure 2.1 above.

Decision areas are considered to be either performance-determining (or facilitating) or decisions which ultimately measure performance results. Our model contains financial elements and considerations in both areas. The reason for this is explained by the fact that *any* decisions to utilise resources originate at the level of financial resource availability, consequently the basic financial 'model' of the organisation is an important element when capacities and capabilities are discussed. Other determining characteristics discussed were innovation, service quality and flexibility. Performance results decision areas were competitiveness and financial performance.

A similar treatment was afforded to the areas of operational and strategic decision-making. Here we discussed some of the options that confront organisations, but again we described these rather than prescribing decisions for particular situations.

Chapter 5 will begin to put structure into the decision-making process by first constructing an interactive model for both operational and strategic performance planning and control and considers the information inputs required to make it effective. Chapter 4 considers the details of margin spread and asset base management.

4 Managing the Margin Spread

INTRODUCTION

The concept of the margin spread was introduced in Chapter 2. It will be recalled that it was suggested there that the margin spread, the difference between the gross margin and the operating margin, was an important feature in performance management because it indicates how well the gross margin covers the operating costs of the business and contributes towards profit.

We have extended the usual definition of margin spread to include the overall margin generated once costs of goods sold and the operating expenses have been considered. The purpose of extending the scope of the margin spread is to consider the impact of increased sales revenues. The reason for this is that retail productivity and profit performance changes with changes in sales revenue. The impact of the changes will have cost implications for both gross margins and operating margins, consequently we should include the changes in sales (see Figure 4.1).

In this chapter we shall discuss the margin spread from the standpoint of performance improvement in two areas: the increase of sales volume and improvements to productivity and profitability. Both strategic and operational issues will be considered.

THE MARGIN SPREAD

Chapter 1 introduced the strategic profit model. The SPM involves identifying the return on net worth (shareholders' equity) by multiplying a company's profit margin by its rate of asset turnover over and its gearing ratio to derive this performance measure. It will be recalled that the components of the model are:

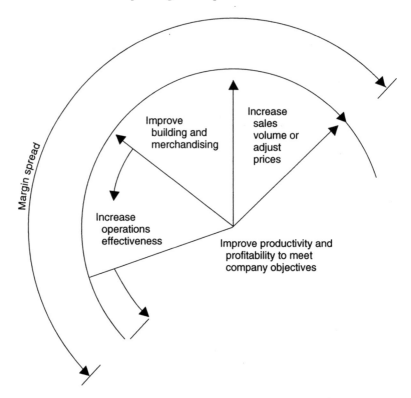

Figure 4.1 Components of the margin spread

Margin management

$$\left. \begin{array}{c} \dfrac{\text{Net profit (operating profit)}}{\text{Net sales}} \\ \dfrac{\text{Net sales}}{\text{Trading assets}} \end{array} \right\} = \underbrace{\dfrac{\text{Net profit}}{\text{Trading assets}}}_{\text{(return on assets)}} \times \dfrac{\text{Trading assets}}{\text{Net worth}} = \dfrac{\text{Net profit}}{\text{Net worth}}$$

Asset management   *Financial management*   *Return for shareholders' interests*

The profit margin measure (profit/sales) indicates management's ability to cover the costs of goods sold (merchandise), operating expenses, depreciation and interest charges *and* provide an acceptable level of return to the shareholders. The profit margin ratio is essentially a *measure of the cost/price effectiveness* of the organisation.

From Figure 4.1, it can be seen that gross margin and operating expenses are the key elements in the resultant profit margin of the organisation. Bates (1990) suggests that gross margin is possibly the most important factor affecting retail profits and that the exact impact of gross margin depends largely on the cost structure of the firm. In a competitive environment the essential challenge for retailers is to generate higher gross margins *without* price increases.

Bates (1990) suggested a number of ways in which this might be achieved. These can be expanded:

- more effective supply chain management – especially through merchandise/supplier rationalisation;
- improved mark-down control through improved merchandise selection and therefore 'sell-through';
- reduced shrinkage via inventory management systems and control;
- improving the merchandise mix by emphasising higher margin items, merchandise and service augmentation and visual merchandising;
- price adjustments; increases on 'monopoly or exclusive' items and others for which price insensitivity can be established;
- an increase in sales volume which is *not* accompanied by an equivalent increase in fixed costs.

Livingstone and Tigert (1987) have demonstrated that the spread between the gross margin ratio and the operating expense ratio has a major impact on return on investment for retailers. They also comment upon the fact that the increase of personnel to make customer service effective reduces operating margins. This explains (they suggest) why the distributive trades have frequently lagged behind manufacturers in productivity increases. However, a counter argument is that the effective use of information now enables retailers to be selective with their labour scheduling, and they may now be able to use customer service as means of both augmentation and differentiation and therefore increase both sales, productivity and profitability.

Though the resultant net profit indicates performance at a given level of sales, it is not an indication of the effectiveness of resource allocation. Therefore though profit performance when compared with sales volume may be acceptable, the sales generated may not be satisfactory when compared with net assets and working capital invested in the business. There is a requirement for management to consider stock turn and the turnover of accounts receivable. If sales have been increased by reducing prices and extending customer credit, the result may well be lower net profit.

Asset turnover (sales/assets) is a measure of the effectiveness of resource allocation in both fixed assets and in current assets. Industry performance will identify over-investment or under-investment in total assets by indicating typical (competitor) asset circulation performance.

The return on assets (profit/assets) ratio provides a more adequate measure of operating efficiency. It also illustrates how quite different businesses may generate much the same overall performance but do so by emphasising either margin management or asset productivity. This point is illustrated in Figure 4.2(a), which shows that the same return on assets (ROA) may be generated by two quite different businesses. In Figure 4.2(b) there has been an increase in ROA due to an increase in either margin or asset circulation performance.

COSTS

Gearing – assets/net worth (equity funds) – indicates the extent of the firms' dependence upon short-term and long-term funds for asset financing. A low ratio (high equity) suggests conservative management with a preference for low levels of risk but with a high degree of liquidity. Depending upon the gearing ratio, the firm has to a lesser or greater degree the opportunity of lowering the rate of interest at which it borrows – an essential feature of financial management.

Finally, the return on investment (or on net worth/equity funds) – that is, profit/net worth (equity) – demonstrates the return earned for the shareholders. A low ratio may indicate poor performance due to management, external conditions or excessive investment in assets. A high ratio may be the result of effective management, favourable business conditions or the effective use of debt financing.

It should also be remembered that firms do have some choice over operational gearing (that is, the relationship between fixed costs and variable costs). There may be a number of alternative ways by which a business may structure its assets, freehold or leasehold, sale and lease back, leasing vehicles rather than purchasing on financial packages etc. It follows that the margin management performance for one company may be lower than that for a competitor, reflecting the fact that assets are leased and lease charges are operating costs being deducted from the profit generated, rather than being regarded as an asset which would, consequently, be reflected in a high rate of asset circulation.

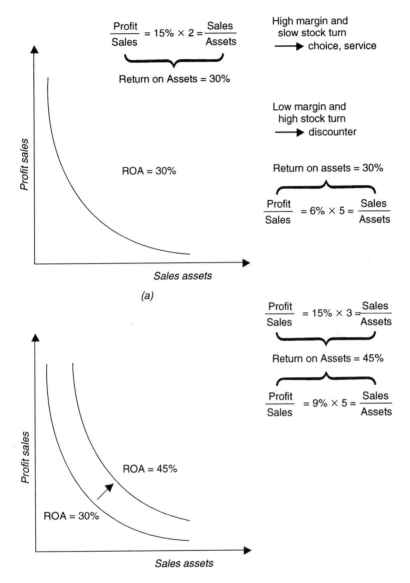

Figure 4.2 The relationship between margin management and asset management

For this reason the ROA concept is particularly useful when analysing comparative competitive performance. It identifies how the individual firm views its business. A company with lower margins/higher asset circulation may take the view that it only invests in its core business, preferring to keep fixed costs low, and thereby gaining flexibility.

As Lusch *et al.* (1992) suggest, the strategic profit model has four important features.

- It identifies the principal financial objective of the business as being to earn an adequate return for the shareholder.
- It offers three 'profit paths' to the firm: the return on equity funds may be improved either by increasing profit margin or by increasing the asset productivity (circulation) or by the planned use of debt.
- The model identifies the principal areas of decision-making and asset management and suggests that an integrated approach may well result in an improved overall performance.
- The model provides a means by which alternative strategies used by different organisations maybe compared.

To these we shall add a fifth feature:

- The model offers a facility to review customer expectations and preferences and to evaluate the likely impact on alternative decision options and on adjacent decision areas. As such, it enables managers to evaluate the effectiveness of alternative resource allocation options upon returns to the shareholder.

This latter feature is important because it identifies the resource elements involved in delivering customer satisfaction and their cost implications and, consequently, their impact on the margin spread.

IMPROVING MARGIN SPREAD PERFORMANCE

From the foregoing discussion it is clear that the margin spread should be planned if *optimal profitability* is to be achieved. We stress optional profitability because many of the decisions confronting managers require them to consider and to choose between short-term profitability and long-term growth as well as between resource combinations. Figure 4.3 illustrates the two decision areas which comprise effective margin spread management. The requirements are to manage the 'spread' to ensure that the company's objectives (both marketing and financial) are achieved: hence the issues concerning short-term profitability through adjustments which may impair long-term customer loyalty can be evaluated prior to implementation.

Managing the Margin Spread 107

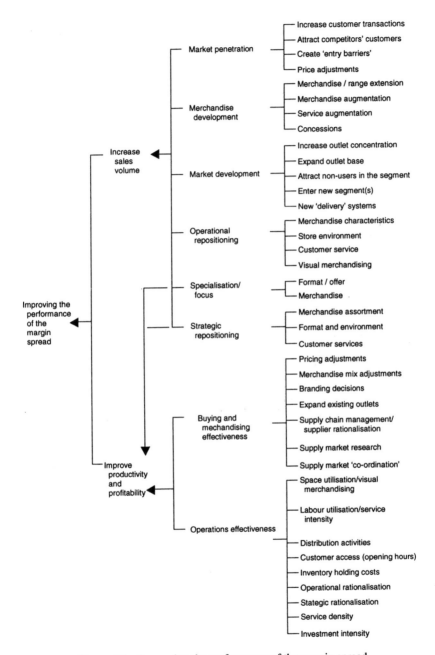

Figure 4.3 Improving the performance of the margin spread

The margin spread concept also permits evaluation between alternatives. As we shall demonstrate later, customer requirements and expectations may be evaluated using a model derived from the strategic profit model. However, to do so first requires evaluation of the implications of the alternatives for resource allocation and the impact on the margin spread.

There is a considerable range of options confronting decision-makers within the two component areas. A review of these maybe helpful with the use of Figure 4.3.

INCREASE OPERATIONAL SALES VOLUME

Market penetration

Market penetration is a low-risk option which comprises four alternatives. An *increase in transactions* with existing customers may have a significant impact on both market penetration and sales volume. This is often achieved by offering 'multi-buys' (Tesco) on a planned basis: high margin items are offered selectively and on a sequential basis to customers, the objective being to influence purchasing behaviour (that is, they *look* for the offers) and to increase their average transaction values.

Competitors' customers (provided the competitor operates in the same – or an adjacent – segment) may be attracted by suggesting and demonstrating a clear differentiation in these 'offer' attributes that are important in the store selection process. For example, a service-led business may choose to offer a very high level of customer service across a selected range of activities and areas to increase the value-added offer to customers.

Entry barriers may be created which will discourage competitive entry. The high level of advertising expenditure by the leading multiples in food, DIY and durables retailing would be difficult to match for potential market entrants. Similarly the capital expenditure on distribution infrastructure and retail outlets would require substantial investment if an effective entry was to be made.

Price adjustments across fast-moving core-range items may increase market penetration and profitability if done selectively. Care should be taken with the size of the price reduction to ensure that it is made to be effective within the price-elasticity sector of the demand curve. If price reductions are made at price levels below this range, neither the volume increases nor the margin requirements may result. Hence both productivity and profitability improvements will not materialise.

Merchandise development

Merchandise and range extensions may be used to increase sales volume by expanding the price, features or size variety of an existing merchandise offer. The 'leading prices' offered by many retailers are examples of this. The purpose is to make a credible, but limited, choice offer to customers with the view that they may be attracted to higher price, higher feature product versions. However, the purpose is twofold, in that it does extend the attraction of the business in a controlled manner: the direction of extension can be such as to position part of the range within a higher growth rate segment and enjoy the benefits of both margins and sales increases. There is also the consideration that extension decisions may be market-led in that they provide market credibility.

Merchandise augmentation is often used to differentiate the merchandise offer by selectively adding features that create value for the customer. At the same time, the objective should be to increase the revenue (and margins) earned by the item. Augmentation may be simple, such as the inclusion of batteries or accessories on durable products.

Service augmentation usually takes the form of features not typically offered (for example, remodelling services for apparel products) which may be applied selectively to high loyalty customers.

Concessions are often used by retailing businesses to extend both merchandise ranges and service activities. For many businesses, the attraction is the credibility that a concession offers (the full assortment offer) without the excessive costs of stockholding.

The decisions made concerning merchandise development have both long-term and short-term implications. In the long term, the issues to be considered are the viability of merchandise offers within the context of strategic positioning: the allocation of fixed capital support for new merchandise ranges (for example, service facilities) and the implications for long-term commitment of working capital (for example, stockholding, credit facilities) may have significant effects on capital requirements. There is also the impact on space allocation (and space performance) and on staffing levels to be taken into account. For these reasons a long-term view of the implications of change should be considered.

Market development

There are five areas to be considered. The first involves *increasing the current outlet concentration*, a low-risk option and one which may improve the productivity of the fixed asset infrastructure (assuming no unnecessary investment is required) and may improve gross margin performance due to the volume increases. This option may also improve the productivity of field management (human resources and promotional activities). Sales cannibalisation is a threat and should be considered carefully before commitment is made.

By *expanding the outlet base*, sales volume will be increased but the incremental benefits should be examined closely. In a fiercely competitive market area the initial costs of establishing a presence may be high in the short run and require a long-term view to be taken. In addition the long-term recovery of fixed asset investment should be appraised, with particular attention being paid to utilisation factors.

The attraction of non-users in the segment (or catchment) may be expensive. Often there are reasons why they are currently non-users and these should be investigated prior to making changes to the existing 'offer'. Not only may changes to the current retail offer be expensive (that is, the resources utilised may not produce an adequate 'return', due to the low level of response) but also the response from existing customers may be damaging. It should be remembered that the profitability and productivity of the business has been forecast and planned around the purchasing activities of existing customers and a decline in either their purchasing visit frequencies or average transactions would present major problems for performance achievement. It would require higher levels of purchasing visit frequencies and average transactions from new customers to compensate for losses due to the reduced levels of activity from existing customers. Clearly, the performance issues should be examined closely.

Sales volume increases achieved by *entering new segments* may require long-term investment in fixed and current assets. It follows that the profitability and productivity performances require a longer-term view and as such may force the business to consider opportunity cost issues. A similar view may be taken before investment into new *'delivery systems'*. However, here there may be a shorter lead time for performance returns. The option suggests that volume of existing merchandise may be increased by increasing the 'delivery' options for customers. This may be necessary as consumer habits change (for example, the growth of home shopping). Next Directory expanded the convenience aspect of shopping to high street customers when it made all of its merchandise ranges available through the catalogue *and* the stores. Clearly the utilisation of *all* of the assets must be considered – because unless the increased volume and margins compensate for the utilisation changes, their overall productivity will be reduced and it is likely that profitability will decline.

Operational repositioning

Operational repositioning is inevitable in a dynamic business environment: the issue is whether it can be achieved with an accompanying increase in capacity utilisation and profit improvement. There are four options.

A change in the *characteristics of the merchandise offer* to match changes in customer preferences, may be achieved without making major changes requiring extensive cost adjustments. Often these changes do incur cost increases for suppliers (for example, a shift of emphasis towards more fashion content may require a change in production methods), and consequently they may need assurance of long-term benefits.

Store environment changes do involve cost. Two aspects should be considered: cosmetic changes and efficiency changes. Cosmetic changes occur often because competitors update and improve store facilities and customers may respond to the improved environment and ambience either by their continued patronage or perhaps by increasing expenditures. Efficiency changes may result in improved productivity, either by increasing the speed of customer transaction handling (with existing numbers of staff) or possibly by increasing the productivity of the selling area following the redesign of the floor space. Again, the increased sales volume must be considered against the cost increases incurred.

A similar argument follows for *changes in customer services*. Here there may be a need to consider opportunity costs, either of space resources or staff. Recent developments in retailing suggest that customer service is an important feature in developing competitive advantage. Despite the impact of the 1989–93 recession there was little evidence of a reduction in the extent or range of customer services.

Visual merchandising has, as its primary objective, the increase of sales and margins. It follows that visual merchandising should be considered to be a management aid for developing both productivity and profitability. Provided that it is successful, the results of a well-designed and implemented programme should be: increased sales, improved gross margins and increased customer transactions. Any increases in operating expenses should be marginal and more than compensated for by the increase in sales and gross margin. In terms of the margin spread, the overall impact is for increases to occur due to the response by management to the shift in operational repositioning achieved by the changes made to visual merchandising.

Specialisation/focus

For a few merchandise areas there often appears an opportunity to develop a specialist activity which has the potential to 'stand alone'. Marks & Spencer and Boots offer examples of this. Boots have developed a specialist activity within the Sainsbury superstore format, suggesting that two non-competitive companies each having very strong individual positioning can benefit from the synergistic effect on costs (as well as revenues) that a joint venture such as this can offer.

The requirements are for the customer response to be sufficiently positive as to produce a frequency and level of transactions that is able to offer a wide enough margin spread to cover the fixed and variable costs. Clearly this occurs in the Boots and Marks & Spencer examples, where the merchandise is the same and the costs are limited to occupancy and staff, as they would be for any store expansion development. This suggests that specialisation requires a strong base from which to expand, which will probably be merchandise-led, but not necessarily so: the growth of direct response and mail order systems may provide an opportunity for specialisation to be operations or delivery-led. An example of this is Past Times, a company using a consumer interest in history, which has combined both store format and mail order as delivery systems. Within this combination Past Times has begun to expand its merchandise offer and is currently attempting to develop a specialist offer in garden and outdoor merchandise.

Strategic repositioning

Strategic repositioning, as with specialisation, has an overlap with productivity and profitability issues. Strategic repositioning suggests that for long-term success a major shift in the merchandise offer, store format and environment and/or customer services is necessary. A look back at the development of food and DIY retailing provides examples of how all three characteristics were developed as consumer interests and preferences changed over the years. Again, both sales and margins must provide strong cover for the success of such a move. This is particularly necessary if the venture is financed by capital from outside the business, this will add interest charges to the fixed costs and require additional cover from the margin spread.

An interesting (and successful) example is provided by Direct Insurance. Here the company detected a willingness by the customer to conduct their business by telephone, rather than through the traditional

Managing the Margin Spread

high street locations. The impact on costs had been demonstrated by the competitive pricing policy of the company. The success of this and similar strategic repositioning requires an understanding of current or future consumer preferences and the impact of these on the cost structures of a repositioned offer.

IMPROVE PRODUCTIVITY AND PROFITABILITY

The previous paragraphs have discussed ways in which the margin spread may be increased by expanding sales. In the remainder of this chapter we shall consider the impact of improved operating effectiveness throughout the business.

Buying and merchandising effectiveness

Pricing adjustments are obvious considerations. The requirement is for either a 'monopoly' or some form of exclusivity in a merchandise area which will reduce customer price comparison opportunities, or, an appeal to the price insensitive sector of a market segment. To be effective in generating margin increases, price adjustments should be made within the positive sector of the price-elasticity pricing area of a demand curve. Often monopoly/exclusivity may be engineered into an offer by combining both merchandise and service, thereby offering a strong value-added package through merchandise and/or service augmentation. A major influence is the ability to develop strong economies of scale or possibly economies of scope (a synergy effect) which increases the effect on margins and the overall margin spread.

Merchandise mix adjustments may also improve the margin spread. Figure 4.4 illustrates how, by seeking to differentiate the merchandise/service offer, gross margin may be increased. The impact can be more effective if the offer can be 'distanced' from the competition by offering exclusivity. Successful 'packages' may be vulnerable to competition, but examples such as Hamleys (the toy retailer) suggest that a 'unique' offer combining range, location and service is often difficult to emulate (and in Hamley's case to replicate). It is quite possible to use this approach in merchandise planning for standard ranges. For example, differentiation may be developed through an augmentation policy based upon price levels or perhaps brands.

Branding decisions, specifically retailer branding, is an obvious opportunity for margin expansion. This is particularly effective when

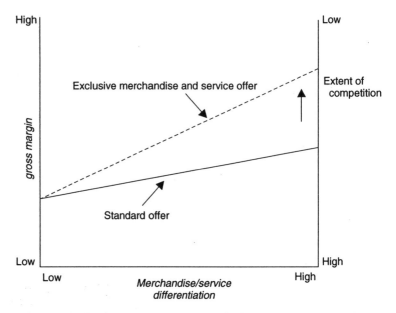

Figure 4.4 The impact on gross margin of differentiation and competition

combined with exclusivity, for example Harrods have been very successful in developing own-brand merchandise which has no obvious equivalent or has a positioning image as strong as a leading exclusive 'label'. However, this is not necessary, as the success of Marks & Spencer and Sainsbury have demonstrated. Strong corporate positioning for quality and reliability has enabled Marks & Spencer to build a successful range of financial services products.

The productivity and profitability implications of *expansion* have been discussed earlier. The sales volume resulting from such expansion activities (replication) is not required to cover those fixed costs already met. However, the impact of increased volumes on the costs of distribution and other support activities should be considered. In particular, the impact of future growth on fixed asset requirements should be part of the decision-making process.

Supply chain management (including *supplier rationalisation*) consists of activities within which scope often exists for improving margins. An evaluation of the stages in the added-value system can be used to direct the analysis. Clearly the potential for improved effectiveness is greater during the 'retailing' activity. It also follows that if resources are limited, the retailers may focus on the retailing activity and 'buy-in' the support activities. Supplier rationalisation often occurs when customer research identifies strong specific brand preference for one product rather than another. The cost savings are extensive throughout the supply chain.

Supply market research is increasingly important. The reason for this is the dynamic environment of the supply markets themselves. Recent political changes, particularly those in Eastern Europe, have exposed a range of skills and labour costs hitherto unavailable, or difficult to access. However, it has already been noticed that these are changing due to inflation and the economic factors accompanying the growth of their economies. For these reasons, a number of retailers, particularly apparel retailers, are planning supplier programmes whereby a sequence of likely supply location shifts will be programmed for two or three years. The plans are monitored by close reviews of key economic trends.

Co-ordination of supply markets is a well-established practice. Rather than make an equity involvement in production and physical distribution, larger multiple retailers will negotiate large production capacity contracts – thereby effectively controlling their suppliers. The benefits are obvious: capital intensity is minimised (if not eliminated) and the capital resource then deployed in the mainstream business. Hence 'vertical co-ordination' is more beneficial to the margin spread than is 'vertical integration' without the capital investment.

Operations effectiveness

The alternative route to improved productivity and profitability is to improve the return on resources invested in the operations of the business. This suggests that the investment intensity should be examined for efficiency: this involves examining the sales yield per unit of resource or questioning the costs of the resource commitment, by reviewing the level of investment intensity (the fixed and working capital) in the business. There are a number of issues.

Space utilisation and the role of visual merchandising in generating sales is an important operational feature. The costs involved include an apportionment of both the investment for development and the occupancy costs, which comprise rent, utilities and associated costs. Visual merchandising costs include dedicated management and staff and possibly materials (including stock for display purposes). A measure of the productivity of space utilisation is given by the sales density (sales generates per square foot) and the merchandise density (the stockholding costs per square foot). These and other direct costs, when deducted from the sales density provide an indication of the profitability of the space.

Labour utilisation may be measured in a similar manner – that is, the sales generated by each full-time (or equivalent) employee. In businesses with a large element of sales the *service intensity* may be measured; this identifies the proportion of service to selling personnel.

Distribution activities also measure operations effectiveness. Typically costs are measured as a percentage of sales, given a prescribed frequency or level of distribution activity. A supporting measure is the level of availability achieved by the stores (that is, the in-stock situation, measured by requests for replenishment services and by the physical and computer and IT checks).

Customer access is measured by hours open for sales. The effectiveness of the customer access is measured by the sales and operating profit achieved during the period when the store is open. Given an effective use of (EPOS) data, both the productivity (sales) and the profitability of each hour can be assessed for effectiveness.

Overall *inventory holding costs* should be examined from the total stockholding view. It is essential to consider the stockholding costs (together with infrastructure costs) required to maintain the level of availability in the stores. To be effective this measure should also consider also supply chain commitments.

Operational rationalisation concerns decisions taken by management to focus resources on core operational activities. Thus they may consider that distribution management and other support activities are more effectively supplied by specialist functions (such as third-party service businesses) and accordingly these become services which are 'bought in' by the company. A recent example, as we have mentioned, is the decision by Mothercare to 'put out' its management information activity. Though there is no one measure of operational rationalisation, it occurs when the operating costs of these activities are seen to increase without accompanying benefits.

Strategic rationalisation is a related concept. However, the purpose is to focus on a strategic direction. For example, Storehouse and Sears have divested themselves of businesses which do not 'fit' their strategic direction. Storehouse is focusing its activities around BhS and Mothercare, volume multiple outlets; while Sears is developing a strategic focus on ladieswear, having divested Hornes and Foster and acquired Richards from Storehouse. Burton has also undergone a similar exercise by questioning the 'relative' positioning of its component retailing companies.

Service density measures the use of sales area for sales and service purposes. Clearly each unit of sales area has an opportunity cost and

Managing the Margin Spread

once allocated to a sales or service purpose cannot be used for other purposes. However, an effective measure of the optimal use of space is to consider the overall productivity and profitability produced by alternative combinations of sales and service areas and consequently the impact on margin spread performance. An increase in service facilities is likely to have a positive increase on the margin spread, but clearly diminishing returns will occur, which may be evaluated by observation and experiment.

Finally, the *investment intensity* of the overall operations activity should be evaluated. Here we are considering the commitment of fixed and working capital within the business and the effectiveness of alternatives. Within this decision area are the questions of operational gearing, the impact of sales fluctuations, and the impact of service flexibility on margin spread performance.

SUMMARY

This chapter has considered the components which influence decisions which have an impact on the margin spread. These are featured in Figure 4.5 and Figure 4.6 includes the determining or facilitating factors discussed earlier.

The facilitating factors are positioned adjacent to the decision areas that are important to margin spread decisions. Some, such as financial

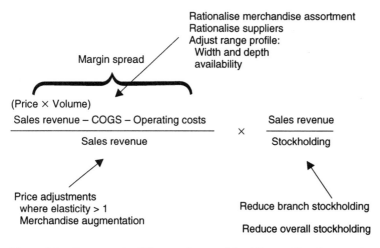

Figure 4.5 Components of the margin spread (and the asset base): managing productivity and profitability

118 *Exploring Concepts and Models*

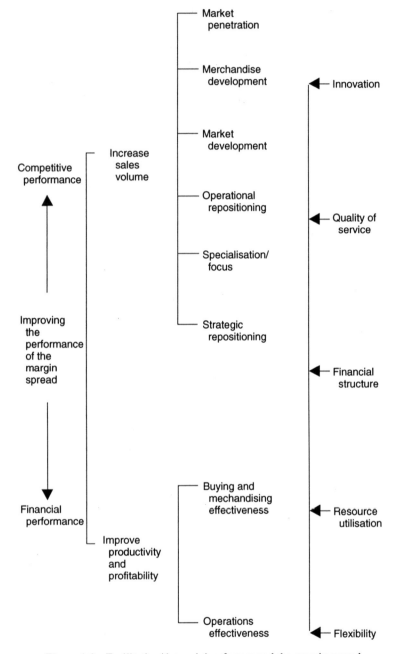

Figure 4.6 Facilitating/determining factors and the margin spread

structure and quality, have a wide influence. The important point here is to consider the role of each factor in contributing to margin spread performance.

A benefit of the strategic profit model is that by viewing margin management and asset management separately not only may productivity and profitability performances be compared, but insight into how the company is structuring its competitive and financial performance is possible.

5 Managing the Asset Base

INTRODUCTION

Asset management was seen to be part of the SPM model and is an integral part of the productivity–profitability–performance activity. The purpose of this chapter is to consider some of the major issues concerning asset management performance. Initially we shall discuss broad aspects of asset management; this will be followed by a discussion on the major elements of fixed assets and working capital (net current assets).

This chapter will also consider asset management issues in the context of the facilitating/determining factors as well as financial and competitive performance requirements.

CHARACTERISTICS OF ASSET PRODUCTIVITY

There are four particular characteristics that are important in this discussion. It will be recalled that overall performance is maximised when both margin management and asset circulation are optimal. Both fixed assets and net current assets can be considered from these performance characteristics (see Figure 5.1).

Fixed capital intensity

Fixed capital intensity is typically viewed as the original value (that is, before depreciation) of property, equipment, vehicles and systems hardware expressed as a percentage of sales. As retailing increasingly utilises more capital in its 'offer', so it becomes important to consider fixed capital intensity as an issue. The expansion by the large multiple retailers (both food and DIY) is an example of how the need for volume sales is necessary as the fixed charges (depreciation and/or interest) are increased. It will be recalled that as fixed changes increase, (that is, as the fixed costs assume an increasingly larger proportion of the total costs) operational gearing increases. Provided sales increase and remain above the 'break-even point' the increase in

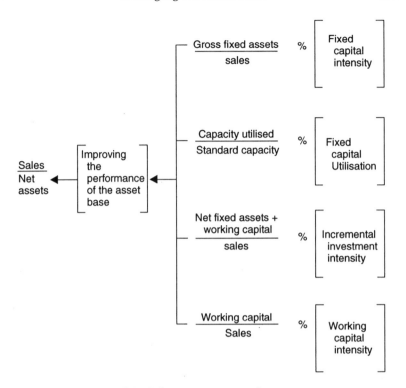

Figure 5.1   Influences on asset performance

profitability is higher than that for businesses without comparable levels of capital in the business.

Fixed capital utilisation

Capital utilisation is the average percentage of standard capacity utilised during a specified period (usually a budget year). Standard capacity is the *sales value* of the maximum output a business can sustain with facilities normally in operation and under normal constraints (that is, technology, working hours and practices, and so on). Fixed capacity utilisation should be at a high level if the capital intensity is high (this was established in the previous paragraph). A number of retailing businesses have expanded their asset bases very rapidly and have changed the structure of their businesses – away from having their assets mostly in debtors and stocks, into property and other long-term assets. The difference is that typically debtors and stocks are usually 'short-term' investments, which are often funded by suppliers' cash, but the more retail businesses expand their long-term fixed assets, the more important it becomes for them to maintain high levels of utilisation to ensure that payment of interest charges will be made.

Investment intensity

Investment intensity is usually measured by expressing the investment in net fixed assets and working capital as a percentage of sales; or equity plus long-term debt as a percentage of sales; or total assets employed less current liabilities in the business. The importance of investment intensity is demonstrated by the trend of the ratio over time. If profitable growth is to be achieved, then the value of the ratio should decrease (as the incremental growth of sales exceeds the incremental increase in investment) or at least remain constant.

For retailing businesses the most appropriate measure would appear to be the investment in net fixed assets and working capital. The reason for this is to monitor the two components, both jointly and as individual values, in order that the growth of the components of the investment can be compared as sales volume increases.

Working capital intensity

If the business could forecast its activities with perfect accuracy, it would have sufficient cash and inventory to meet its sales requirements and have exactly the level of debtors to meet an optimal customer credit programme. However, uncertainty enters into the process and management must take a view concerning the minimum balances required for each asset, together with a level of safety stock to account for imperfect forecasts.

If we compare working capital increases to sales increases (working capital to sales) we can see that as well as a theoretical optimum we can have a conservative measure where the working capital to sales ratio is high and in which risk is low but so too are returns. By contrast an aggressive working capital ratio (lower ratio of current assets to sales) will result in unpaid bills to suppliers, stockouts because of low availability and lost sales. See Fox and Limmack (1989) for a detailed discussion.

Management's policy should be based upon decisions concerning in-store merchandise availability, credit policy for customers, its number of suppliers and the terms of trade, together with a view of the amount of cash required for operational purposes and contingencies.

All four aspects of asset management are important. A balance between ideal performance (competitive and financial) and customer satisfaction should be made. The underlying decisions for both fixed assets and net current asses will be considered below.

FIXED ASSETS

There are four groups of fixed assets which can have an important impact upon asset base performance. These are:

- property
- fixtures
- systems and
- distribution facilities.

It is important to note that they do interrelate with each other and the important aspects will be discussed (see Figure 5.2).

Property

There are four aspects to property which are particularly important in this discussion. The *sales/service format* (the allocation of space between sales and customer service functions) has an obvious part to play in both financial and competitive performance. From a financial performance aspect the sales and operating profit contribution made by unit space (and aggregate totals) is a major consideration when considering the profitability of the business. Competitive performance, specifically positioning (and customer purchasing and perceptions responses), is influenced by the appropriateness of 'fit' that the sales/service combination has with customers' positioning perceptions.

The *location effectiveness* of property has a very large impact on the return made to the investment in property. A number of retailers calculate a catchment potential (an average transaction value per head within a viable 'drive' time) and from this measure a catchment effectiveness index is calculated, which is the actual transaction value divided by the calculated potential transaction value. The purpose of doing this is that because the cost of researching, developing and building on a site is now extensive, the catchment effectiveness index gives a useful indicator of the extent of the recovery or under-recovery of the investment. It is also proving useful for comparing existing performance levels across a range

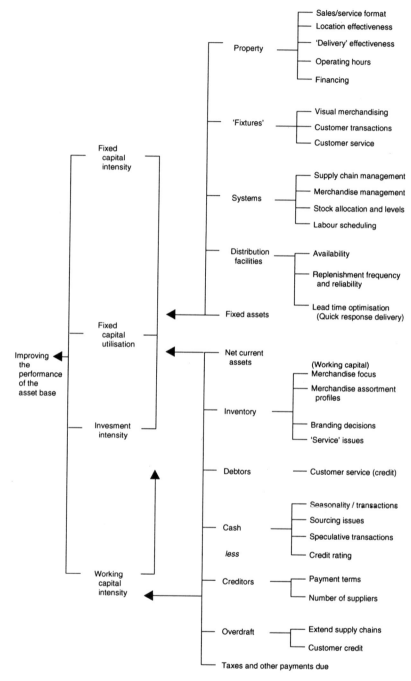

Figure 5.2 Components of fixed and net current assets

of locations, as well as an evaluative (and predictive) tool when comparing new location alternatives. An important consideration is one concerning the viability (not simply the effectiveness) of many existing locations; this is useful when considering rationalisation.

'Delivery' effectiveness is a measure of how well a location is delivering the 'retail offer'. The effectiveness can be measured by monitoring customers' perceptions and comparing these with their expectations. Tracking studies and a transactions monitor (a measure of the value and composition of purchases made by 'target customers') are useful monitoring devices. Retailing is operating in a dynamic environment and is probably the one sector which responds rapidly (if not immediately) to customer and consumer changes. In recent years the effects of the 1989–93 recession and changes in preferences have had noticeable impact on retail offers. For example, the growth of delivery alternatives encouraged by a consumer preference for convenience and information technology as a facilitator, has brought about a growth in home-based shopping. If this trend continues, some shopping mission activities will change and retailing management may need to reconsider the structure of its 'retail offer' if a cost-effective investment is to be maintained. Often concessions offer a cost-effective means of completing the 'delivery' offer. The attraction of this alternative is that no capital commitment is made over and above the existing space and facilities.

Operating hours have increased for many retailing businesses. In general, the impact had been on operating costs. However, the contribution towards fixed occupancy costs (a notional market rent based upon the freehold asset value of the location) is an important consideration. Though it may at first appear that extended operating hours will expand sales revenues, this should be reviewed against any incremental operating costs that may dilute the overall return on the property investment.

Financing methods are also an important consideration. Whatever the 'ownership' features of the property portfolio (leasehold, freehold, and so on) the property is seen as an asset. Accordingly financing decisions can have significant impact upon the return to the asset. In recent years (1989–94) property values and leasing arrangements have undergone changes as retailing has rationalised its property portfolio. Major retailers such as Next, Burton and Sears have reduced the number of locations now operated and this, together with a lack of expansion by other retailers, has resulted in a less than buoyant property market. It follows that leases and rents have decreased in many locations, reflecting lower freehold values; furthermore the premiums sought by many developers and agents have disappeared in many areas. Clearly there has been a significant impact on financing decisions; a general view is that evaluation will continue to be rigorous and financing approached with a continued risk-averse caution.

Fixtures

There are three issues to be considered in the context of the impact of decisions on generating a return to the asset value to fixtures. We have to consider fixtures from the viewpoint of opportunity cost as well as their cost. The opportunity cost consideration concerns the impact of fixtures on the sales density and productivity of alternative fixture options.

Visual merchandising decisions are (or should be) aimed at increasing the value of customer transactions. Visual merchandising is a means by which advice on merchandise style and colour co-ordination is given to customers. It follows that, though it may require additional sales area for display purposes, along with increased investment in fixtures, if an impact upon customer transactions and profit (that is, an increase in both the value *and* the range of purchases) is the result, then the incremental increase may be considered worthwhile. Visual merchandising is a major test of the innovativeness of a retailing business.

Handling customer flows at *transactions* points is an important flexibility issue. There has been research evidence for a considerable time suggesting that many shopping missions and destinations are influenced by the capability of the retail store to handle customer purchase transactions rapidly and effectively. Investment in POS systems and redesigned store formats has been considerable and will continue for as long as customers indicate fast and efficient cash-handling as an important factor in store selection. Again the overall impact of operating costs on return on assets should be considered. A system offering labour savings but maintaining target levels of service (time spent in the checkout queue) has attractions for many large multiple retailers where the volume of customer traffic is large but *average* transactions (throughout the entire period of operations) is low.

Customer service is an aspect of retailing which has been used extensively to create competitive advantage. Exclusive service aspects may identify the company as being innovative, but clearly investment in the assets required for effective customer service requires close evaluation. The extent of any investment will depend upon the service offer intended and the customer expectations the company wishes to meet. Often there is little choice. For example, durables require an after-sales support activity without which few sales would be made. The extent of services offered, the response and the commitment all create an image of service quality, one of the facilitating, determining factors discussed earlier. To conserve capital and to avoid committing it to assets that may not produce satisfactory revenues and profitability, service facilities may be franchised (consumer durables and personal computers are two examples among many) to specialist companies or, if the company wishes to maintain control of the service function, these could be moved to a lower-cost location.

Systems

Systems have become a large part of retailers' investments and consequently are a significant part of the asset base. For most retailers the increase in systems assets is assumed in order that costs elsewhere may be reduced. For example, an investment in EPOS systems provides more effective inventory management (lower stock levels and more effective merchandise allocation): in addition to these substantial benefits there are economies available from improved use of labour. To these can be added the space or cube planning facility that CAD (computer-aided design) software packages offer. *Supply chain management* systems linking stores with suppliers through the retailers' distribution facilities are systems assets that are proving to have a major impact on costs and managerial effectiveness. It follows that *merchandise management*, inventory management (*stock allocation and levels*) together with *labour scheduling* activities have each benefited by investment in system assets.

Distribution facilities

Effective distribution activities are essential if an efficient level of distribution service is to be maintained in the stores. *Availability* is an essential (but expensive) feature of the merchandise service to customers: effective distribution service planning (requiring resource allocation), together with a programmed cycle for *replenishment frequency and reliability*, can optimise the stock levels required. The impact of supply chain management systems linked to distribution facilities now provides retailers with a selective *quick response* facility which optimises lead times based upon merchandise rates of sale *and* their importance within the merchandise offer. A current trend is for retailing management to prefer to contain their investment in main core assets, those which drive the business and generate sales and profit. It follows that many companies are opting to use third-party distribution services as part of this strategy.

NET CURRENT ASSETS

The management of net current assets (or working capital) is an important aspect of financial management in retailing. As Figure 5.1 illustrates, the typical structure of retailing net current assets is for high levels of trade creditors and strong cash balances. Usually the large number of outstanding trade creditors results in negative values for net current assets. The term 'negative working capital' relates to this situation where, because of high stock turns, merchandise is often sold once or twice (possibly, in the case of perishable products numerous times) before it is paid for; hence the negative balance. We shall discuss five out of the six components shown in Figure 5.2; the sixth 'taxes and other payments due' is more of a financial than a retailing management concern.

Inventory

There are four areas of interest in this category. *Merchandise focus* concerns the decision to use the merchandise offer to make a positioning statement. Thus whether the business is a specialist retailer, a department store or whatever, the focus selected will identify this positioning for the customer. Accordingly the merchandise decisions will be made such that the focus will stress depth across the range of merchandise that customers would expect from a specialist retailer; or as wide a range of merchandise with sufficient depth to offer choice of colour, style finish and so on, in the case of the department store.

Issues concerning focus also include decisions concerning core product areas and core products. These are groups of products (or specific products) for which there are typically high levels of demand and which, if out of stock, would damage the credibility of the business with its customer base.

Merchandise assortment profiles detail the structure of merchandise groups around customer-determined 'shopping' characteristics. For example, if customer choice is price-led, then it follows that price point intervals should be used to display merchandise. Similarly an 'end use' choice should be recognised by displays demonstrating a range of potential end uses. Other shopping selection characteristics such as quality, style and colour may be important, and as such would form the basis on which an assortment profile might be structured.

Both merchandise focus and merchandise assortment profiles have an important influence on inventory decisions. Given that both require inventory stockholding support if the 'offer' is to be perceived as credible, it follows that the greater the number of characteristics the larger will be the amount and value of inventory required and the higher the value of net current assets.

Branding decisions have similar implications. The specialist retail offer will require to offer a range of recognised brands across the 'shopping' characteristics whereas, by contrast, a department store may select only those brands which are important to the target customer group. Another view of the brands option includes retailer own-brand merchandise. The attraction of this option is twofold: first, the breadth (as represented by choice alternatives) and the depth (variations within choice categories) may be reduced, due to the fact that only one overall brand is offered; secondly, there are usually larger gross margins attributed to retailer brands.

'Service' issues concern inventory decisions in the respect that they reflect the level of availability seen as being required by the target customer. It is widely accepted that as availability increases so too do stockholding costs: the problem is that at very high levels of availability the cost increase is exponential and may not be cost-effective. Other aspects of service include the location of inventory in order that sensitive aspects of the 'offer' may be optimised. For example, a problem for furniture retailers was always to minimise damage to merchandise during delivery from store to customers' homes. A solution was found which required co-operation between furniture suppliers and their stockists. The retailer holds minimum stock levels, usually one display item of each piece of furniture; once a sale has been made an order is transmitted to the supplier who dispatches the item directly to the customer's home. There are a number of benefits. First, damage is minimised by reducing the number of times each item is handled; secondly the problems of obsolescence are minimised and thirdly, the overall stock holding requirements' (for both retailer and supplier) are reduced throughout the supply chain.

Customer choice has always been an essential part of many merchandise offers. The home improvement markets have been moving towards 'design and fashion' for some time. Part of their offer has been an extensive choice of colour in decorative materials such as paint, wallpaper, and so on. Until recent years there had been a problem with the amount of stock and space required to 'service' the range of choice seen as necessary to satisfy customer requirements. This problem has been solved by the development of colour agents which require the retailer to maintain a limited range of base colours and a range of small containers of colorants. The result has been a significant reduction in inventory holding, in-store space and distribution warehousing facilities and an increase in this aspect of customer service.

Debtors

For almost all retailing businesses the cost of credit has been reduced by relying upon credit card services operated by the clearing banks. However, the cost of customer credit, debtors, may increase as the benefits of customer information on purchases becomes available through store credit cards and loyalty cards. The favoured move would appear to be the use of loyalty cards (without a charge card or credit facility). This would offer the benefits of tracking customer purchasing activities without carrying large amounts of debt. Clearly credit adds to customer service, but its cost effectiveness in so doing does require close scrutiny.

Cash

There are four aspects of cash management which have interest. The first concerns having sufficient cash on hand to meet the *transactions requirements that seasonal patterns of sales demand*. This may be significant for 'gift' and seasonally orientated retailers for whom buying ahead of peak demand periods requires large cash levels (or access to overdraft facilities).

Another requirement for cash increases as the supplier base is extended geographically. *Sourcing issues* are becoming more complex as markets expand. The 'new Eastern European' countries are offering sourcing opportunities at labour rates close to, or below, those prevailing in the Far East. Adjacency has benefits and a number of retailers are using Eastern European suppliers to bring the source markets closer to demand markets for both cost and control purposes. Quite what impact this may prove to have eventually is unsure. Theoretically it should shorten lead times and therefore the period over which transactions take place.

Speculative transactions may be important for some retailers. Gift and craft products are typically purchased in this way and buyers in these merchandise groups require large open-to-buy budgets if they are to take full advantage of the exclusivity and variety offered them to offer the customer an innovative range of merchandise.

Credit ratings are of concern to financial managers. Whereas the larger retailing businesses are well established, small and medium-sized companies do need to maintain sufficient cash balances to meet regular (and forecast) operating expenses. A reputation for 'slow payment' of regular expenses and merchandise suppliers may lead to a poor credit rating, which may discourage new suppliers.

Creditors

For most retailers, creditors form very large amounts in their working capital balances. The characteristics of negative working capital have been discussed earlier. The size of the negative working capital depends very much on *payment terms* negotiated with suppliers. The importance of negative working capital in the expansion plans of retailers varies. It has been observed that in the 1970s a number of customer goods retailers used suppliers' cash for expansion. Clearly this was seen as a source of interest-free cash and was expanded by innovative merchandise range planning and creditor management. A similar view can be seen operating in many retail businesses. The view of suppliers is usually philosophical: it is a cost of doing business and often is worthwhile, particularly for large regular transactions.

The *number of suppliers* can influence the management of supplier transactions. A large number of suppliers will increase the balance of trade creditors, but in doing so will also increase transactions costs. By contrast a lower number of suppliers will have the benefit of increasing gross margins due to the larger purchasing volumes.

It should be remembered that there is a 'cost' to the firm if trade creditors are used as sources of short-term finance. Not only are settlement terms in the form of cash discounts forgone, but it is likely that persistent practice will result in higher prices from suppliers.

Overdrafts

Overdrafts are used for short-term financing requirements. The problem of *extended supply chain* sourcing management was discussed above (see p. 114). As the number of locations and distances is extended, it is often necessary to use short-term financing facilities to meet transactions requirements. This is particularly of concern for retailers, whose merchandise is *not* characterised by fast stock-turns; furniture, jewellery and apparel merchandise groups are examples of this. Overdrafts have the benefit of interest being charged on the outstanding balance (often daily) and as such may offer a cost-effective way in which slow moving inventory may be financed.

Another aspect of overdraft financing concerns the provision of *customer credit*. It may form a useful method of credit control. Usually customer credit balances are charged at interest rates in excess of bank charges for credit, the difference in rates compensating for risk and administration. Financing customer credit by using overdraft facilities does protect trading margins and is clearly an option if the costs are found to be acceptable by customers.

SUMMARY

This chapter has considered the components of the company's asset base which influence the size of that base and its effectiveness: The purpose

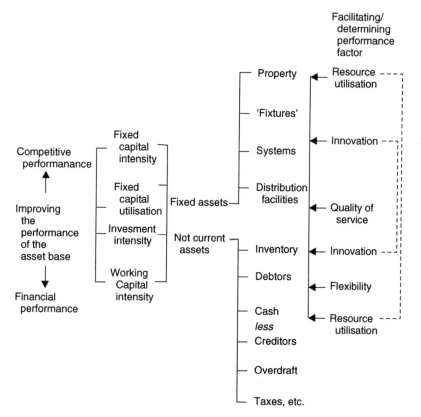

Figure 5.3 Facilitating and determining performance factors and the asset base

of fixed assets and working capital is to generate productive revenues and hence profitable returns for the business.

As net assets may therefore be considered to be determining or facilitating factors, they should be considered within the context of the model established in Chapter 2 and used to explore margin spread characteristics discussed in Chapter 4.

As with margin spread management, an analysis of asset base characteristics permits comparison of alternative asset structure on productivity and performance and to explore the structures on competitive and financial performance (see Figure 5.3).

6 Modelling Performance Options

INTRODUCTION

The previous two chapters have discussed margin management and asset management in detail. This chapter brings them together using the strategic profit model (SPM) as the co-ordinating medium. It will be recalled that the SPM uses both margin management and asset management to explore performance options and has the facility to identify trade-off options between the two in an attempt to optimise the return on assets. We are using an expanded version of the model to identify the operational and strategic aspects of the decisions. In Figure 6.1 the facilitating/determining factors appear as activities requiring decisions; those decisions relating financial management issues are also included. One other item to be included are customer expectations which is an important input into the decisions to allocate resources. The SPM is used to optimise both customer satisfaction and corporate performance.

CUSTOMER EXPECTATIONS

Customer satisfaction is a function of customer expectations: if customer satisfaction is to be maximised, then customer perceptions should equal, or exceed, customer expectations. This can be described by:

Customer perceptions < Customer expectations = Customer satisfaction not realised.

Customer perceptions > Customer expectations = Customer satisfaction achieved.

However, if customer perceptions are clearly in excess of expectations and suggest relative preference over and above competitive offers, we may assume an element of competitive advantage has also been achieved.

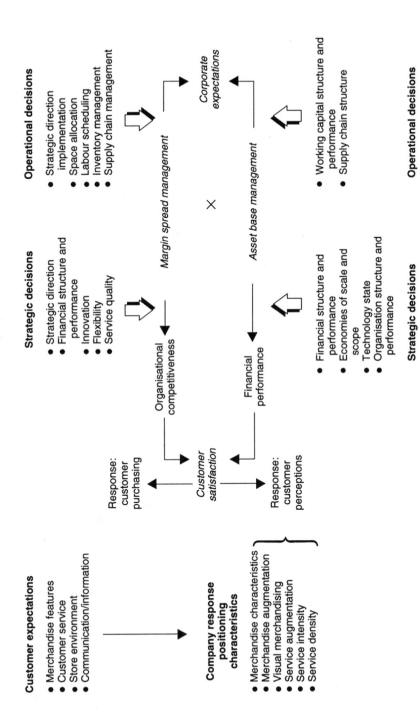

Figure 6.1 Strategic and operational decisions using the strategic profit model

Customer satisfaction response may be measured in two ways. First, customers' purchasing activities may be monitored to ascertain:

- visiting/purchasing visits;
- transactions
  - size and composition
  - value;
- repurchasing activities.

Second, and equally important, is a measure of customer perceptions of the offer being made to meet their expectations. The offer components or positioning characteristics, listed in Figure 6.1, are discussed in more detail here.

- **Merchandise assortment characteristics** – merchandise features that meet customer expectations for: choice, quality, exclusivity, style, availability, and so on,. at competitive price levels. (A service company would establish service assortment characteristics.)
- **Merchandise augmentation** – features that add value to the merchandise by the selective addition of accessories and product-services that are relevant. It creates for customers benefits that are not available from competitors and thereby creates competitive advantage through merchandise-led differentiation.
- **Visual merchandising** – reinforces the company's positioning statement. It uses merchandise displays to inform customers, arouse interest, encourage comparative shopping and to move the customer towards a purchase commitment. Visual merchandising should coordinate the merchandise offer into an integrated message which reflects customers' expectations. It should also classify merchandise into related groups (or departments) which reflect customers' applications of the products to end-uses or perhaps their specific shopping mission requirements.
- **Service augmentation: (i) information** – is a combination of both service and customer communication. The communications task is twofold: it both persuades and informs the customer. It should be directed towards that aspect of communication which is identified as most effective and is preferred by customers – research will identify their preferences but often it is the information content which is most influential. **(ii) facilities** – the interest here is the range of supporting facilities that are offered to customers. These are not directly supporting the merchandise offer but are indirect service features

that can influence customer store selection because of the value added during customer visits.
- **Service intensity** – relates to the number of staff (sales and service dedicated) within a department or within the store. The trade-off considerations between sales and service staff concern the implications on sales and profitability of additional levels of staff.
- **Service density** – measures the proportion of store floor space allocated between service facilities and sales area. Again the trade-off considerations concern the implications on sales and profitability of the optional configurations or combinations. These in turn are determined by the service needs of the merchandise offer and the planned 'positioning statement'.
- **Store ambience** – should reflect the planned positioning in the store's 'mood', character, quality and atmosphere. It should be tailored to the target customer group. It has no specific components but the store ambience reinforces the merchandise and service offers. Customer communications should be co-ordinated to enable a 'transfer' of the ambience to the customer by the creative and subtle use of media and design.

Having defined the offer components in qualitative terms, it follows that if we are to make use of them in planning and controlling productivity and profitability, some quantitative measures are required. The following are suggested as being workable:

Merchandise choice (index)	$\dfrac{\text{Stock-keeping items per product group } (\%)}{\text{Stock-keeping items per product group of nearest competitor}}$
Merchandise quality; exclusivity and style (index)	Customer relative perceptions expressed as a percentage of nearest competitor
Merchandise availability	In-stock position of selected merchandise items, expressed as a percentage
Merchandise augmentation (index)	$\dfrac{\text{Sales value of products and related accessories}}{\text{Sales value of product}}$
Visual merchandising (merchandise density)	$\dfrac{(\pounds) \text{ Inventory holding}}{\text{Sales area of merchandise group or department}}$

Service augmentation – information	Advertising and promotion awareness measurements
Service augmentation – facilities	Customer use of facilities (that is, use of service facilities, number of information requests, and so on)
Service intensity (ratio)	Proportion of service staff dedicated service staff to total staff
Service density (%)	Proportion of stores space dedicated to service facilities compared with the total space available (assumes the remainder is dedicated to sales)

These quantitative values will prove to be useful as we examine resource allocation decisions while attempting to optimise customer satisfaction. Clearly we shall have to consider the fact that customer preferences may differ across a spread of store types resulting in a range of rank ordering of these components. For example, department store customers may favour visual merchandising more than they do some aspects of merchandise characteristics such as availability. For individual businesses it is important that such issues are identified and research findings incorporated into planning decisions. We shall return to customer expectations and their role in customer satisfaction.

CORPORATE PERFORMANCE EXPECTATIONS AND RESOURCE ALLOCATION

Corporate performance expectations are implicit in the 'model' expressed by the strategic profit model. Figure 6.2 illustrates the primary areas of performance objectives. It is from these that detailed performance expectations for productivity and profitability can be developed. They will also be used to decide upon resource allocation.

Resource allocation will take place at two levels: strategic and operational. Strategic resource allocation is the concern of the 'executive' and involves consideration of alternatives in reaching decisions concerning the allocation of capital to fixed and current assets. At an operational level the allocation process charges branch (and field) management with optimising productivity and profitability from allocated resources, com-

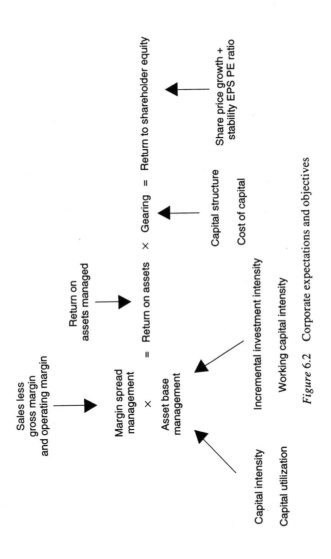

Figure 6.2 Corporate expectations and objectives

140   *Exploring Concepts and Models*

prising space, stock, staff and service facilities. At this level of decision-making management's role is to produce productivity, profitability and customer service outputs to meet customer satisfaction objectives.

STRATEGIC PERFORMANCE

The task confronting the company executive is to meet shareholders' expectations for profitability (and objectives and so on; see Figure 6.3) and concurrently, to meet the requirements for a long-term return on strategic resources and to establish the means by which customer loyalty will be developed and from this long-term customer satisfaction. In Figure 6.3 the 'strategic resources' of fixed assets and net current assets are featured, together with capital employed components of debt and equity. The resource allocation process at this level poses choices for management in order that optimal profitability and productivity be maximised.

A basic and underlying choice concerns the target market segment because this determines both the level of sales achievable and the resource requirements necessary to compete successfully in the segment. For example, the resources required to compete successfully as a department store are clearly different to those required for success as a food discount multiple. Figure 6.3 considers resources in a conventional financial management context – however, it should be noted that fixed assets would include both tangible and intangible components.

At this strategic level of decision-making, resources are allocated to achieve sales and profitability performance and the 'executives' focus is on how best these may be achieved.

In Figure 6.4 we consider the specific decisions that are made. At the executive level there are two aspects to these decisions: one concerns the structure of the company's financial base – this is influenced by the requirements of functional management's needs for 'production capacity'; the other concern is the return to shareholders that is realised by the business and this is very much influenced by capital structure decisions.

As we saw in Chapter 2, a company whose objectives prioritise growth of the business (taking a long-term view of shareholders' returns) may emphasise internal funding for growth. Thus the re-investment rate and retentions policy are aimed at providing low-cost capital for expansion. Alternatively the view of the executive may be that expansion funds are obtained externally using debt to obtain tax benefits and thereby enhancing shareholders' wealth. Should the decision to obtain

Modelling Performance Options 141

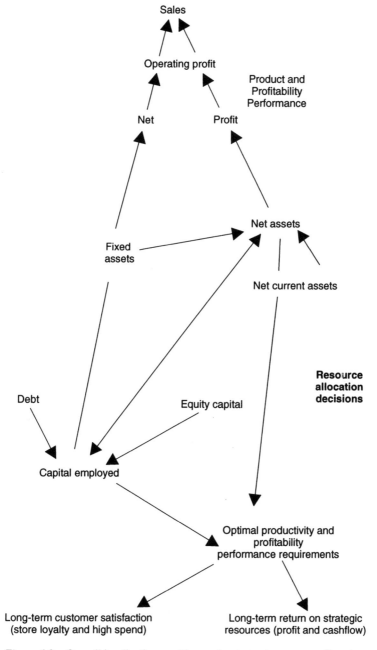

Figure 6.3 Overall implications and issues for strategic resource allocation

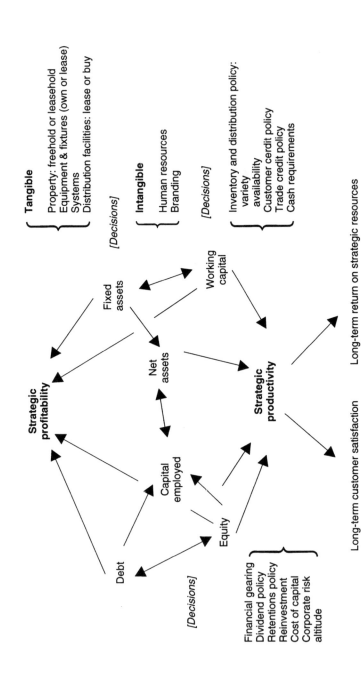

Figure 6.4 Strategic resource allocation: decisions and options

funds favour external sourcing, the options are wide and this is of particular interest at the present time. Currently a number of retailing companies are reviewing their activities and some are deciding to focus exclusively on their core business, with the result that there is reluctance to consider investment in peripheral activities. It follows that a range of financing alternatives are being utilised together with an increasing range of bought-in services, and this has seen a growth in distribution service companies and, latterly, information management bureaux. The implications are that inter-company performance comparisons are likely to become both difficult and pointless. However, our interest is primarily in the performance and control of the business.

At a more detailed level the decisions confronting management concern the choice of assets required to achieve objectives. Figure 6.4 identifies some areas of decision-making. It suggests that not only are there decisions concerning funding options – for example, internal versus external funding, and all that this entails for retentions and dividend policy decisions – but that there are decisions concerning capital intensity and the requirements for flexibility. Other decisions concerning fixed assets involve the allocation of funds between tangible and intangible assets.

The decisions concerning capital intensity and flexibility are important. The ability to be able to respond to changes (for example, in volumes, sourcing, product mix, and so on) requires an equally flexible asset structure. It follows that a number of fixed asset decisions may reflect such a preference and that a number of leasing arrangements may be preferred. Much the same thinking influences distribution facility decisions where flexibility for volume and delivery frequency may be increased by using distribution services. The use of leasing does of course facilitate the decision to focus on the core activity of the business.

Intangible asset decisions are influenced by issues concerning positioning. For example, a retailing business positioned to offer a high level of customer service will require personnel and development infrastructures which meet the requirements of customer expectations responding to the 'offer'. Branding has the same considerations: the accounting literature now considers that brands and logo style characteristics have value as fixed intangible assets. Thus a decision to invest in developing the retail company as a brand requires attention to the long-term considerations (and implications) for funding issues.

Working capital decisions are also influenced to a degree by positioning. Both inventory and distribution policy and customer credit policy are directly influenced by the 'executive's' decisions concerning positioning and the subsequent merchandise and customer service issues. The funding requirements of positioning alternatives should be evaluated and included in the strategic resource allocation decision.

OPERATIONAL PERFORMANCE

Operating management implements strategic decisions. In many companies this requires managers to meet the cost and performance objectives established by the 'executive' by using the resources allocated within overall budgets. Increasingly field and branch managers have control over how budgets may be allocated to achieve cost-effective performance within the context of local circumstances and requirements.

However, it remains necessary to consider how operational resources may best be utilised if the market positioning decisions are to be implemented and operating profit objectives met.

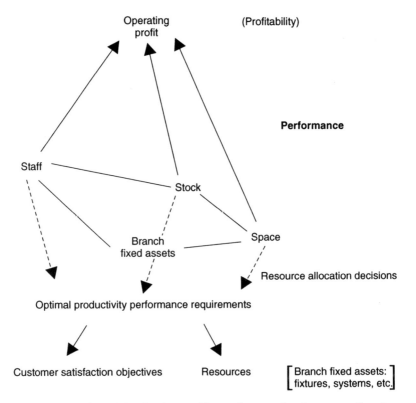

Figure 6.5 Overall implications and issues for operational resource allocation

At the operational level we consider resources to reflect the requirements to implement the strategic directives of the board. Thus we have space, stock, staff and service facilities as the resources. Essentially these are physical resources but clearly they can be regarded in financial terms (and should be when profit performance is considered). See Figure 6.5, which suggests that resource allocation productivity performance and the customer satisfaction objectives should reflect the strategic decisions concerning positioning and profitability requirements. Performance measurement considers both profitability and productivity measurement and within the context of productivity performance the measurement of physical resources productivity is featured.

As with strategic performance, so we can consider the components of operational performance, and this is the topic of Figure 6.6. The suggestion is that to achieve an optimal level of performance there are a number of options available. These are both of an intra-resource group nature as well as of an inter-resource nature. The resulting resource allocation will be a response to customer expectations and reflect productivity performance requirements that will in turn meet profitability objectives.

Examples of decisions that may be taken concern, for instance, the combination of merchandise characteristics such as availability, choice, exclusivity in proportions that respond to customer expectations. Another example, which is related to the mainstream merchandise decision, concerns visual merchandising. Here the resource decision concerns the cost-effective use of both merchandise and space to make an overall combination that will both inform customers and encourage to make purchases that increase the average transaction size.

Customer service-'led' decisions such as service density involve the choice of the use of space for *either* sales *or* service facilities. Here the influence upon the eventual decision concerns how effective combinations may increase both customer traffic (that is, how store selection may be influenced) *and* how customer transaction frequency and value may be influenced.

TIME PERSPECTIVES: OPERATIONAL AND STRATEGIC TRADE-OFF CHOICES

It is conceivable that management is faced with options that involve resource allocation decisions forcing them to choose between short-term *or* long-term objectives. For example, assuming resources are not finite,

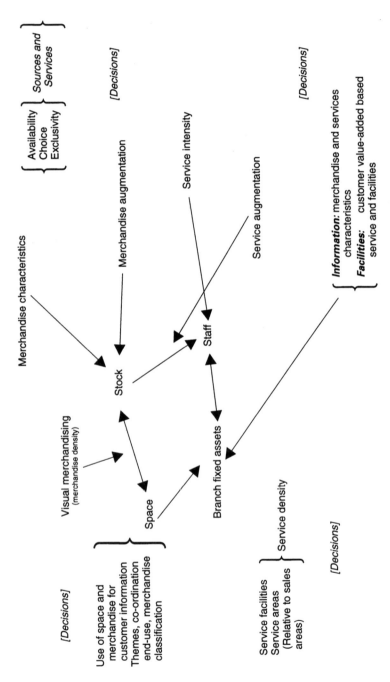

Figure 6.6 Operational resource allocation: decisions and options

there are often investment alternatives available to a business for which the returns not only differ in terms of magnitude but also in terms of time. An example of such alternatives could be an expansion of the existing business which might offer low-risk short and medium returns from the existing format: an alternative might be to direct the resources into developing a new format or perhaps a new concept, where the risk might be high and the returns long term.

This might appear to be a problem that could be resolved by using discounted cash flow investment appraisal techniques. However, it may be seen to be more complex, particularly if the *means* by which funding is to be achieved differ. Thus we may opt for a strategy that expands the cash generation capability of the existing business, which would provide cash resources to make an acquisition, or perhaps to expand the profit generating capabilities over a period of time from the organic expansion which might take place. Alternatively the development of a new format would require considerable investment in fixed and working capital with *additional* fixed costs. Both have implications for productivity and profitability performance. See Figure 6.7, which illustrates the effect of increasing the size and scope of the existing business. As volume increases and with it buying margins increase, then with fixed costs and overhead increases at a minimum trading profit increases are large and cashflow will increase.

A 'profit generation' resource allocation decision (illustrated by Figure 6.7) may lead the company into either market penetration or market development (see Figure 4.3 above) with an increase in sales volume and with this an increase in operating and net profit as the volume is amortised over a static (or at most, nominally increased) fixed-cost base. Alternatively we might see increases in cash flow generated by merchandise assortment adjustment or perhaps a rearranged supply chain: both options would provide an increase in cash flow (and margins).

The same objectives may be achieved by improving the utilisation of fixed assets and working capital (see Figure 5.2 above). The use of EPOS systems and a change of distribution policy can result in lowering stockholding requirements (in both levels and locations); consequently stock turns may be improved and negative working capital increased. Specific attention to creditors and payment policy, together with the use of customer credit in the customer service package, can also result in an improved cash flow situation.

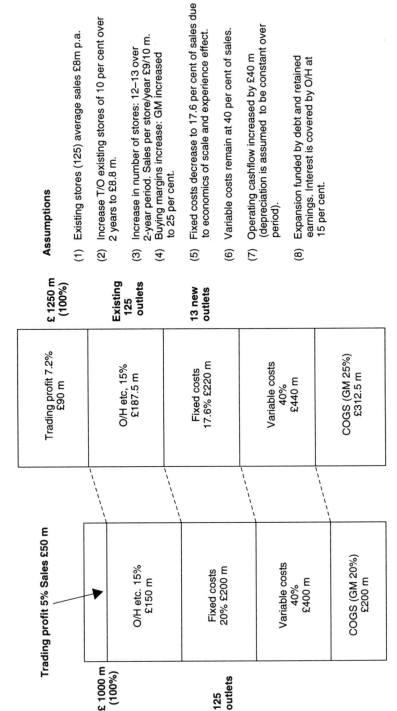

Figure 6.7 The effect of a volume increase in sales (25% over two-year period) on profitability and operational cash flow

DEVELOPING A PERFORMANCE MEASUREMENT MODEL

The model we are proposing has been developed using the Strategic Profit Model. A number of other attempts have been made at using the Dupont approach to performance measurement. Early models such as those by Dalrymple *et al.* (1966) were largely focused on relating sales, gross margins and stock levels. Subsequently Lusch (1980) extended these to consider the gross margin return on space and employees as well as stockholding; Figure 6.8 describes Lusch's approach. The expansion of the model identifies the relationships of space and employees with sales area which, as we have seen, can be used as components in the measurement of visual merchandising and service density (these will be developed later in this chapter).

However, for it to be effective we need to expand the model to include both strategic and operational performance measurement, together with the facility to probe interrelationships at the operational level and to explore the impact of changes made (or being considered) on the financial structure of the business. This is the subject of Figure 6.9.

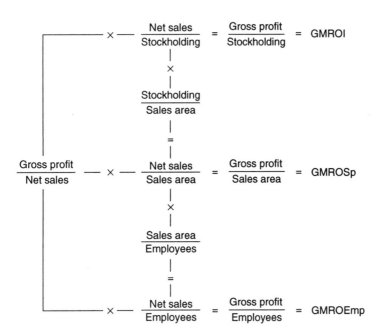

Figure 6.8   The SPM expanded (from Lusch)

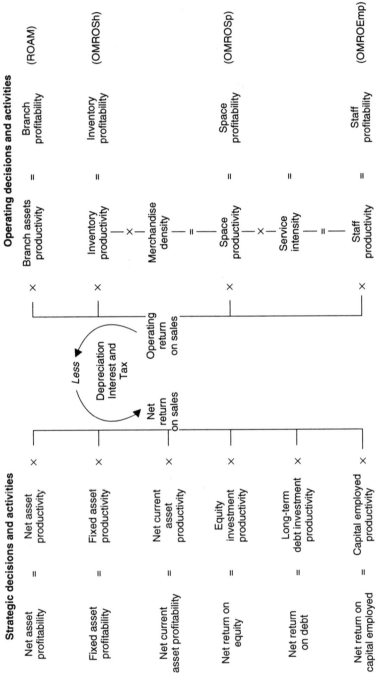

Figure 6.9 An overall view of the productivity/profitability performance model

Central to the measurement of both productivity and profitability is the operating return on sales:

$$\frac{\text{operating profit}}{\text{sales revenue}}$$

And this, it will be remembered, is a function of the margin spread:

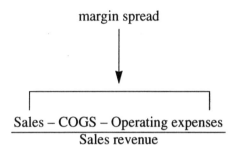

The model offers management the facilities of monitoring current performance and exploring the impact of potential changes (the 'what ifs?') at both an operational and a strategic level. It can also be used to consider alternative funding options as well as changes in policy concerning asset structure. A particularly interesting application is the facility to consider the impact of changes in customer expectations in terms of the likely changes to productivity and profitability. Should it be decided to make changes to the business to meet expectations, then the model is able to consider the impact of these changes at both the operating level *and* the strategic level. Examples will be discussed in subsequent chapters.

STRATEGIC DECISIONS AND ACTIONS

At the strategic level we have already established a number of performance requirements. Figure 6.10 shows the linkages between the central performance measure (operating return on sales) and the components of assets and funding structures and the decision options that can influence performance.

There are some obvious issues to be considered at this level and these concern the capital structure of the business. The lower portion of Figure 6.10 is concerned with financial structure and management. It suggests the funding alternatives to be either the shareholders equity

Figure 6.10 Strategic decisions and alternatives

or external long-term debt. The topics which will influence the outcome are the cost of capital subsequent to the decision; the implications of the interest charge on profit and tax; and the risk accompanying the investment.

The funding requirements are identified in the top half of Figure 6.10. Decisions here are both strategic and operational. They can include major changes to the number of stores operated, extensive changes to existing stores or perhaps investment in an alternative delivery system (for example, investment in database development and catalogue operations). At an operational level the decisions which influence financial performance are suggested to be changes in the merchandise profile, visual merchandising, customer credit and settlement policy.

The decisions and actions considered at the strategic level would include:

- the impact of a change in policy towards own assets on the return on net assets, fixed assets and capital employed;
- the impact of an increase in the number of branches on profitability – or alternatively the level of profitability required if a specified investment in branch expansion is made;
- an indication of the level of profit that must be generated from an alternative delivery format;
- the increase in operating return sales if investment is made in distribution and/or systems;
- the profit requirements of a major 'branding' strategy;
- Changes required in merchandise, service and store environment characteristics to meet specified profitability criteria.

Clearly there are numerous options and more will be explored in subsequent chapters. The ratios that form the basis for the analysis of strategic decisions are displayed in Figure 6.11.

OPERATIONAL DECISIONS AND ACTIONS

Operational decisions and alternatives are shown in Figure 6.12 and identify the linkages between the central performance measure (operating return on sales) and the operational resources.

There is an obvious requirement to measure branch management performance and this is measured in both productivity and profitability terms. Branch assets should only include those resources that can be con-

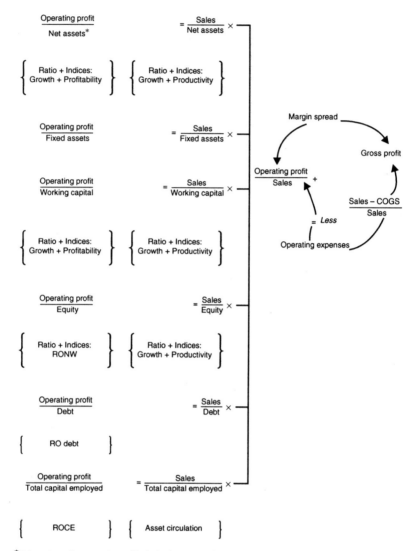

Figure 6.11 Ratio analysis of strategic decisions and alternatives

*Net assets are those assets *used in the business* to produce revenues

trolled by local management. As Figure 6.12 suggests, there are links between the key resource areas of space, stock, staff and service facilities.

Inventory decisions that will affect inventory performance include merchandise and assortment range profiles which respond to customer expectations. Thus increased variety and availability will be reflected in higher levels, of inventory. Policy decisions concerning core product

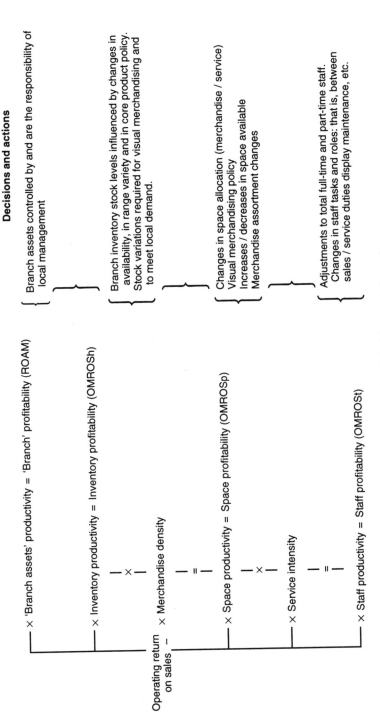

Figure 6.12 Operational decisions and alternatives

range specification and visual merchandising themes will have an impact on inventory levels, as will assortment variations to meet local demand. Again, we can approach these issues from the performance objectives perspective; that is, we can ask: given a required level of performance (operating return on sales) and given customer expectations, what are the resource allocation options available such that customer satisfaction *and* performance are optimised?

The decisions and actions at the operational level would include consideration of the following:

- the impact on performance of increasing resources in response to changes in customer expectations;
- an evaluation of alternative resource allocation actions which may be required if the margin spread is to be maintained or expanded;
- the implications of changes in service resources – for example reduced distribution frequency – on space productivity and profitability. (A reduced distribution service implies that higher stock levels will be required at branch level. This leads to a number of alternative actions. For example, it may be decided to rationalise low-performing merchandise groups or items within groups. Alternatively availability may be reduced, overall or possibly differentially, or perhaps variety may be addressed in a similar way.)
- the resource requirement issues that accompany the decision to increase sales volume (that is, market penetration, merchandise development, operational repositioning and specialisation and the implications of a target operating return on sales – see Figure 4.3); and similarly
- the resource requirement issues of productivity and profitability performance, by focusing on buying and merchandising and operations effectiveness with *the same* performance requirements constraint (again see Figure 4.3).

As with the strategic decisions and actions there are a number of options to be explained in subsequent chapters. The ratios that form the basis for the analysis of operational decision are displayed in Figure 6.13.

MANAGING CASH FLOWS

Strong positive cashflow is a vital element of retailing management. Figure 6.14 proposes a range of cashflow measurements that are appropriate for performance measurement.

Modelling Performance Options

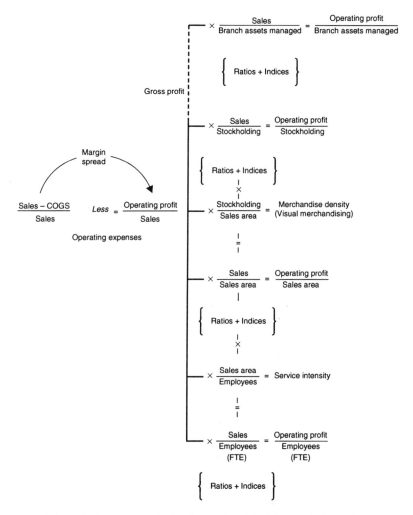

Figure 6.13 Ratio analysis of operational decisions and alternatives

The difference between strategic cashflows and operational cashflows reflects the time span and level of responsibility of managers (see Figure 6.14). Essentially we are considering cashflow increases over specific trading periods compared with increases in resources, interest payments and depreciation, together with an expansion of the capital base (ensuring that it is not 'double counted').

The decisions and actions at both levels would include considering the implications for cashflow of the following:

158   *Exploring Concepts and Models*

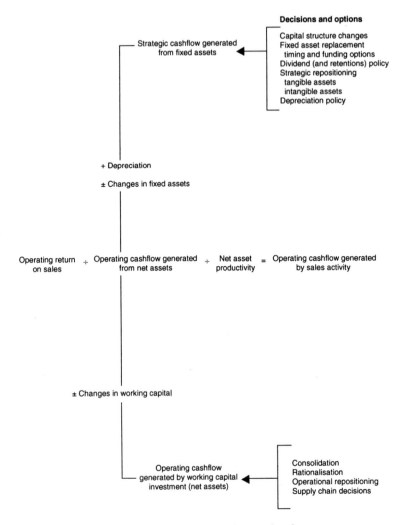

Figure 6.14   Cashflow decisions and options

- acquiring new locations (new businesses through acquisition);
- changing a 'buy' policy for major assets to one of leasing;
- launching a loyalty card backed by a customer credit facility;
- the cashflow benefits derived from a supplier rationalisation programme within which extended payment periods may be negotiated for larger purchasing commitments;
- outlet rationalisation or range rationalisation;

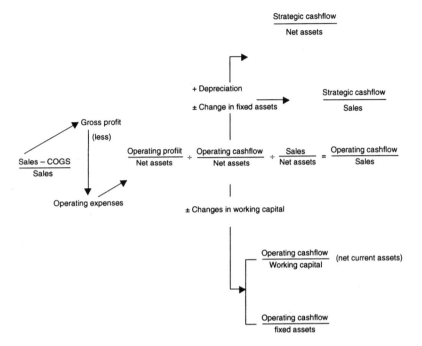

Figure 6.15 Ratio analysis of cash flow issues – strategic and operational decisions

- funding developments from retained earnings over a period of say, five years, as opposed to alternatives such as a rights issue or perhaps loan stock funding.

There are a number of other issues that will arise during subsequent chapters and they will explored in context as they occur. Meanwhile, the ratios that form the basis for the analysis of cashflow decisions and alternatives are displayed in Figure 6.15.

SUMMARY

This chapter has constructed a model capable of exploring and evaluating the impact of actual and proposed decisions to meet customer-based demands on the retail offer.

At an operational level the model can evaluate the performance outcomes of changes in merchandise, service, format and other activities requiring resources. It can of course be used to optimise resource allocation in order that a pre-determined level of performance be met or approximated while undertaking changes in the customer offer. This will result in an optimal solution whereby alternatives are evaluated to offer management a selection of outcomes of operating returns, levels of customer satisfaction achieved and operating format and performance data.

For example, the recent recession (1990–4) has changed consumer purchasing patterns and expectations. For many retailers the implications have been that buying frequencies and transactions have been lower. The model constructed during this chapter (and summarised as Figure 6.15) enables management to evaluate the impact of the lower overall value of customer response and offers the facility for management to explore a number of options to maintain a value of operating profit close to its objective. Furthermore, the impact of the change in customer purchasing may be considered within the strategic context, thereby suggesting long-term performance problems should the rate of visits and level of transactions continue.

Another example of how the model may be very helpful to management is in the context of consumer change or perhaps in a proactive move involving repositioning.

For example, assume that there is research evidence suggesting an opportunity is emerging for a specialist activity in the homeware sector. The opportunity is based upon style and design for both merchandise and store environment. Merchandise ranges, in terms of user functions are largely unchanged, but the emerging consumer segment has a strong design sense and is prepared to pay a premium for functional style and design and for 'knowledgeable staff who are friendly and helpful'. Clearly there are cost implications for both the merchandise offer and the level of service offered at the point of sale. There are also likely to be cost implications for store environment changes such as visual merchandising and the use of space: there may well be a requirement for a customer service facility (such as wedding list administration, gift wrapping, and so on).

With the help of the model we can explore the costs of designing and implementing the offer concept, the level of customer response required to meet an acceptable operating return on sales and the implications there might be for strategic productivity and profitability performance.

Having established the model in this part of the text, Part II will consider its use under a number of operational and strategic circumstances. The situations described as examples (and worked through) will be hypothetical but based upon actual situations identified through research.

7 Productivity and Profitability: Planning and Control

INTRODUCTION

A number of companies use gross margin as a planning and control objective. Their rationale is based on the fact that if the gross margin objective meets budget then the cost of goods sold, operating expenses and contribution to fixed costs and overhead will be covered. The approach developed in the previous chapters adds the dimension of 'investment'. The availability of more detailed information (in terms of currency and accuracy) enables the performance measurement perspective to include dedicated resources and to consider performance as a 'return on investment'. The earlier discussion considered the different viewpoints of productivity and profitability. This chapter considers how the model developed in Chapter 6 may be applied across a range of strategic and operational decisions.

The early application of the 'strategic profit model' was to merchandise management decisions. For examples of these applications see Doody and McCammon (1969), Sweeney (1973), Dalrymple *et al.* (1966) and Walters and White (1989). The direction of the argument of these authors is that a retailing company's eventual success is ultimately evaluated in terms of generating profit from resource 'investment'. Their emphasis is on merchandise and its related issues of merchandise costs (COGS), payment cycles (terms of payment) and assortment planning to provide customer service (choice and exclusivity).

The availability of information facilitates the expansion of the SPM. We take 'assets' to be strategic and operational resources. These were discussed in Chapter 6, in which we discussed the relationships between resources and attributes (or customer expectations). This chapter extends the discussion by developing an integrated approach to the model which may be presented visually to aid decision-making.

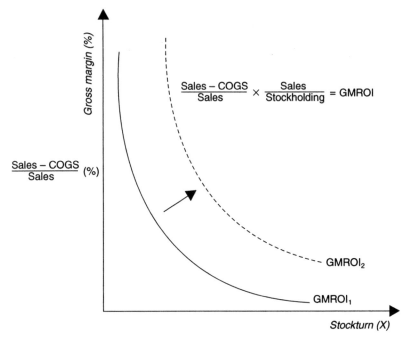

Figure 7.1   The GMROI model

A VISUAL APPROACH

The earlier work in this area resulted in gross margin return on inventory investment (GMROI) profiles. These could be presented graphically (see Figure 7.1). The two inputs of information are gross margin and stock turn. The use of this model for planning and control merchandise management decisions was extended by considering payment terms (discounts and payment periods) and product participation in overall assortment sales performance. The model was modified to use contribution margin (operating margin), rather than simply gross margins. The model illustrates the fact that GMROI value is constant for each GMROI curve (or isoquant); the values may change – that is, margins may decrease while stockturn value increases:

Gross margin (%)	GMROI	*Stockturn*
25	GMROI	6
30	150	5
50		3

For the business to increase its GMROI performance it is necessary to increase the efficiency of buying (that is, to achieve higher gross margins and to *maintain* stockturn values, or increase stockturn (sales volume) and *maintain* gross margin). Thus we could see situations where firms increase margin performance by price increases, or perhaps by a more effective merchandise mix, and maintain sales volume performance. Alternatively, the firm may increase sales volume without an adjustment of prices: in both situations a higher GMROI results.

Gross margin (%)			*Stockturn*
25	29.1	$GMROI_1$	6
30	35.0	175	5
50	58.3		3

Or alternatively:

Gross margin (%)		*Stockturn*	
25	$GMROI_2$	6	7
30	175	5	5.8
50		3	3.5

Expanding the 'assets' base

If we are to incorporate the topics discussed in earlier chapters, the horizontal axis requires to expand its coverage to include other resources. Figure 7.2 suggests an expansion to include other operational resources or assets. The vertical axis has been modified to enable the components of the margin spread to be included. Thus we have an operating margin return on investment (OMROI) which considers: branch fixed assets; stocks; space and staff. The argument concerning performance increases follows that for GMROI: an increased OMROI (that is, from OMROI $(0)_1$ to OMROI $(0)_2$ and subsequently to OMROI $(0)_3$ may only be achieved while the other remains constant (or for that matter also increases).

The argument for strategic performance follows in similar vein. Figure 7.3 suggests that operating margin is now compared against an expanded asset base which includes supporting assets as well as those in use at an operational level, together with intangible assets such as human resources and branding investment. The operating margin also requires modification by ensuring that interest, depreciation and trading overheads are included and a trading net margin realised.

164 *Exploring Concepts and Models*

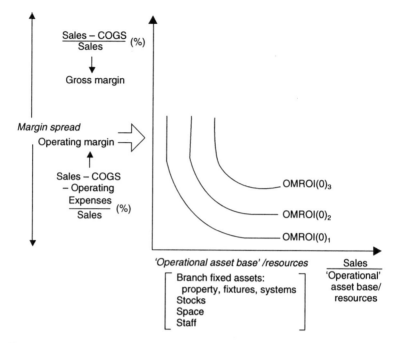

Figure 7.2 Expanding the GMROI model to consider the resource/asset base at an operational level

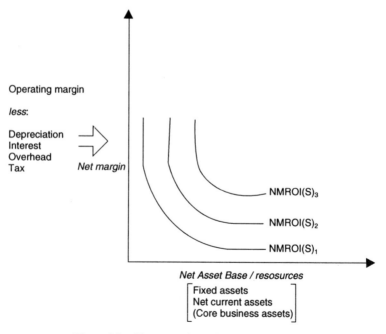

Figure 7.3 The strategic performance model (SPM)

165

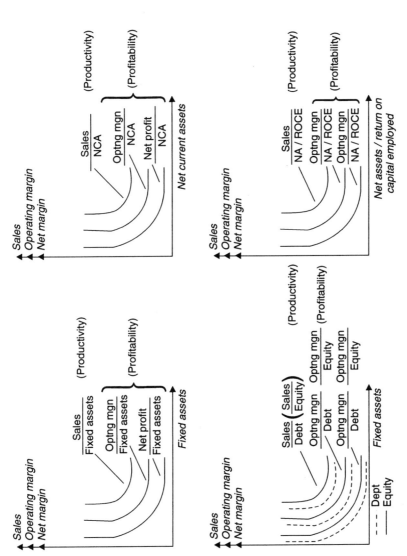

Figure 7.4 Graphical representation of strategic performance

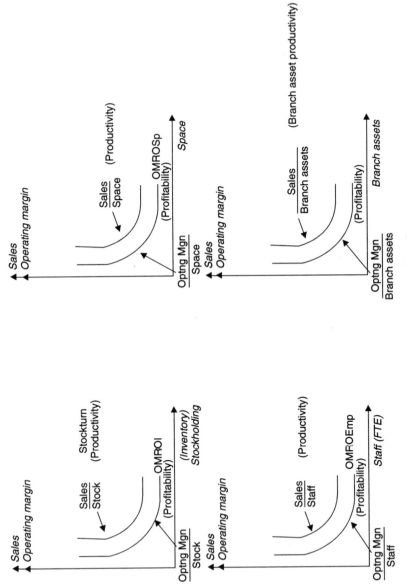

Figure 7.4 (continued)

AN OVERALL APPROACH

To be useful the model should be able to identify changes *across* the activity of the business: ideally the impact of an increase in sales (or operating profit) should also be seen in the context of space and staff as well as stockturn (the original aim of the model). In Figure 7.4 the principle of this is illustrated. The isoquants used by Walters and White (1989) are again a feature of the analysis, but the model is extended to provide the indication of change and influence across the resource base. An important feature of the approach is the ability to consider its 'what if?' exploratory facility: given customer expectations, it is possible using the model to evaluate the impact of meeting them such that:

Customer perceptions > customer expectations = customer satisfaction is achieved.

or the situation that may result in:

Customer perceptions < customer expectations = customer satisfaction is *not* realised.

For both, the implications on sales and profit may be projected and thus the operating requirements of an offer which will respond to customer requirements (that is, merchandise characteristics, merchandise augmentation, service intensity, service augmentation, service density, and visual merchandising) may be evaluated, not only at an operational level, but also for its strategic implications. Figure 7.4 simply provides a graphical presentation of the major variables, which should be used with the model developed in Chapter 6. Detailed variables may be examined by using the relationship models represented by Figures 6.8, 6.9, 6.10 and 6.11.

Performance topics within each of the quadrants are indicated in Figure 7.5, while the detailed decision topics are shown on Figure 7.6 (strategic decision topics) and Figure 7.7 (operational decision topics).

The strategic decision topics in Figure 7.6 can be seen to be based upon balance sheet topics. Typically these decisions are policy decisions aimed at responding to customer expectations (in a proactive sense) or perceptions (if they are a response requiring repositioning or any macro-reallocation of resources). The upper-left quadrant determines (and measures) the overall performance.

The operational decisions featured in Figure 7.7 are those typical for an ongoing retailing business. In addition, Figure 7.7 identifies a range

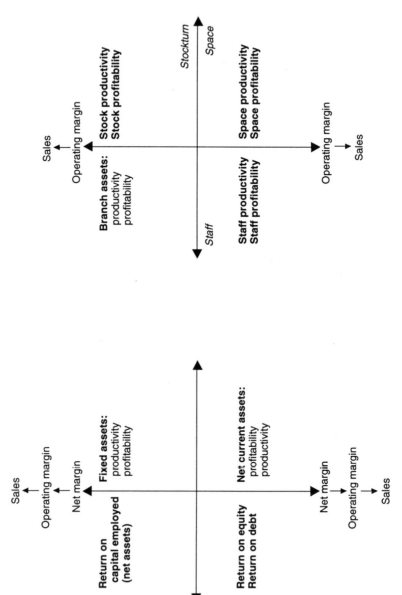

Figure 7.5 Strategic and operational performance: an overall perspective

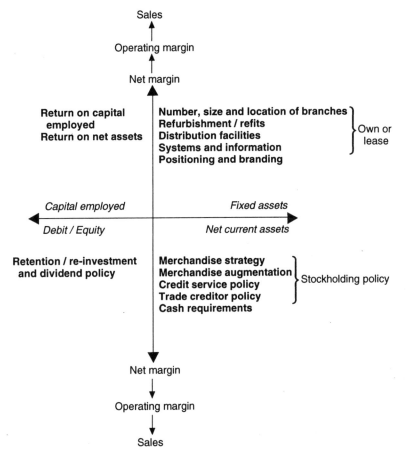

Figure 7.6 Strategic decision topics

of associated issues and topics, including the positioning characteristics introduced in Chapter 6.

AN ILLUSTRATIVE EXAMPLE: ARGOS PLC

Argos Plc announced its 1993/94 performance (*Guardian*, 22 March 1994). The report suggested that gross margins for the second half of the trading year were lower by about 0.1 per cent than they were in the previous, equivalent period. Argos' positioning is based upon a clear competitive pricing offer and this result clearly reflects a decision based upon a knowledge of price elasticity, because its sales increase through

170

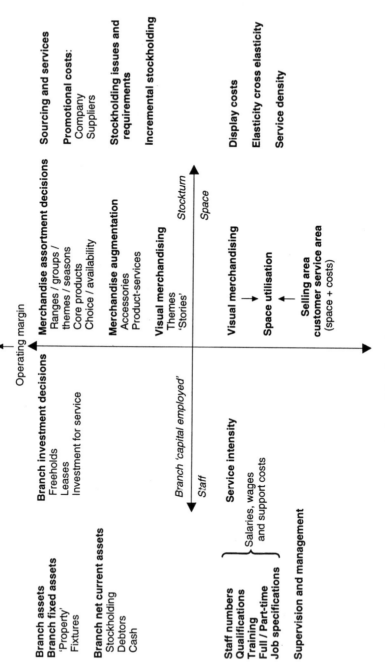

Figure 7.7 Operational decision topics

Productivity and Profitability: Planning and Control

existing stores was 8.1 per cent, overall sales increased by 10.6 per cent (£ bn 1.0 to £ bn 1.11) and profit (pre-tax) by 57.8 per cent (£ m 52.9 to £ m 83.5).

In addition to substantial sales and profit increases, there have been considerable costs savings, which have clearly contributed to the profit increases. These include closing a warehouse and a reduction of stock-holding costs and storage costs by increasing the number of product items which are delivered direct to customers from Argos Warehouses. Efficiency has also been increased by increasing the number of products which are imported directly by the business (rather than through an intermediary): this has the effect of increasing gross margin and through this operating profitability (which shows a 21.4 per cent increase year on year).

The effects of Argos' management expertise can be shown in Figure 7.8. The elasticity effect of the price reduction across a selected range of items has resulted in a volume increase, thereby moving the company from $OMROI_1$ to $OMROI_2$. The cost reductions and buying margin improvement have also resulted in increased performance and a move to $OMROI_3$.

It is likely that other productivity and profitability performance improvements will have resulted. An increase in both space productivity and profitability are almost certainly likely to have occurred; similarly staff performance for both aspects (sales and profit per employee) will have followed. It follows that branch assets' performance will have shown an increase. Provided with relevant information we could trace the performance changes through to the strategic framework. Figure 7.9 illustrates the effects of these decisions on the margin spread.

SUMMARY

The foregoing chapters have explored the basis for an approach to measuring productivity and profitability performance within retailing businesses.

Central to the measurement of performance are the *operating return on sales* for operational productivity and profitability and *net return on sales* for strategic productivity and profitability performance measurement. Resource allocation is influenced by customer expectations. Hence corporate expectations for operational performance (that is, the productivity and profitability of branch assets, space, inventory and staff resource commitments) and for strategic performance (essentially the

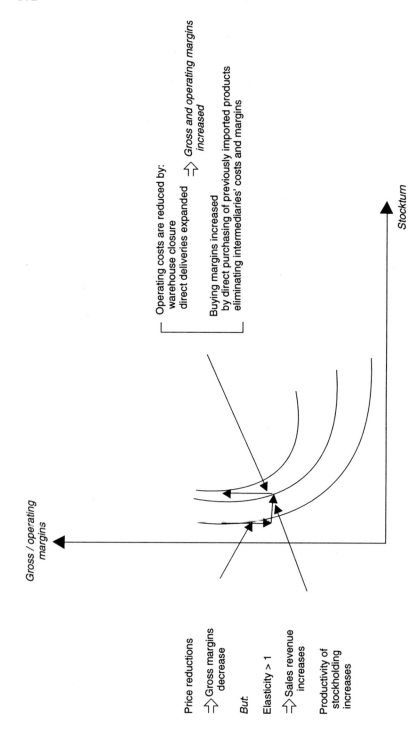

Figure 7.8 Improving productivity and profitability: an example

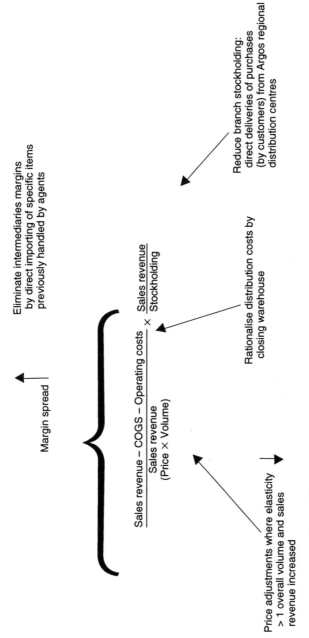

Figure 7.9 Increasing margin spread performance: an example from Argos Plc (1993/94)

capital employed and the net assets this represents) are a function of the response represented by merchandise, customer service, store environment and customer communications decisions. Clearly there are numerous combinations from which customer expectations may be accommodated.

Operational decisions (and performance measures) are indicated in Figure 7.9. The resource allocation process is directed towards specific expenditures for store environment elements (such as fixtures and visual merchandising) sourcing and stockholding (which will be determined by the type of merchandise response the customer expects). Space allocation decisions involve the consideration of service facilities requirements, visual merchandising (merchandise density) and opportunity cost issues. Operational resources performance is measured by the 'return on assets managed'; the costs of goods sold (gross margin); stockturns; availability, merchandise density (for display and customer availability); merchandise sales per unit of space and service sales per unit of space and sales per employee. Strategic performance measures should include sales and operating profit compared against fixed and net current assets employed. Measurement should also include: the overall return on capital employed; the return to shareholders (ROE) and measurement of the level of financial gearing.

Overall performance measures include the conventional profit and loss and balance sheet items together with a frequent review of the 'margin spread'. Of particular interest is the relationship of changes in the size or rate of change of the margin spread compared with similar changes in the 'spread' components. In addition there should be regular monitoring of *customer sales responses* and *customer perceptions* of the company's response to customer expectations through the regular use of tracking studies.

PART II

Productivity and Profitability, Planning and Control: Decisions and Information

8 Productivity and Profitability Decisions and Information Requirements

INTRODUCTION

Chapter 7 concluded with an overview of the productivity and profitability process. A summary of the main components of the process is:

- identifying customer expectations and potential response options;
- appraising corporate performance expectations for strategic and operational productivity and profitability;
- identifying the performance criteria for strategic and operational productivity and profitability; and
- setting objectives for customer and corporate responses.

We continue with these issues in this chapter. In Figure 8.1 we introduce the decision flow process whereby corporate response to customer expectations is examined and during which the issues of competitors' activities and responses are considered, together with other external influences such as technological development (a major concern for productivity decisions) and social and economic trends (both of which have a strong influence on shaping customer expectations). Given that these are important and within the decision-making process are assumed to be so, they will be reflected in both the response options and in the corporate expectations emerging at this stage of the process.

Corporate expectations will be expressed in sales revenue, profitability and cashflow terms together with target performance parameters for strategic resources. At an operational level the productivity and profitability response to resource allocation will be expressed as the performance of specific resources such as space, stock, staff and the 'branch assets'. Customer responses will be expressed in terms of sales responses (purchasing activities and amounts) and perceptions (of the overall retail offer).

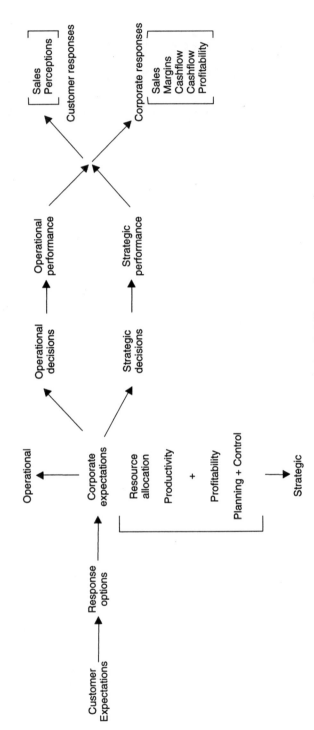

Figure 8.1 The overall productivity/profitability performance approach

ESTABLISHING OBJECTIVES

If productivity and profitability planning is to be effective, a set of overall objectives is necessary. Figure 8.2 proposes interrelated objectives for the retail offer components *and* for the resulting resource allocation requirements. The 'offer' objectives overlap in the sense that each contributes towards *making* the positioning statement explicit. They also have individual constituents.

- **Merchandise objectives** should reflect variety, quality, exclusivity and availability expectations but should also attempt to add value for customers and the company by increasing the average value of transactions and the margin realised.
- **Customer service objectives** may also prescribe product areas which become specialist activities: the growth of Marks & Spencer's financial services package into a specialist profit centre is an example here.
- **Store environment objectives** are suggested to be time based. The value added by customer convenience may be quite broad. It can include location (close to a large proportion of customers homes); parking (for those customers making regular large purchases) and convenience in the sense that the store layout or design facilitates transactions. the objectives should also consider the selection and purchasing process by using relevant visual merchandising which reflects customer preferences. This in turn should be supported by a store layout which ensures that customers are encouraged to 'shop' the entire store.
- **Customer communications** has both a persuasion and information role. The persuasion role should ensure that the customer is taken through the purchasing decision effectively (and this may necessitate extending the communication activity backwards into the customers' homes – for example, through catalogues (such as Argos and Littlewoods) or perhaps by using direct response and direct marketing (Racing Green and Lands End). Communications objectives should also be seen to exploit the differentiation strengths of the business.

Having explored the tasks of the offer components and having made their objectives explicit, the objectives for resource allocation may then be considered. Figure 8.2 infers that resource allocation productivity (and profitability) objectives are determined at whatever levels are seen

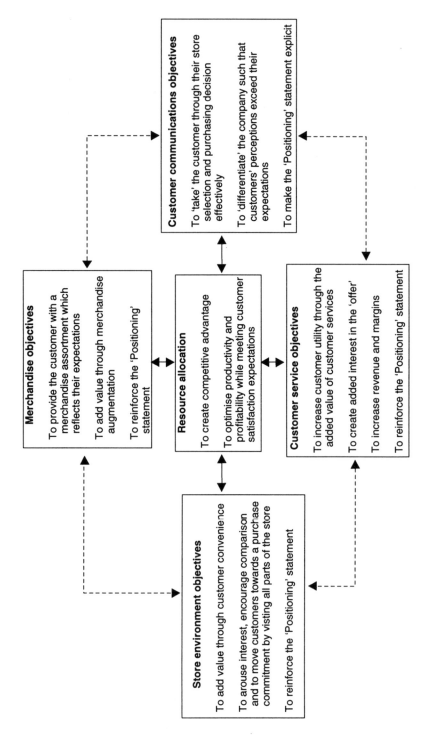

Figure 8.2 Establishing overall objectives

as necessary. Typically these will relate to the strategic and operational areas described in Chapter 7 in which decision areas are matched with resources performance measures. They should correspond with the measures featured in Chapter 6 because they are major inputs into the planning model.

The model that has been developed offers a 'two-way' method of deriving objectives at both strategic and operational levels. By being able first to set 'ideal' objectives at both levels for a specified target market, the alternative 'ways and means' (strategies) of achieving customer and corporate satisfaction may be investigated. In Figures 6.10, 6.12 and 6.15 the 'decisions and options' suggested strategic and operational actions that will influence specific performance items. The benefits of the model are that not only does it facilitate the exploration of alternative responses or formats (provided both revenues and costs are estimated with accuracy) but it also offers a trade-off facility. This can operate at both levels or between levels.

Trade-off options between options *at* a strategic or operational level may occur as consumer expectations are seen to change. For example, the preference for out-of-town locations over high street facilities or an increasing preference for customer service facilities would be seen as a strategic change requiring evaluation not simply on the impact on existing revenues and resources but also on fixed assets' productivity, and on return to equity and on capital employed. At an operational level a shift of emphasis between merchandise or customer service characteristics would require an examination of the impact of the changes on revenues and margins, and on the operating return on sales.

Trade-off issues *between* strategic and operational levels require a more detailed analysis. The type of problem confronting management concerns the choice between short-term and long-term productivity and performance *and* the allocation of resources. It follows that for most businesses there is a limit to the allocation of funds to resources. Chapter 2 discussed at length the conceptual approach of portfolio planning and the underlying requirements of generating both cash *and* profit. These are precisely the choices to be made here. It is the selection between investing in current and potential merchandise and/or offer formats that confronts management. Should an existing format be funded in order to maintain cashflow and profitability, or should resources be applied to the new (question mark) projects and growth (star)projects in order that their progress through their individual cycles is managed and their *future* cash and profit generation activities brought on stream? Clearly the decisions require a view to be taken that should be based upon external information concerning market trends and competitor activities.

The decision process described earlier (see Figure 8.3) has been expanded. In Figure 8.4 strategic decisions and topics are illustrated, together with decision areas and options and performance considerations. Figure 8.5 deals with operational decision. In subsequent chapters the discussion will be expanded in order to consider each of the 'offer' components in detail and at strategic and operational levels.

It is interesting to revisit the margin spread at this point (Figure 8.6) and to consider the decisions that can be made at both the strategic and operational level and how they impact on the margin spread components and the asset base.

Figure 8.7 aligns the decision features with the components of the margin spread and the asset base. As the figure suggests, there are a number of dual influences where a topic will have an impact on both sales revenue and the cost or asset components of the relationship. Figure 8.8 repeats the exercise for operational decisions. Both figures are helpful in that they provide the decision-maker with an indication of where the influence on productivity and profitability will occur and how large it will be.

Decisions require information and the remainder of this chapter considers the nature of the information required, its sources and its delivery. This latter topic is important. It considers frequency, currency, accuracy and format. As we shall discuss, information should be delivered in a meaningful, informative and useable format if it is to provide *the vital input* for decision-making.

INFORMATION FOR PLANNING AND CONTROL: A DECISION SUPPORT APPROACH

Effective business planning requires a datum point from which to measure both inputs and outputs. For most types of business an *audit* of some type is usually the basis for this. In this chapter we propose an audit system together with a means by which data may be presented to both levels of management (strategic and operational). This is designed to make decision-making more effective at both levels.

Figure 8.9 presents the basis for such an approach. It considers both corporate and customer expectations and incorporates measurement of both aspects of performance before and after changes have been made. To be effective an audit system should possess a number of features.

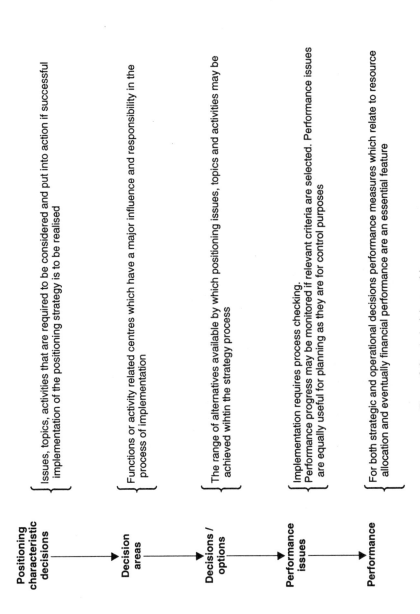

Figure 8.3   A decision-making process

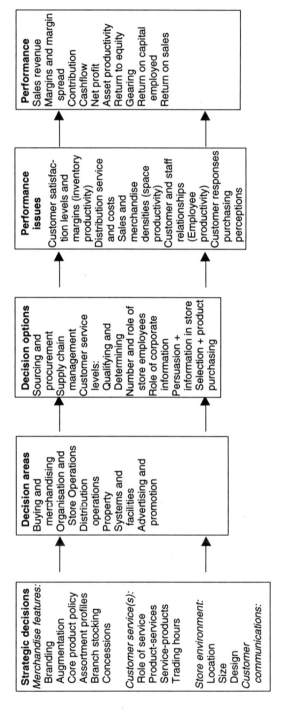

Figure 8.4 Strategic decisions for productivity and profitability performance

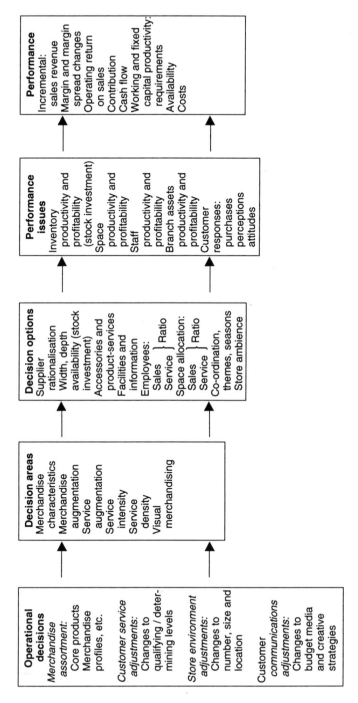

Figure 8.5   Operational decisions for productivity and profitability performance

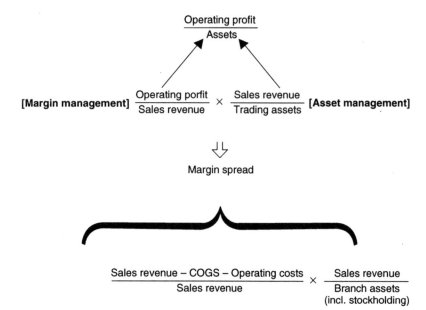

Figure 8.6 Revisiting the margin spread and asset base

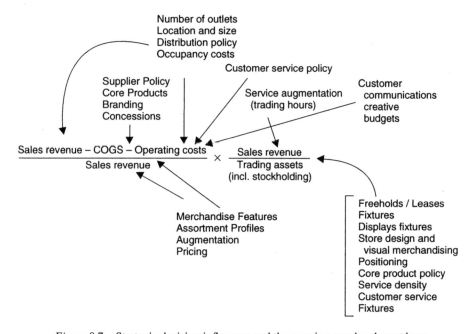

Figure 8.7 Strategic decision influences and the margin spread and asset base

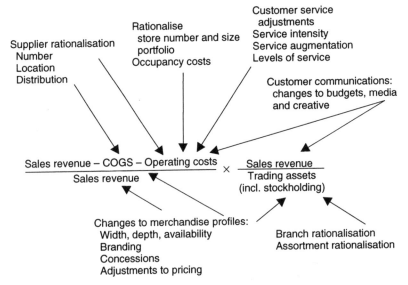

Figure 8.8 Operational decision influences and the margin spread and asset base

- It should monitor activities using a decision-related content and time base. In other words, the information supplied to managers should reflect the type and nature of the decisions they make, following a time schedule that reflects the decision cycle. Information should be sequenced so that it reports the results of a decision taken, but provides sufficient lead time for subsequent adjustment.
- Information delivery requires to be selective. The information presented to a decision-maker should be sufficient and relevant for the purpose required.
- Information should be market-led. Customer responses to the 'offer' made require to be quantified (where possible) in order that a corporate response may be considered and implemented.
- In order that the long-term implications of short-term decisions (and vice versa) may be considered, the information needs of both levels of decision should be linked through an interactive decision/information model (such as that described in Chapters 6 and 7).

This chapter continues by identifying information issues and suggests a presentation method by which the information assembled may be disseminated.

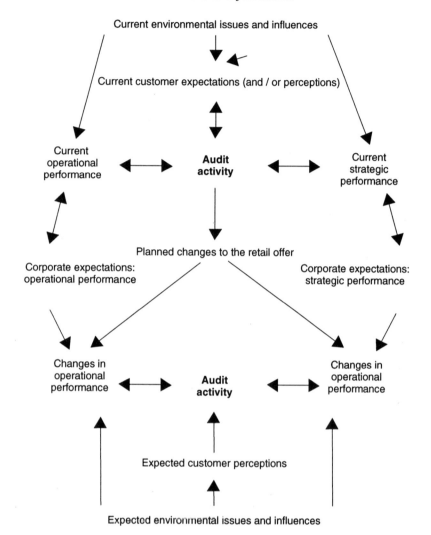

Figure 8.9 'Auditing' customer expectations and responses and corporate performance and response

INFORMATION CONTENT FOR PRODUCTIVITY, PROFITABILITY AND PLANNING AND CONTROL

The topics discussed in Chapters 4 and 5 provide the basis for detailing information requirements. These are the components of the *margin spread* and the *asset base*.

Within the margin spread there are sales, cost of goods sold, and operating expenses; each of which can be disaggregated alone as

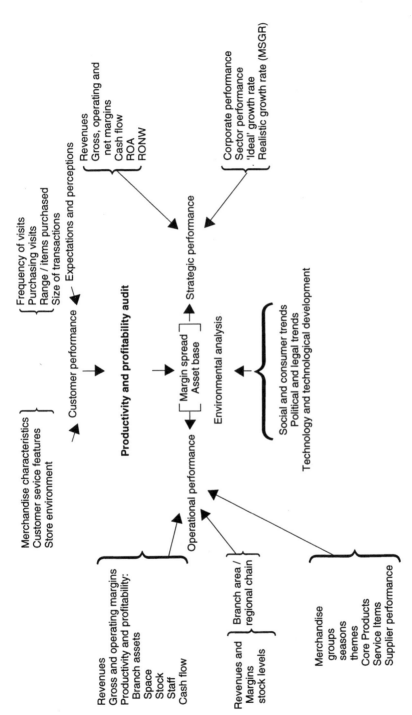

Figure 8.10 Information content for strategic and operational decisions

performance data requires to be related to resource inputs if a worthwhile interpretation of any activity is to be obtained. Both productivity and profitability are relative and comparative measures. Therefore the information items presented in Figure 8.10 require some datum points if they are to be useful in planning and control. Planning and control in its simplest form is a process by which alternative uses of resources may be evaluated. Evaluation implies a comparison of resource uses if an effective use of resources *and* customer satisfaction is to be achieved. This may be achieved if the objectives for customer satisfaction (and performance) are clearly defined and, just as important, expressed in a format that reflects their use of resources. The information content described by Figure 8.10 identifies sources and information topics; however, for effective decision-making they should be related to the areas and resources they influence.

The margin spread and asset base 'model' is also useful for this purpose. Figures 8.11 and 8.12 indicate the information topics required to make margin and asset management decisions. Two points should be considered and these are connected: the expectations for margin and asset performance should be clearly understood and with this, the extent of the impact of changes in any specific influence should be anticipated. This is important because it determines the extent of the currencies, accuracy, frequency and format of the information delivered to the decision-maker. In other words, though collection of all the data identified may be ideal, it is not all going to be used. Some topics will have much more influence on performance output (for example, core product gross margins – COGS) and as such should have priority in the context of frequency, accuracy and currency. Managerial experience and judgement together with a broad 'sensitivity analysis' approach will evaluate and identify information needs at both levels of decision-making.

INFORMATION PRESENTATION: A DECISION SUPPORT SYSTEM

The approach suggested is for an 'audit' of essential decision activities and information gathering and distribution to be focused on the broad areas that have emerged during the development of the model:

- strategic productivity and profitability
- operational productivity and profitability
- competitive analysis.

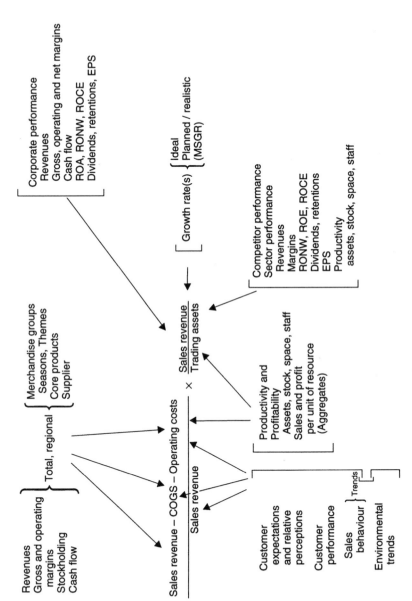

Figure 8.11 Information for strategic productivity and profitability decisions

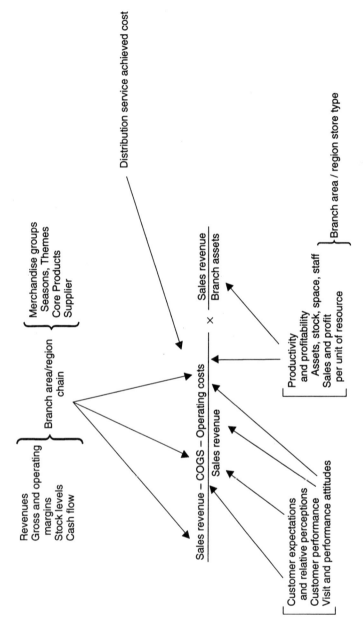

Figure 8.12 Information for operational productivity and profitability decisions

Decisions and Information Requirements

The information presentation format is important; if it is complex it will be confusing and perhaps not be used, if it is superficial it will be found to be 'lacking' and ignored. Accordingly some thought should be applied to the design of a format which will maximise the utility of the information generated.

(a) Current and past performance: inputs and outputs

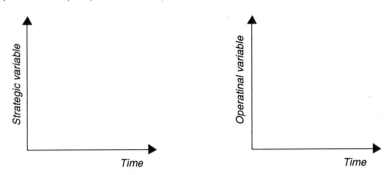

(b) Current performance and performance options

(c) Graphical presentations

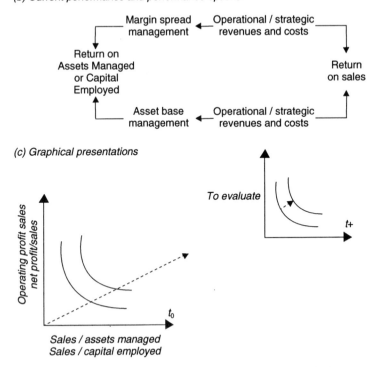

Figure 8.13   Structuring information: content and displays

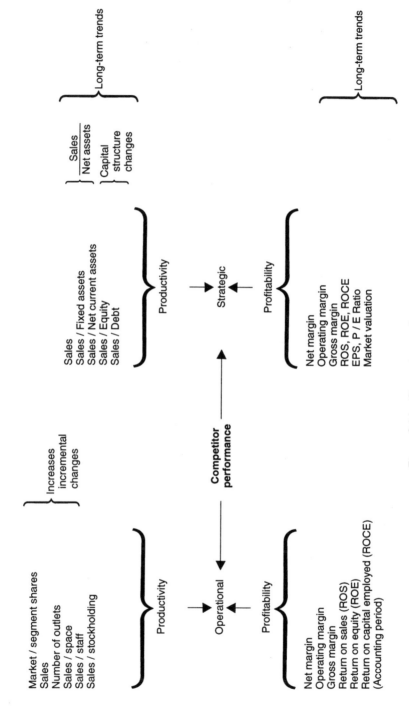

Figure 8.14 Competitor performance measures

Decisions and Information Requirements

A suggested format for the information given to managers appears as Figure 8.13. Current and past performance comparisons and trends are monitored and presented to decision-makers. The level of data presented is a function of the needs of the decision-makers. Competitive analysis is shown as Figure 8.14.

Returning to Figure 8.13(b),: at this second stage of information presentation the data which appeared at the first level – see Figure 8.13(a) – is used to identify relationships between decisions and return on assets managed at the selected level of decision-making. The key areas for which information will be required is implied by the 'decisions and options' identified in Figures 6.10, 6.12 and 6.15.

Clearly management should consider funding alternatives within the context of strategic decisions. Figure 8.15 models likely interrelationships between strategic business decisions and financial structure and management. This particular information presentation is unlikely to be required by any other than the executive level of management. Its usefulness to them is that it may be used as a primary input for long-term decisions where discounted cash flow (DCF) solutions are sought.

Finally the information presentation includes a graphical 'solution' of the options selected at each level. Figure 8.16 indicates an ROCE isoquant along which the value of the ROCE is constant. It is influenced by positioning issues: there are expected (anticipated) levels of performance for the return on sales and asset productivity associated and acceptable when specific strategies are pursued.

Similarly at an operational level there is an arc on the operating return on operational assets managed which prescribes the acceptable (ideal) levels of performance for the components associated with a specific positioning option.

SUMMARY

This chapter has combined the decision-making process with management's requirements for information during the decision-making process. We have adopted an *approach* which makes two basic assumptions.

- The first assumption follows through the thesis of this work, which is that strategic and operational performance achievements are essentially based upon productivity and profitability decisions.
- The second assumption concerns the premise that decision-making may be improved by providing a decision support system which

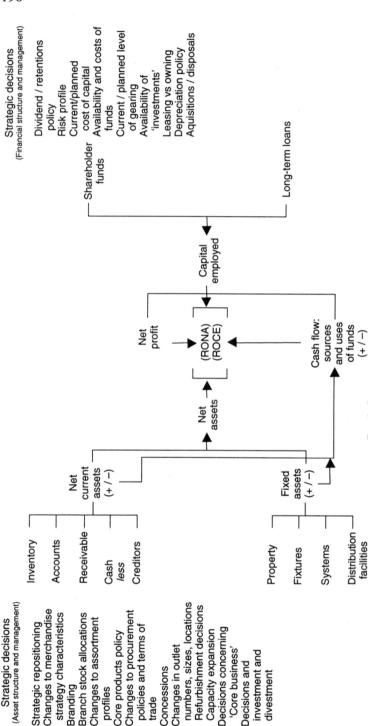

Figure 8.15 Strategic decision making: funding options

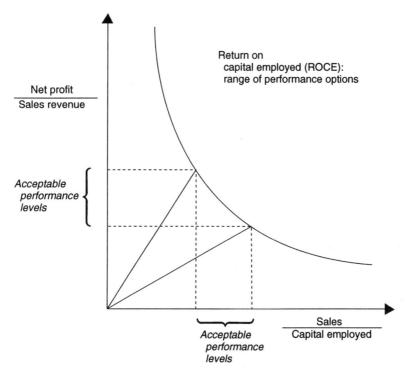

Figure 8.16 Strategy decisions: alternative values

enables the manager to ask 'what if?' questions and then decide upon a course of action from a range of decision outcome alternatives.

The components of both the margin spread and the asset base are important issues within the decision/information set. Primary measures of productivity and profitability performance are the operating return on sales together with the operating return on assets managed and the net return on capital employed.

9 Productivity and Profitability Planning and Control: Decision Types

INTRODUCTION

Chapter 8 established a decision/information format for making productivity and profitability decisions. We have argued throughout this text that productivity and profitability decisions have strategic *and* operational perspectives. In this chapter we shall explore the nature of these decisions.

In this chapter we shall use a number of approaches (based upon the discussion and models developed in earlier chapters). We shall be using

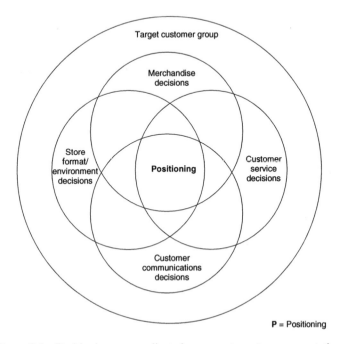

Figure 9.1   Positioning: a co-ordinated response to customer expectations

those that seem appropriate to the examples used in this chapter such as the models from Chapter 6 (Figures 6.10, 6.12) and the margin spread performance components (Figures 4.3 and 4.6). In addition to these there will be another approach introduced, the Issues/Objectives Summary. This is explained and used in some of the examples.

The effectiveness of decision making at both the strategic and operational level can be considered graphically. In Figure 9.1 the decision process is shown to be an integrated activity with decisions concerning: merchandise; customer service; store format and environment; and customer communications 'overlapping' to provide reinforcement for the selected positioning response. Figure 9.1 also suggests that the more effective the positioning is then the better the 'fit' with the expectations of the target customer group.

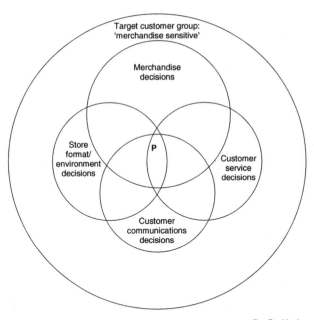

P = Positioning

Productivity and profitability emphasis will be on ensuring that features such as choice, availability and exclusivity generate target sales and profit (gross) and operating profiitability.

The merchandise offer is seen as the most important element in the retail offer. Customer service, store enviroment and customer communications support the merchandise offer. Specialist stores (such as sportswear) are examples.

Figure 9.2(a)   Merchandise-led positioning

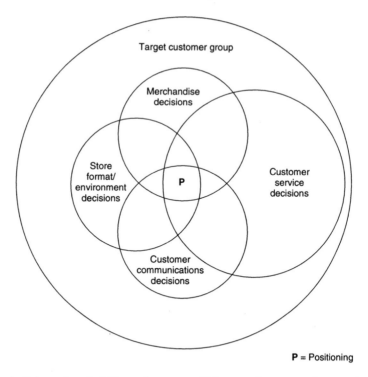

Productivity and profitability performance will focus on the space and personel used to 'deliver' customer services.

No strong merchandise differentiation is either required by customer (or competitively viable). Differentiation is therefore achieved by product-services, service-products and personel services. Department stores are examples.

Figure 9.2(b) Customer service-led positioning

We should also consider the possibility (if not the certainty) that the positioning response may require a particular direction or differentiation. Hence we may expect an emphasis on one or more of the positioning response options where research establishes an implied requirement by customers for a more specific response – a specific 'lead' by merchandise, customer service and so on. This is the role of management: to identify the need for editing the retail offer and providing focus on a particular component. Figure 9.2 suggests how each component may be used in this respect, with examples.

Clearly this situation will influence the resource allocation decision and the productivity and profitability performance expectations. These are outlined in the figures. A more detailed discussion follows.

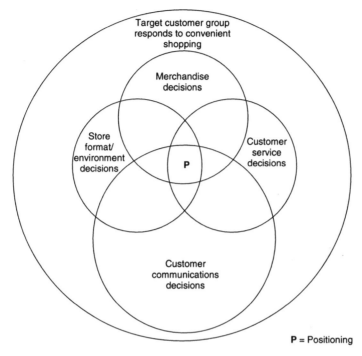

Productivity and profitability will focus on transactions generated by data base activity. The growth of data bases for customer communications has led to a number of retailing companies extending and/or adding sophistication to their existing offer. Racing Green is an example of a company whose initial offer was communications-led.

Figure 9.2(c)   Customer communications are used to focus positioning

PLANNING AND CONTROL FOR MERCHANDISE DECISIONS

Strategic merchandise decisions

Some of the **decision topics** and **decision areas** likely to be encountered are suggested in Figure 9.3. They are by their nature long term and potentially far-reaching throughout the business. As we suggested earlier in this chapter, positioning may be merchandise-led – in which case the question branding (either which suppliers' brands are offered or what characteristics are to be featured in a company own brand) becomes a major issue. The role of concessions is also important because they may enable the company to extend its merchandise offer much more cost-effectively than by 'investing' in merchandise, space and staff only to

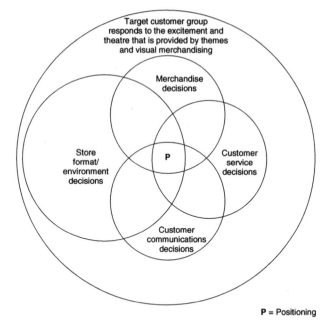

The effective use of both merchandise and place will be primary measures of productivity and profitability. Measures will be made across traditional department 'territories' and based upon joint stock and space performance measures, for example OMROI, OMRO space.

Adding theatre or exciment through the store enviroment is the basis of this approach. Themes and 'end-use' applications with opportunity to try the product is a justifiable use of space. Early Learning Centre, sports equipment specialists and DIY retailers are examples.

Figure 9.2(d)   Store format and environment-led positioning

achieve a less than acceptable return on the investment. Concessions benefit from economies of scale and consequently there is a mutual advantage for both parties.

Core product policies are equally significant. Not only do they prescribe the basic offer to be made in response to customer expectations but they also indicate the space required for effective visual merchandising and support stock, together with the levels of working capital required to offer service to customers. A longer-term consideration concerns the development of the business around specialist merchandise areas; therefore what may initially appear to be an excessive working capital investment may have a long-term benefit.

Assortment profiles should reflect initial customer demand centre characteristics. For example, price-led offers usually use price points and

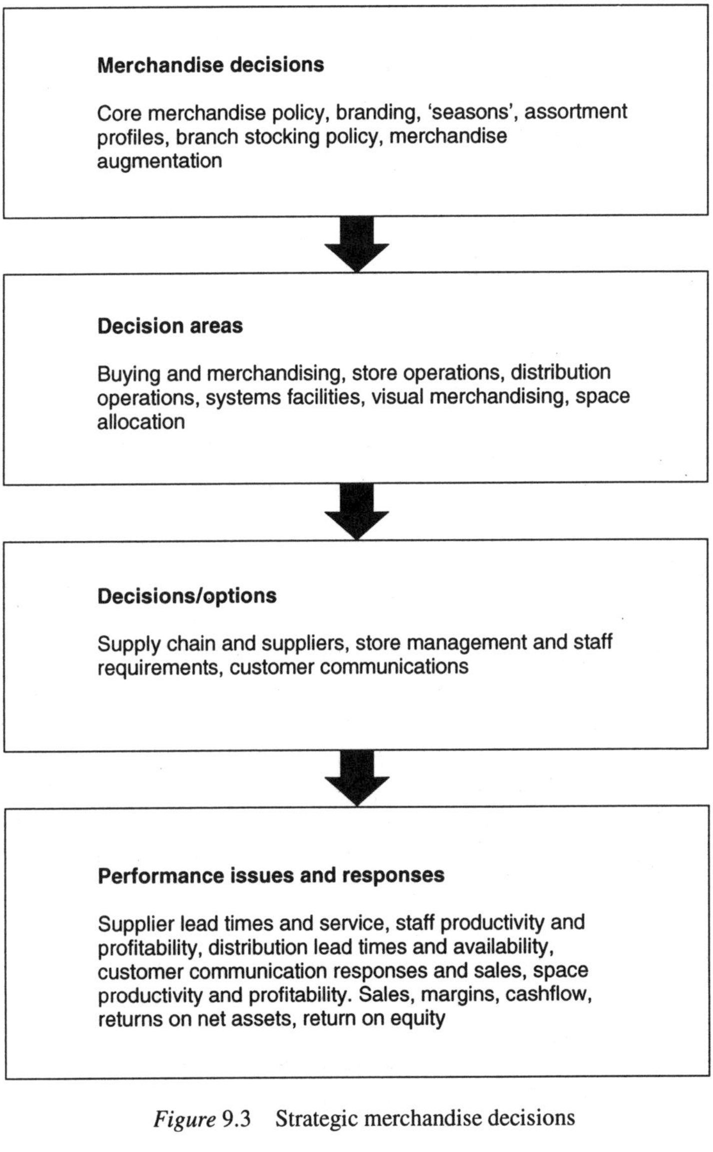

Decision Types

Merchandise decisions

Core merchandise policy, branding, 'seasons', assortment profiles, branch stocking policy, merchandise augmentation

Decision areas

Buying and merchandising, store operations, distribution operations, systems facilities, visual merchandising, space allocation

Decisions/options

Supply chain and suppliers, store management and staff requirements, customer communications

Performance issues and responses

Supplier lead times and service, staff productivity and profitability, distribution lead times and availability, customer communication responses and sales, space productivity and profitability. Sales, margins, cashflow, returns on net assets, return on equity

Figure 9.3   Strategic merchandise decisions

leading prices as the consumer attraction or focus. Merchandise stocks are allocated around a range of price points which are known to be those generating most customer interest and transactions. Similarly branch stocking profiles should reflect local demand characteristics, with stock allocation following both the merchandise groups and characteristics, indicated by customer research. A similar approach is required for other demand characteristics. Choice can be expensive (from a stockholding costs viewpoint) if it is not managed by a similar method. For example, price points, colours, end-use or 'brands' may be the demand centre characteristics used by customers: whichever is the initial demand centre it should be used as the focus for merchandise assortment decisions, in this way stockholding levels may be managed to meet customer expectations *and* company targets for working capital investment.

Merchandise augmentation decisions will reflect the overall merchandise strategy. Essentially it aims to expand the value of transactions and the gross margins generated from the merchandise, but can only do so if the customer sees value-added and responds accordingly.

Clearly there may be other important topics. It is likely that specific merchandise categories or perhaps positioning formats will have particular topics (or even critical success factors) that are recurring issues. It is essential that these are identified and researched because effective management of recurring issues suggests that it may lead to sustainable competitive advantage.

The **decision areas** most frequently involved in strategic merchandise decisions are identified by the activities described in the earlier paragraphs. It is important to identify the relevant decision areas for a number of reasons. The first concerns organisation structure. It is obvious that organisation structure should reflect decision-making, if this is to be effective. By so doing it permits a responsibility/accountability structure to develop which not only facilitates effective management, but also enables expertise to be developed. Another important issue concerns the management of costs. By identifying the important **activity centres** we also identify the important **activity costs** and by doing so are able to allocate overhead costs more accurately to both merchandise and operations functions within the business. (See Walters, *Retailing Management*, 1994, for a more detailed discussion of this topic.) The decision areas suggested to be important include: merchandise and buying; distribution operations; store operations; system facilities; and visual merchandising. However, as with the **decision topics** these may differ across a range of businesses.

The **decisions/options** available will reflect overall productivity and profitability objectives. For example, a merchandise strategy decision concerning merchandise quality may require the buying and merchandising function to re-evaluate suppliers' abilities to meet increased quality requirements. These may also require a review of margin expectations (assuming that COGS will increase if product quality and quality control costs are increased). A more far-reaching implication may be involved if the motivation for the decision is based in changing consumer requirements rather than a detected decrease in quality by existing suppliers. If the emphasis is upon meeting customer expectations, an extensive review is required not only of suppliers but also of stock profiles to meet the consumer changes.

It is not difficult to think of examples for each of the other **decision areas**. For example, an increase in the competitive intensity in a segment may require more effective visual merchandising *and* space utilisation. A hypothetical situation may be envisaged in which in order to meet increased competition the number of seasons is increased together with a decision to make visual merchandising more persuasive (that is, to increase the value of transactions *and* the gross margin yield) and to increase, merchandise availability. A number of decisions require attention. Clearly stock levels will increase as will the demand for space in store. In essence the company would be attempting to offer increased choice in terms of merchandise group changes (the increase in seasons) and *within* the merchandise groups. In addition the stock levels in the stores will increase to ensure availability levels are increased to prevent customer disappointment if a colour or size (or both) is not available. **Performance issues** now become important. An increase in stock levels will increase working capital, decrease stock turn and change the space utilisation profile (that is, space productivity and merchandise density factors together with overall space allocation/utilisation performance levels). Two essential factors should be considered: the rate of sale of the merchandise and, associated with it, the elasticity of the space resource.

The competitive response can only be justified if it improves revenues and contribution – that is, productivity and profitability. It follows that a number of considerations emerge. The increase in the number of merchandise seasons will impose higher stock levels and *may* result in lower stock turns, higher mark downs and therefore decreased performance. Sales revenue may increase but the margin spread could well decrease. Furthermore, changes in space allocation may result in a reduction in productivity and profitability due to the fact that the sales response (sales per space unit) decreases sooner than is forecast.

Clearly there are a number of decisions required and to reach the most effective for the company both the decisions and their likely outcomes require a thorough analysis. Two steps are proposed for this. first an issues/objectives summary should be drafted (see Table 9.1) in which the cause of the strategy re-evaluation is examined and during which a range of decision options and their implications are identified and explored. Following on from this a decision/performance trace can be

Table 9.1 Identifying a strategic response to changes in the competitive environment

Issue:	Increasing competitive activities in the target customer segment is causing a loss of sales revenue and is challenging the company's position as the premier 'destination shopping' outlet.
Objectives:	To maintain/increase credibility and customer loyalty To maintain/increase sales revenue and cash flow To maintain/increase customer purchasing visits and average transactions To maintain return on capital employed (and shareholders funds): expansion of facilities should not dilute earnings To maintain/increase strategic productivity and profitability
Decision options (sales revenue):	S1. Increase the number of seasons from five to eight each year. S2. Expand the high performance/specialist merchandise groups (width and depth). S3. Increase the participation from 'customer attraction' and 'support' merchandise groups. S4. Expand core product range cover of high performance specialist merchandise group. S5. Introduce core product concept into the 'customer attraction' merchandise group. S6. Increase the effectiveness of visual merchandising. S7. Expand merchandise augmentation.
Implications:	1. Stockholding will increase significantly, requiring an increase in distribution storage and/or transportation facilities. 2. Space allocation between merchandise and customer service will require adjustment, as will space allocation between merchandise groups. 3. Expansion of buying and merchandising groups is *not* required. 4. Store personnel will require training to understand, introduce (and sell effectively) any 'new' merchandise concept. 5. Visual merchandising activities will increase and increased staff costs may be expected.

Decision options (gross margins):	G1. Increase buying terms by:
	    • renegotiating discount structure and/or distribution services;
	    • negotiating increases in buying terms for core product ranges (to be expanded);
	    • rationalising supplier numbers.
	G2. Expand merchandise augmentation.
	G3. Rationalise 'service' merchandise groups.

Implications:	1. The risk of mark-downs will increase due to the increase in specialist range coverage (the range of fashion merchandise will increase); supplier rationalisation will restrict buyers' selection ranges.

Table 9.1 *Continued*

	2. Merchandise availability may be reduced if the company reduces the number of suppliers. 3. A small decrease in gross margins will occur in 'service' ranges.
Decision options (operating margins):	O1. Sales productivity may be increased by changing the allocation of space used for sales and customer services. O2. Merchandise density may be increased if current availability levels are to be maintained. O3. Subsequent to reformatting the merchandise offer (that is, expanding the number of merchandise seasons and planning to increase merchandise participation of the specialist, customer attraction and support merchandise groups) it is to be expected that some stores will be unable to produce the productivity and profitability performance expected and may require a decision concerning rationalisation. O4. Staff numbers may be increased if specialisation is increased (alternatively staff hours may be re-scheduled to provide more cover at peak trading times – and less when trading is low). O5. A reduction of customer service facilities will release both space and staff. O6. Availability may be maintained by increasing distribution service to the stores either through expanding facilities by using distribution service companies or the distribution services of suppliers. O7. An increase in promotional/advertising spend will be required to support strategy direction changes.
Implications:	1. There may be a negative impact on sales (and profits) if customer services and facilities are withdrawn. 2. An increase in merchandise density may restrict customer traffic flows and reduce sales (and profit) as average transaction levels decrease. 3. Rationalising stores will have a negative impact on distribution utilisation; the capacity increases may or may not be used to compensate for increased capacity demanded by the increased activity levels: some may be regional. 4. Staff re-scheduling may prove to be difficult in small stores due to low numbers of staff and, therefore, low flexibility. 5. It follows that operating margin changes may be both positive and negative and decision options should be carefully examined for situations whereby cost increase cannot be compensated either by increased productivity and profitability from the increased activity or from cost savings realised by a reduction in activity levels.

Table 9.1 Continued

Decision options (trading assets):

A1. Pressure in selling areas may be reduced by increased distribution facilities (expansions, additions or third-party services).

A2. Future location acquisitions may require to be larger and located in higher customer traffic density areas if the new strategy is to succeed.

A3. Refixturing may increase sales productivity and profitability and merchandise density (for example, merchandise displays that utilise wall space currently not in use; fixtures that improve visual merchandising effectiveness.

Implications:

1. Any increase in fixed assets will require compensatory increases in productivity and profitability of ROAM and ROCE are to be maintained.
2. Distribution facilities may be expanded 'off-balance sheet' but only with a reduction of the operating margin.
3. Freeholds and leaseholds for alternative locations may prove to be significantly higher than those of existing locations.

Overall Implications:

1. A shift in strategic direction is accompanied by an increase in risk. Specialisation offers higher returns and higher risk. It follows that the changes made should be such that existing customer loyalty is both maintained and increased to ensure that customer purchasing activities (and loyalties) are increased and to compensate capital expansion.
2. Both fixed assets and working capital are likely to expand. Initially fixed assets may be funded 'off balance sheet' but working capital requirements will need overdraft funds unless supplier relationships may be structured to avoid this.
3. Mark-down policy will require careful consideration. A well-planned 'sell through' policy will be required if gross margins are not to be eroded and the margin spread expanded.
4. From 2 and 3 it follows that the margin spread must be expanded if the strategy is implemented. Not only are there mark-down considerations but operational activities may increase some costs which cannot be compensated for: hence both buying and merchandising and store operations' activities will require careful planning and control.
5. An overall concern for the business is to determine its investment strategy. This will be determined by the view held concerning the nature of the business and the extent to which it desires to own and operate 'service' functions and activities.

designed, which places the decision options into their context within the model established in Chapter 6 (see Figure 6.10). The 'trace' for this particular example is described by Figure 9.4.

The next step is for management to allocate costs to the options and to evaluate the performance implications for relevant productivity and profitability characteristics. In the example we have used there are three relevant factors: fixed asset productivity and profitability; net current asset productivity and profitability; and capital employed productivity and profitability. The example suggests that 'management' requires the performance in each of the six characteristics to remain as it is or, if possible, to improve. Figure 9.5 considers the implications for margins and trading assets.

These broad areas are the basic performance criteria. They may be expanded to identify elements of each, depending upon their importance. We shall discuss these measures in some detail within the context of the examples/case studies in subsequent chapters.

Operational merchandise decisions

Operational merchandise decision-making follows the format established above for strategic decisions. (See Figure 9.6 and Table 9.2.)

The **decision topics** will include changes to:

- assortment expansion/contraction; assortment characteristics (such as width, depth and availability profiles);
- core product items within the 'basic' and 'model' stock lists;
- merchandise augmentation cover;
- product-service support; and
- branch stockholding listings.

Whereas the strategic merchandise decisions were concerned with policy matters, operational decisions deal with detailed (tactical) changes *within* the overall strategy.

Decisions areas at the operational level are likely to be more specific. Suggestions include:

- sourcing and procurement;
- stockholding profiles;
- visual merchandising;
- service augmentation; and
- implications for operations activities.

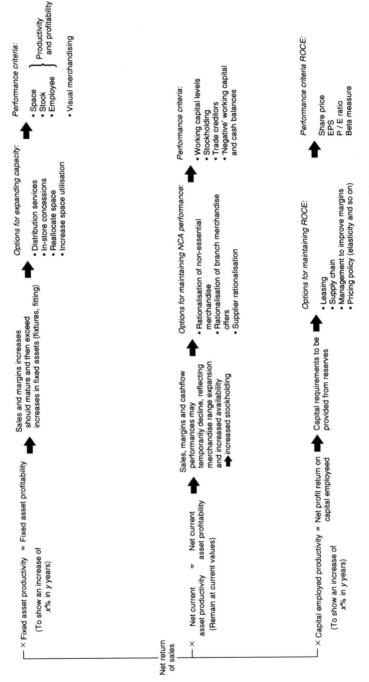

Figure 9.4 A strategic decision/performance trace: merchandise-led decisions

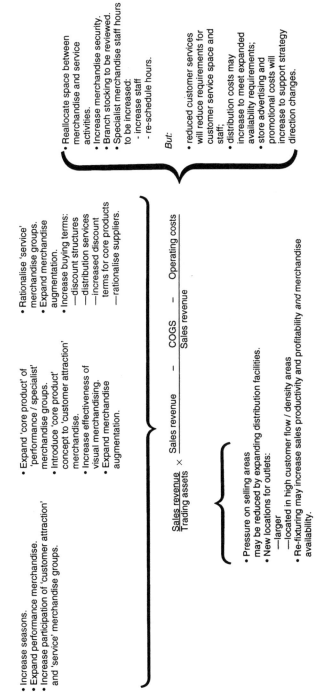

Figure 9.5 Decision options strategic merchandise changes and the margin spread

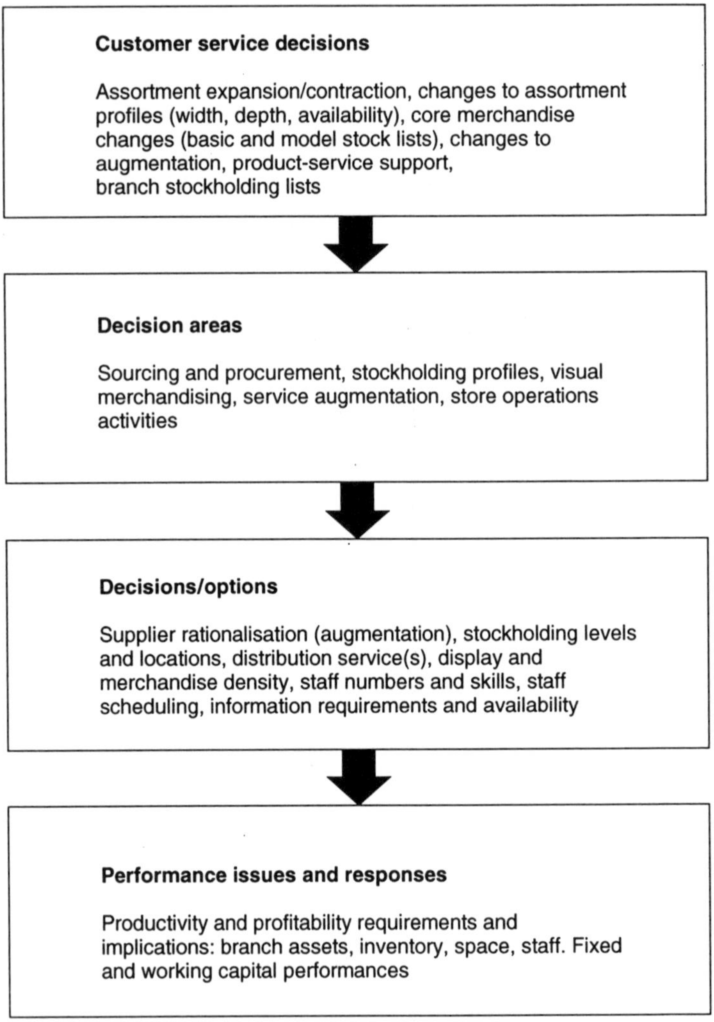

Customer service decisions

Assortment expansion/contraction, changes to assortment profiles (width, depth, availability), core merchandise changes (basic and model stock lists), changes to augmentation, product-service support, branch stockholding lists

Decision areas

Sourcing and procurement, stockholding profiles, visual merchandising, service augmentation, store operations activities

Decisions/options

Supplier rationalisation (augmentation), stockholding levels and locations, distribution service(s), display and merchandise density, staff numbers and skills, staff scheduling, information requirements and availability

Performance issues and responses

Productivity and profitability requirements and implications: branch assets, inventory, space, staff. Fixed and working capital performances

Figure 9.6 Operational merchandise decisions

From the decision areas a number of **decisions/options** are derived; as with the strategic decision example, not all of them are feasible or desirable. **Performance options** identify the range of productivity and profitability performance outcomes possible by the resource inputs of:

- branch assets;
- inventory;
- space; and
- staff.

Table 9.2 Identifying an operational response to changes in the competitive environment: an operational merchandise decision

Issue:	Consumer expectations are becoming dominated by price concern during a prolonged period of recession. For both of the company's 'offers' there is now significant margin erosion (as prices are lowered to meet competitors price offers) and there is a noticeable, but as yet not damaging, decline in sales revenues. There is also a differential market share performance across both regions and stores.
Objectives:	To maintain/recover margins in both chains To return both businesses to their planned levels of productivity and profitability performances, thereby maintaining profit and earnings and shareholder returns
Decision options (Sales revenues):	S1. Maintain or increase revenues by selective promotional and advertising activities, such as: • price reductions based on previous purchases (consider elasticity issues); • Selective price reductions (loss leaders) • related purchases: 'special' prices for products usually purchased together (for example, 80 per cent of customers are known to have purchased products A and B at the same time, and 40 per cent of transactions include A, B and C); • multi-buys: specially priced quantities of selected products throughout the assortment. S2. Increase advertising expenditure selectively: • in areas where stores are within the coverage of successful media, thereby increasing the economies of scale; • in selected areas where stores are underperforming due to competitive pressures. S3. Review core product ranges and items. Evaluate the success of the core product concept with a view to making effective changes (these may have to expand or reduce the coverage of the concept): customer research will be required. S4. Reduce the ranges offered in both offers: this would enable lower prices to be offered (through improved buying terms) and thereby increase sales. (Offers to become 17,500 and 1500 SKUs, they were 20,000 and 3000 respectively).
Implications:	1. Price reductions may not increase overall sales volume and revenues. Careful analysis of all previous price reduction exercises should be considered to evaluate elasticity effects. 2. Loss leaders can be counter-productive. Once customers realise that the items are priced lower than those of competitors they will purchase only those items and reduce overall purchases by buying other requirements from competitors if they offer price deals.

Table 9.2 Continued

3. Related purchases will require inventory support; stock-outs of any of the featured merchandise will result in an overall reduction of sales (and margins) far greater than might otherwise occur. However, in the larger stores, where ranges are wider, the options may prove to be more cost effective.
4. 'Multi buys' will raise stockholding requirements and costs and result in lower subsequent customer purchase volumes. However, if the concept is introduced on merchandise which is a regular purchase item, offering high margins (or for which supplier contributions might be obtained, such as discount terms or distribution services) it has relevance as an option in the current circumstances.
5. Increasing advertising expenditure will clearly increase costs of the stores featured in the promotion programme. *Also* it is accompanied with covert cost increases within distribution and store operations activities ensuring 'delivery' of the advertised offer.
6. Core range review offers two possible outcomes:
    - if it is proving to be successful, then it follows that an expansion of concept would enhance revenues and possibly margins;
    - if it is not proving to be successful, then a phased withdrawal will reduce costs and not be particularly damaging towards sales.

Decisions options (Gross margins):

G1. Renegotiate buying terms:
- across the range for both 'offers';
- for selected promotional items;
- for core product range items;
- for one 'offer' only.

G2. Rationalise assortment and thereby increase margins but decrease customer choice. Ranges to become 17,500 SKUs and 1500 SKUs

G3. Rationalise suppliers: select those who offer a number of items in the assortment.

Implications:

1. Renegotiated terms will not be obtained without concessions. Suppliers may require:
    - exclusivity (which would restrict choice);
    - access to stores (which would interfere with space allocation and performance);
    - a rearrangement of distribution services which may add to company costs, not help reduce them, together with availability;
2. A rationalised assortment (unless conducted with utmost care) will result in a lower appeal for customers and possibly lower sales (and therefore margins).

Table 9.2 Continued

	3. By rationalising suppliers the company may expose itself to offering customers lower choice and increase the risk of out-of-stock situations.
Decision options (operating margins):	O1. Sales productivity increases will result in improvements in operating margins due to range rationalisation: • lower range 'in-store merchandising' costs; • Increased merchandise density (which in turn will increase availability but can decrease distribution costs). As sales increase (or are maintained) the impact on operating margins of lowered costs will be to improve operating margins. O2. Space reallocation may need to reinforce the range rationalisation activities.
Implications:	1. Operating margins can be increased by lowering staff requirements (in-store merchandising) following range rationalisation. 2. Distribution service requirements are likely to be obtained at lower cost levels due to the fact that packing and order assembly activities will be con solidated and stockholding costs lowered subsequent to the range rationalisation activities.
Decision options (trading/branch assets):	A1. Pressure on selling areas may be reduced by reducing width and depth profiles of merchandise assortment. A2. Future store development decisions may be influenced: range rationalisation may suggest smaller selling areas and consequently smaller stores. A3. Range rationalisation may offer an opportunity to reconsider fixturing decisions.
Implications:	1. A reduction in range offers (both stores) will require an increase in sales from the remaining merchandise offer if sales productivity *and* space productivity is to be maintained. 2. The return on branch assets will be improved due to reduced stockholding (and reduced operating costs). 3. Long-term investment may be reduced if merchandise rationalisation proves to be effective. 4. If only the price incentives are used, there may be a large increase in throughput requiring increases in distribution facility capacities.
Overall implications:	1. A decision concerning price differentials between the two offers is an essential issue and one which should be addressed initially. If the difference and

Table 9.2 Continued

  the offer itself is allowed to narrow, customers may drift towards the lower-priced offer, thereby increasing the problems of the 'up-market' business.
2. Within both businesses the price adjustment decisions should consider price elasticity as well as choice.
   Range reductions should be made where it has been established that choice is not an important issue for customers: but if the purpose of range reductions is to increase margins and lower prices, then consumer response to price reductions should be explored.
   If it is seen that sales volume does not increase to a level sufficient to increase revenue and profit within a reasonable time period, the decision clearly cannot be seen to be successful and alternative measures considered.
3. The full cost-implications of range/price adjustments should be considered. Very large price differentials may result in very large shifts in customer demand; the inability to respond may present problems for customer retention.
4. Supplier rationalisation should be undertaken only after all issues have been considered. Mistakes can prove to be costly as and when negotiations are re-opened.
5. The success of the option selected will have long-term implications for future developments of both store offers. Less selling space may reduce overall development costs *but* efficient and effective distribution facilities to provide quick response systems and service may introduce alternative investment considerations.

In addition the conventional financial measures for **performance** are measured.

As we suggested above, operational decisions are concerned with tactical events. They may be proactive or reactive but are essentially decisions taken within an already determined set of policies concerning the overall strategic direction of the business. An example may prove helpful.

Consider the problems of a national food multiple which operates two different retail offers. One chain competes with the two major national companies and here the offer comprises a merchandise offer based upon width and depth, offering a wide range of choice, in large superstore format, supported by a range of customer service products and facilities. The other 'offer' comprises a range of low-price, low-service outlets.

Prior to the recession both were well-positioned in their respective segments. To maintain margin differentials a range of retail brands was offered in both store groups and in the discount store costs were constantly monitored to meet productivity and profitability objectives. The SKU coverage (stock-keeping units) for the superstores is approximately 20 000 items, whereas the discount operation has managed to contain assortment expansion to 2500–3000 SKUs.

Increasing competition for both 'store brands' has intensified and both volumes and margins are under pressure. The response is to consider short-term options that will prevent further loss of revenues (market share) and margin erosion. As well as declines in overall profitability, there are reasons for concern for the productivity performance of space, staff and inventory investment. To evaluate a competitive response to what the 'executive' considers may become a long-term problem a similar procedure to that followed for the strategic example would be necessary.

A decision/performance trace and a margin spread profile would also be constructed.

PLANNING AND CONTROL FOR CUSTOMER SERVICE DECISIONS

Strategic customer service decisions

A common problem for retailing management is the extent to which customer service is becoming a permanent feature of retailing. For many it is becoming a strategic positioning issue. Typical of the decision options facing management is the extent to which customers consider specific aspects of service as 'given': these are credit facilities, fitting (changing rooms), delivery and installation, and so on. Many of these service characteristics have appeared over recent years but almost all are expected by customers: hence they are 'qualifying' services – features that are essential if customers are to consider a particular retailer as a *potential* supplier. Determining features of service are characteristics which are adding extra value to the offer. Often they are exclusive and as such provide competitive advantage. They are service features that influence the customers strongly such that they consider the store an essential component in their 'shopping' activity (see Figure 9.7).

It follows that customer service requires investment in fixed-cost facilities and human resources and often additional service products

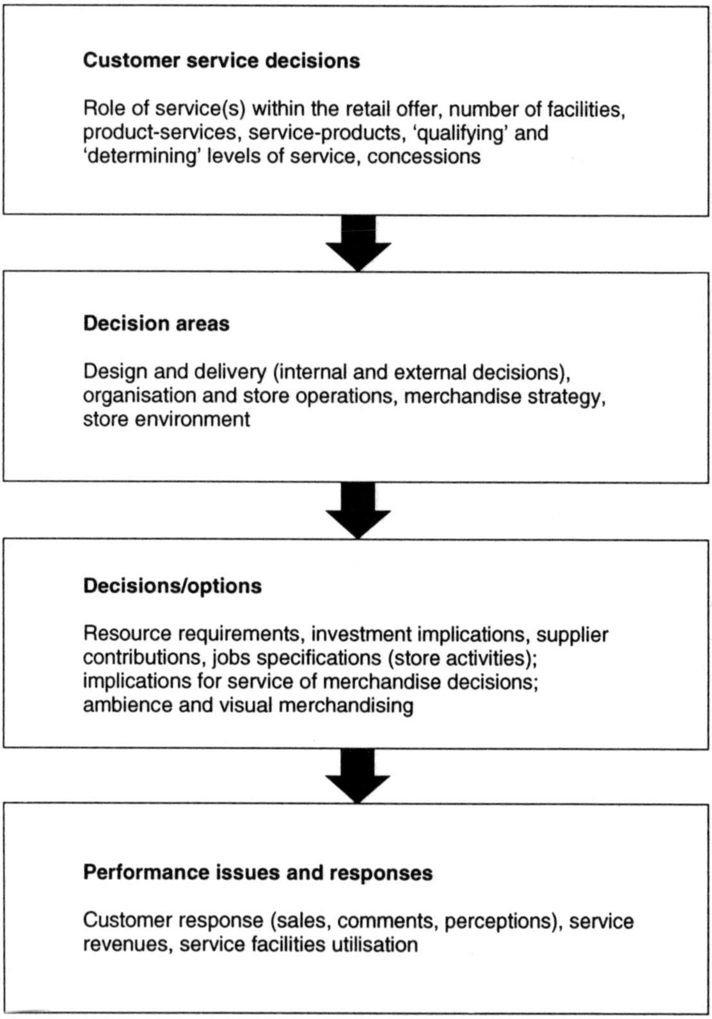

Customer service decisions

Role of service(s) within the retail offer, number of facilities, product-services, service-products, 'qualifying' and 'determining' levels of service, concessions

Decision areas

Design and delivery (internal and external decisions), organisation and store operations, merchandise strategy, store environment

Decisions/options

Resource requirements, investment implications, supplier contributions, jobs specifications (store activities); implications for service of merchandise decisions; ambience and visual merchandising

Performance issues and responses

Customer response (sales, comments, perceptions), service revenues, service facilities utilisation

Figure 9.7 Strategic customer service decisions

are required. In addition to these considerations others are equally important: the opportunity costs of space; the changes required in merchandise augmentation; adjustments to the existing service offer, and so on.

The decision should be approached in a similar way to that for allocating resources for merchandise-led decisions. Table 9.3 identifies decision issues (and options) and their implications. These are considered within the context of a decision performance trace and this analysis is extended using the margin spread/asset base model.

Table 9.3 Strategic Repositioning: a response to a customer trend for 'service facilities'

Issue:	Over time there has been a noticeable increase in customer awareness of service facilities. Competitors who have met this demand satisfactorily have increased sales and profits. The 'executive' could decide (following extensive research) to increase the service facilities in its largest stores. These include crèche/child care areas, wardrobe (fashion/style) consultants and health and fitness centres.
Objectives:	To increase the differentiation of the larger stores, each of which operates in a segment comprising high spending, highly discerning and service sensitive customers. To expand the penetration within this group and thereby increase volumes and profitability To increase the number of visits and purchases made by existing customers To become the destination purchase store (first choice) within this segment To maintain the current level of ROCE and ROE: funding to be from reserves To maintain/increase the company's performance across selected strategic productivity and profitability criteria
Decision options (sales revenue):	S1. Expand coverage of merchandise augmentation in non-price sensitive/high levels of sales response merchandise groups. S2. Expand coverage of service augmentation: service facilities which encourage customers to extend their 'in-store' stay and 'information' facilities which either expand customer interests and encourage trial purchases or expand the benefits of products already owned and which can be 'added' to (sport/leisure products, home improvement, education/development toys). S3. Consider service facilities that are ex-store on a strategic alliance basis in order that economies of sale may be achieved from overall operations (for example, service and maintenance facilities for consumer durables). S4. In-store service facilities may be more effectively offered and managed using a concession or external specialist.
Implications:	1. The increase of service functions will increase service density and decrease merchandise density: 'trade-off' decisions between sales/service areas and between and within merchandise groups. 2. Additional merchandise items may be required: for example, child care areas require both fixtures and a range of disposable products. 3. Service availability and delivery issues are critical: capacities and capabilities requirements differ widely across service functions and require understanding. 4. Distribution operations costs may change due to changes in the patterns of merchandise offers and their rates of sale and stockholding requirements.

Table 9.3 *Continued*

Decision options (gross margins):	G1. Where possible, perceived value-added should be enhanced by the addition of service facilities: for example, the overall margins generated by a children's toys department should be capable of generating adequate gross margin to compensate for the loss of sales area used for *product* demonstration (play areas/crèche). This suggests that merchandise groups for which customers are *not* price-sensitive are likely 'candidates' and that the service augmentation is credible.
	G2. Strong, successful, own-brand merchandise groups for which price comparison is not feasible, are candidates for service augmentation.
	G3. Merchandise and service synergy are preferable combinations. Often suppliers may be persuaded to contribute to costs.
Implications:	1. Value-added perceptions and costs are typically a function of *qualifying* and *determining* levels of customer service. Costs may be investment costs with differing levels of fixed and variable costs. There are numerous issues concerning the structure of break-even volumes and margins to be evaluated.
Decision options (operating margins):	O1. Service intensity increases (service dedicated staff/total staff) as service facilities are expanded. However, options may exist for the substitute of costly specialist labour with IT-based systems which increase fixed costs.
	O2. An alternative is to seek high variable costs (specialist labour) which are available (and therefore only charged) on demand.
	O3. Differences in staff abilities and availabilities may result in differing rates of pay and working practices. These should be considered not only from a costing point of view but also for their implications on staff–employee relations.
Implications:	1. Store operations systems may be insufficiently flexible and therefore difficult to adapt to the management of service activities.
	2. The addition of service facilities will result in changes in store design and layout. It follows that unless care is exercised, integration may not result and the previous effectiveness of visual merchandising may be diluted.
Decision options (trading assets):	A1. An increase in facilities *will* require investment and the issue is to ensure that the quality of the facilities is acceptable to customers. Here the service design/delivery concepts of qualifying services (and determining services) are fundamental to the investment decision.

Table 9.3 Continued

	A2. The decision to expand service facilities across the range of outlets (after evaluation of customer responses) may require careful consideration. Not only is the size of the investment an important consideration but the opportunities to develop and take advantage of economies of scale feature as prominent factors.
Overall implications:	1. The decision to expand service augmentation, density, and/or intensity is one which may result in positioning not actually planned. Careful research should be undertaken at all stages. 2. Because of (1), supervising cost profiles may emerge. An effective method of control is to estimate the necessary level of customer visits and transaction values that will be required given the changes to the merchandise offer, space allocation changes, additional staff costs and the investment required (and the method of funding). 3. The implications of changes in cash flow levels may be significant, particularly if merchandise rationalisation has been extensive.

The **decision area** issues suggested concern the

- design and delivery of the customer service package;
- organisation and store operations implications;
- changes required to the merchandise strategy and
- store environment factors.

Each issue may have two or more **options**. Decisions in this area are essentially concerned with facilities and staff and how these may be combined in the most cost-effective way to achieve the type and level of service required. Again these may be considered graphically as a decision/performance trace and a margin spread profile.

Operational customer service decisions

Operational customer service decisions typically involve aspects of operational repositioning whereby current customer expectations are demonstrating an incremental shift towards a particular aspect of service. For example, food multiples responded for the demand for more in-store customer service by: training merchandising staff (shelf replenishment) to respond effectively to requests for product location information; shortening check-out queues; and making information generally more

Customer service decisions

An increase of service facilities together with an increase in service-products; changes to qualifying and/or determining levels of service; changes to merchandise related issues

Decision areas

Design and delivery of 'service' availability and quality; merchandise strategy and characteristics; space requirements, organisation and store operations; implications for distribution and information systems

Decisions/options

Qualifying and determining service 'level' changes; maintaining 'levels' of service targets; service issues arising from changes in merchandise characteristics and profiles; sales/ service area costs and benefits; opportunity costs; changes in staff numbers and skills; training schedules

Performance issues and responses

Customer response (sales, comments, perceptions); revenues; service space productivity and profitability performance

Figure 9.8   Operational customer service decisions

readily available by installing customer service facilities. Essentially this involved a small addition to staff numbers, labour scheduling and staff training.

We can see the effects of these types of decisions through Figure 9.8. The **decision areas** concern (as for strategy decisions) design and delivery; merchandise strategy changes; organisation and store operations. To these topics are added space requirements together with the implications for distribution and systems facilities. These are important considerations. Whereas they are implicit in the original overall design of the offer, an operational change may be accompanied by significant implications for both activities. The **decision options** concern levels of service and how these may be delivered to achieve service outputs at acceptable cost inputs. The **performance issues** relate productivity and profitability output levels to basic resource inputs of branch assets, space and staff. **Performance responses** are those described earlier.

As with the earlier examples, Table 9.4 identifies the issue, objectives and decision options and implications. These may be considered in the context of a decision performance trace and the margin spread/asset base model.

Table 9.4 Operational customer service decision to increase staff response to customers requests for in-store information concerning use of products

Issue:	Staff have been asked for advice and information concerning the use of products for specific applications. This has largely been brought about by changes in product technology and applications.
Objectives:	To provide customers with advice on the suitability of products for specified tasks and on the application of the products To ensure that sales and margins are increased to cover adequately the cost increases imposed by additional staff and management and staff training
Decision options (sales responses):	S1. Increase point of sale (POS) information by: • Installing video cassette recorders in each major department featuring tapes demonstrating how major tasks may be undertaken: — customers select tapes for viewing; or — the topics appear on a rotation basis; or — a member of staff supervises the operation. • Increasing written communication at the POS. This may be achieved by using fixture installations to carry 'step-by-step' instructional diagrams supported by take-away leaflets. S2. Increasing the number of staff in-store who (already) have training and expertise in plumbing, joinery and electrical matters, and so on. S3. Review merchandise options, selecting items which are either 'easy to use' (user-friendly) or carry explicit instructions for use. S4. Review supplier options, selecting those who either have the customer information required, or are willing to consider contributing (staff or cash [discount]) to the problem.

Table 9.4 Continued

Implications:	1.	The service issue is to build confidence in the customer who, once having made a purchase and a successful installation/application, will:
		• establish the store as a destination purchase store; • become more adventurous and attempt more DIY activities.
	2.	The cost issue concerns how this may be achieved cost-effectively:
		• VCRs are limited in the amount of information they can deliver: often they may raise more questions than they answer; • VCRs need supervision, updating and replacement (when stolen); • in-store staff are expensive but can respond and therefore amplify explanations.
	3.	The convenience issue concerns delivering relevant information that is helpful *when* it is required. This suggests flexibility and quality are important service aspects.
Decision options (gross margins):		As an increase in costs may be expected, viable measures to increase gross margins should be explored.
	G1.	Investigate merchandise groups with a view to identifying those in which the following characteristics exist:
		• strong price-sensitivity • low price-sensitivity • strong choice expectations • low choice expectations.
		Range rationalisation of merchandise with strong price/low choice expectations will offer an opportunity to increase buying terms in merchandise areas where price competitiveness is essential but where choice is relatively unimportant.
	G2.	In-store information services should be developed around products for which:
		• margins are high; • merchandise augmentation can be achieved relatively simply.
Implications:	1.	Though it may be argued that range rationalisation is *not* the issue, there are two important aspects to be considered: the increase of the service offer will require an increase in space *and* staff resources. Both are not easily found and therefore logical readjustments to the offer that are unlikely to create dissatisfaction should be pursued.
Decision options (operating margins):		Without careful research into how, when and what is required by the customer base, considerable cost may be incurred. The research should consider the following issues:
		• the nature of the information and advice sought by customers – this will determine the method of delivery;

Table 9.4 Continued

	• time periods for demand – this will enable the company to estimate the number of staff hours required and the management implications; • The merchandise groups for which information/advice is sought should be identified in order that the impact upon the merchandise group profitability may be assessed.
	From this information a number of options may emerge. O1. Employ specialist staff on a full or part-time basis to provide the service. O2. Develop training packages for store section heads who become 'resident specialists'. O3. From the research identify important merchandise groups and approach suppliers with a view to obtaining support. O4. Develop an IT-driven package for customer use in store. This will require a facility to select *specific* information and to *take away* a printout of the advice.
Implications:	1. Additional staff will put pressure on operating costs and staff cost/sales should be monitored. 2. Training packages may become obsolete quite frequently as product technology changes rapidly. 3. Customer use packages may require costly maintenance if not supervised, as well as replacement (in-store shrinkage problems), again a supervision issue.
Decision options (trading/branch assets):	No major investment or expansion of assets is expected that will require large capital sums. Some issues/options should be addressed. A1. Pressure on selling areas may increase if the information/advice offer proves to be a popular feature, therefore location of either the service function or the overall activity may require investigation. A2. If the information/advice activity requirement is extensive, it may be necessary to 'deliver' the service at the customers' home. A3. An alternative is to consider developing a series of 'how to …' videos loaned free of charge.
Implications:	1. An increase in the branch assets is likely to occur with either option and the effectiveness in terms of revenue and volume increases should be established. 2. The overall implications on return or branch assets should be identified: an investigation into cause/effect will help with deciding upon the extent to which the information/advice service is developed.
Overall implications:	1. There is a clear need to add information/advice to the customer service package as part of an ongoing operational repositioning exercise. 2. The competitive advantage offered should add value to the customers purchases and *increase* revenues and operating profit.

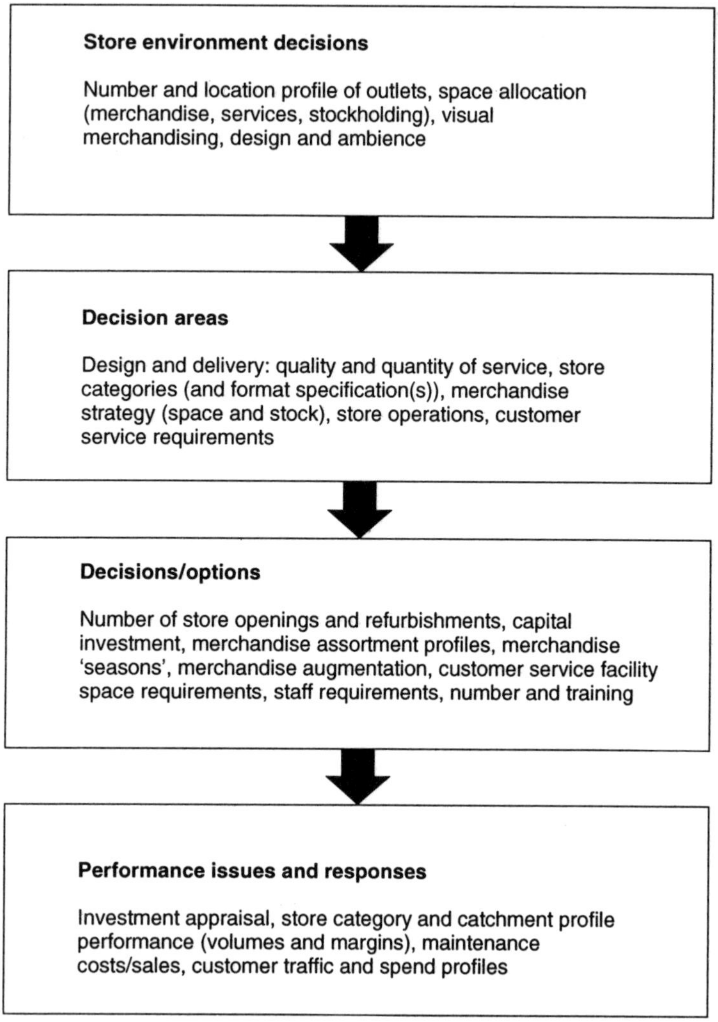

226 Decisions and Information

Store environment decisions

Number and location profile of outlets, space allocation (merchandise, services, stockholding), visual merchandising, design and ambience

Decision areas

Design and delivery: quality and quantity of service, store categories (and format specification(s)), merchandise strategy (space and stock), store operations, customer service requirements

Decisions/options

Number of store openings and refurbishments, capital investment, merchandise assortment profiles, merchandise 'seasons', merchandise augmentation, customer service facility space requirements, staff requirements, number and training

Performance issues and responses

Investment appraisal, store category and catchment profile performance (volumes and margins), maintenance costs/sales, customer traffic and spend profiles

Figure 9.9 Strategic store environment decisions

PLANNING AND CONTROL FOR STORE ENVIRONMENT DECISIONS

Strategic store environment decisions

In Figure 9.9 the decision topics are concerned with strategic store environment decisions. They are essentially based on long-term investment and the decision areas reflect this nature by featuring store format and store category decisions which would consider the number of stores but also the range of 'offers' the company should make. For example Sears and Burton have a range of fascia brands which are targeted options to a range of customer segments. Merchandise strategy is important in this decision because of the application of space and stockholding resources in the visual merchandising decision. Store operations considerations are important too: the number of stores and the scope of the stores' activities makes management a major consideration, while operating and maintenance costs can differ widely. Customer service options have a large influence on the design of the store environment.

A typical strategic store environment decision is that involved in major repositioning. Dickens and Jones in 1985 (see Walters, 1988) faced some far-reaching decisions when they decided to shift their focus on to the major segment of the ladieswear market. The decision required considerable capital for refurbishment and working capital for merchandise.

A hypothetical situation is described in Table 9.5. The situation facing this company is a common occurrence; strategic repositioning is necessary if revenues and profitability are to be increased. Often this response requires new (and perhaps) larger outlets because the market has shifted geographically as well as in the context of segmentation. Recent growth of retail parks and the predominance of durables retailers is an example of how this occurs. Clearly the investment implications (and divestment implications) are significant.

Symptoms of the need for change are usually the decline of sales revenues and customer transaction values. In addition mark-downs are seen to increase and competitors begin to erode the company's segment share.

The response may take a number of forms. It may be necessary to launch a new retail brand into the market positioning opportunity or, if the existing brand is resilient enough and can carry the changes required, redesign of the format/store environment and ambience. Table 9.5 identifies issues, objectives and decisions/options. A decision/performance trace will identify relevant issues, while a relevant margin spread/asset base model will consider important factors for these factors.

Operational store environment decisions

The previous topic described changes that could be far-reaching for the long-term functioning of the business. They typically change the customers' view and use of the store and usually the customer base. Often such changes are accompanied by large capital expenditure.

Table 9.5 Strategic store environment decisions: a repositioning response (a ladieswear retailer)

Issue:	The company's offer has become 'dated' and has little or no appeal to the major segments of the market where significant spending occurs.
Objectives:	To restore the ROE (return to shareholders)
Decision options (sales responses):	S1. Redesign store environment to reflect customer expectations for communication, information *and* convenience – for themselves, partners and children (if applicable).
	S2. Relocate (if appropriate) into more relevant catchment situations.
	S3. Re-brand the offer: if appropriate, segment the offer, thereby meeting specific expectations with clearly differentiated appeal. Introduce well-known 'labels' from suppliers who are familiar to target customers.
	S4. Review the merchandise assortment and replace unpopular labels with those of contemporary style suppliers: evaluate merchandise augmentation. Evaluate concessions.
	S5. Increase the number of seasons: this will increase viability and credibility and generate customer interest, traffic and transactions.
	S6. Consider concessions which complement the positioning. Include relevant and complementary customer services: evaluate service augmentation.
Implications:	1. Both fixed and working capital will require considerable expansions, with significant implications for capital structure and management of capital performance.
	2. Risk is high: it increases steadily with the size of the investment *and* the further the company changes its positioning. Concessions may reduce this problem.
Decision options (gross margins):	G1. Review the mark-downs/sell-through options available using alternative visual merchandising options: end-use, seasonal collections, colour collections, and 'interests' (such as culture, geography, 'technology'; topics that may not have direct linkage but are perhaps topical).
	G2. Focus on non-price sensitive (style) merchandise groups and labels.
	G3. Use merchandise augmentation to enhance margins.
	G4. Consider concessions.
Implications:	1. An increase in the number of seasons is likely to increase the mark-downs. A 'sell-through' plan (progressive mark-down) will minimise the impact of the inevitable.
	2. Margins can be enhanced by increasing customer transactions through relevant augmentation.
Decision options (operating margins):	O1. Staff number and quality may offer a means by which the re-positioning may be reinforced.

Table 9.5 Continued

	O2. Staff development and training/concession staff.
	O3. Expand distribution facility/third-party services to service merchandise/visual merchandise changes.
	O4. Specific services, in-store or out-of-store, may add to the differentiation (such as in-store; 'wardrobe' services; out-of-store; sales visits) to customers 'too busy' to visit the store.
	O5. Service concessions may be attractive.
Implications:	1. Repositioning will increase operating costs. The issue is: how to contain the increases.
	2. Concessions may contain costs.
	3. 'Trade-off' research (conjoint analysis) to identify merchandise and customer service alternatives may optimise both gross and operating margins by identifying optimal combinations of merchandise, service and store environment.
Decision options (trading assets):	A1. Store relocation and refurbishment may be required to meet customer preferences for convenience (such as off-centre locations and ample parking) or particular in-store 'comfort' (space and ambience). A change in visual merchandising policy together with the changes in merchandise strategy (see above: decision options; sales responses) may also be necessary.
Implications:	1. Though it may be possible to achieve a favourable solution to the problem of repositioning by changes the interiors of existing stores and adjusting space allocation and priorities, the most effective solutions are likely to require capital expenditure.
	2. Thus the availability and cost of capital together with its implications for capital structure (even corporate control) are important considerations.
Overall implications:	1. Capital will be required to meet inevitable fixed and working capital expansion.
	2. Supplier involvement may be possible for working capital requirements (for example, sale or return arrangements or extended payment terms). However, the financial involvement of suppliers in fixtures and other aspects of the store environment may prove dysfunctional: not only will the suppliers expect concessions concerning space allocation and a preferred location in store, there may prove to be difficulties in co-ordinating the store design.
	3. Although considerable costs are involved, the 'costs' involved by ignoring the need to undertake repositioning may be considerable, if not fatal!
	4. A delay will undoubtedly place the company at a disadvantage: it may be left so far behind its competitors that it loses total credibility!

Store environment decisions

Space allocation adjustments (merchandise/service, between and within merchandise groups), store expansion/contraction, changes to visual merchandising, changes to merchandise assortment profile (seasons, themes, and so on)

Decision areas

Store opening/refurbishment, visual merchandising, store organisation and operations, merchandise changes, distribution and information infrastructures

Decisions/options

Number and locations of stores, sales distribution, stockholding patterns, changes in support capacity, changes in staff numbers and skills, store design (display, space and costs); distribution service requirements, alternative 'delivery' methods, information

Performance issues and responses

Productivity and profitability requirements and implications: branch assets, inventory, space, staff; fixed and working capital implications

Figure 9.10   Operational store environment decisions

Operational store environment decisions are a more tactical response to current, short-term, changes that may require adjustments reflecting changes in customer expectations that may be seasonal or incremental. Both can be accommodated within the context of the existing business.

Often store environment adjustments are part of an overall response within the business. A typical influence is the incremental change to merchandise strategy (for example, choice may be increased) or perhaps to a visual merchandising approach. Figure 9.10 suggests a number of **decision topics** and **decision areas**.

An example of an operational change to the store environment may be described by some of the home furnishing retailers' activities. Many have responded to the preferences of existing customers for 'ideas' and co-ordinated interiors. Room settings are now the usual way in which furniture is presented, but not many years ago display was product-based: the assumption was that customers preferred to compare product items, that purchases were for single items (an item being a chair or perhaps four chairs and a table) and there was no requirement by customers for an 'overall' view.

The influence of Terence Conran through Habitat (and later Heals) is reflected across home furnishing retailing. Department stores who, hitherto, had displayed product types rather than 'rooms' followed his lead. It was also used by 'home improvement' retailing where company offers such as those of MFI and Magnet became linked sets of interiors. Magnet offered a computer, two-dimensional computer room design service, while Heals offers a team of interior designers. It is important to note here that the changes made have been to the operational positioning of the business, not to the strategic positioning.

However, as we can see from Figure 9.10 even at an operational level the changes may bring about an extensive range of activities. Often the changing expectations of existing customers can result in significant changes to a business: the evolution of edge-of-town food retailing shows such a change. The customer base has not changed but preferences for merchandise characteristics and customer service are reflected in current offers.

The example used is based upon observations of the home furnishings sector. As with previous examples, Table 9.6 identifies response options and a decision/trace and margin spread/asset base topic will explore the options in more detail.

PLANNING AND CONTROL FOR COMMUNICATIONS DECISIONS

Strategic customer communications decisions

Arguably customer communications is an area in which there have been most changes in retailing. The increasing application of information technology to problems (and opportunities) is one of the more interesting aspects of retailing and without doubt the role of IT in customer communications qualifies as the growth area for the next few years. Customer communications can extend the store offer to the home by providing the

Table 9.6 Operational store environment decisions: responding to customers' preferences for merchandise co-ordination and ideas

Issue:	As competition expands and intensifies, the home furnishing sector has seen competition increase from new entrants (IKEA) and from complementary store groups (DIY operators; B & Q, Texas, Homebase, and so on). It follows that the traditional home furnishing retailer should attempt to move closer towards customer needs. Merchandise co-ordination, design advice and information on furniture care are services that are currently expanding. It is a component within an attempt to achieve competitive advantage through differentiation.
Objectives:	To meet customer requirements for merchandise co-ordination To increase the level of interest in-store To increase customer traffic and visit frequency To increase the range of customers' purchases and, therefore, transaction values
Decision options (sales responses):	S1. Increase the range of style/design options. S2. Increase the width and depth of existing and new options. S3. Expand the notion of 'themes' to incorporate all 'rooms' within the home rather than individual room settings.
Implications:	1. Stockholding will increase, necessitating a review of working capital needs. Space allocation requirements will increase, suggesting stock/merchandise rationalisation in the short term.
Decision options (gross margins):	G1. Review opportunities for merchandise augmentation: for example, table top items, lighting, and other high value/low density items. G2. Consider service augmentation opportunities: for example, design services (both in-store and out-of-store consultants), installation services, and so on. G3. Identify opportunities for expanding buying margins with suppliers through more effective supply chain management.
Implications:	1. The increased use of themes and so on is likely to offer an opportunity to increase the size of the average transaction. Consideration should, therefore, be given to the provision of credit facilities, etc.
Decision options (operating margins):	O1. The increased attention to merchandise co-ordination will require more attention to be given to availability *across* the merchandise group. This may be achieved by increasing company stocks and storage facilities *or* by involving suppliers more closely with company distribution activities. O2. Customer services may be necessary. A range of options includes in-store design advice and installation and so on. These may be company-based or sub-contracted.

Table 9.6 Continued

	O3. Delivery services to customers will become more complicated (multi-sourcing of the entire customer order) and co-ordination and control will become an essential feature of the service.
Implications:	1. Costs are likely to increase and for each option the company would be well advised to consider service company activities. Not only is this likely to prove to be more cost-effective, it will enable the company to apply capital and managerial time (and effort) to the core business.
Decision options (trading branch assets):	A1. The change in store environment may require additional design work and refurbishment. A2. Space allocation processes will require review: productivity and profitability performance profiles of merchandise groups are likely to change as the focus shifts from merchandise groups to themes.
Implications:	1. Additional capital expenditure may be required to meet implementation requirements. 2. While overall return on assets is a major objective the components are likely to differ with the changes in merchandise and service mixes.
Overall implications:	1. The benefits from introducing co-ordination into visual merchandising may be identified both easily and rapidly. 2. Furthermore, future resource allocation becomes easier: customer style preferences and so on are more easily tracked and thus space, stock and staff resources are more accurately deployed.

facilities for selection and transactions and with both considerable convenience.

The growth of 'direct' banking and insurance services is an example of how customer confidence problems may be overcome. For some time, purchases of financial and insurance services were considered to be 'personal service' issues and required a one-to-one personal selling approach. The success of the banking and of the insurance service options of the major banks suggests that others may follow.

Within consumer and durable goods retailing the opportunities to apply IT are immense. Of particular interest is the development of loyalty systems which are aimed at developing and maintaining customer loyalty. Typically these are card-based and may (but not necessarily) offer a credit facility. Often the most successful focus on customer store visit and purchasing activities and develop a rapport or relationship with customers based upon responses to the offer: they accept the fact that store credit is often considerably more costly for customers than the credit card systems operated by the banks. Loyalty cards, therefore, are easier (and less expensive) to operate and can build a useful link with core customers.

In recent years the recession has made the competition for customer expenditure a keen and vital activity. It follows that if a strong competitive position is to be achieved, then a very detailed knowledge of customer motivation is necessary, particularly those customers who comprise the loyal, frequent spending group. By 'tracking' purchases and interests customers can be advised of developments in merchandise and service ranges and indeed they may be offered specific incentives to increase both their spending with, and commitment to, the retailer. The concept of 'data base marketing' has become important in a number of retailing sectors. The example here, again hypothetical, is typical of the issues facing many companies questioning the allocation of resources. Figure 9.11 identifies decision topics areas, options and performance parameters; Table 9.7 the issues and objectives. A decision/performance trace and margin spread/asset base model analysis will explore the strategic implications of the decision options.

Operational customer communications decisions

There are occasions where short-term issues arise which require a communications solution. Examples of these include promotional events, new store openings, product launches and so on.

An example of a short-term issue is that of responding to price competition. Customer perceptions of price offers vary, often being influenced by the strategic intentions of price led competitors. The recent (1993–4) events in the UK food retail sector is one such example. Aldi and Netto, major competitors entered the UK from their Continental market bases. The responses of UK major companies was initially cautious, with KwikSave becoming more aggressive in its expansion (presumably taking the view that it could make use of the Aldi/Netto situation – that is, Aldi/Netto promotions *and* the overall public relations activity surrounding the situation), particularly in the south-east of England. The larger (major) multiples began to find core product ranges under pressure and responded with price offers: either price reductions or promotional packages, such as multi-buys, 'essential for the essentials', and so on.

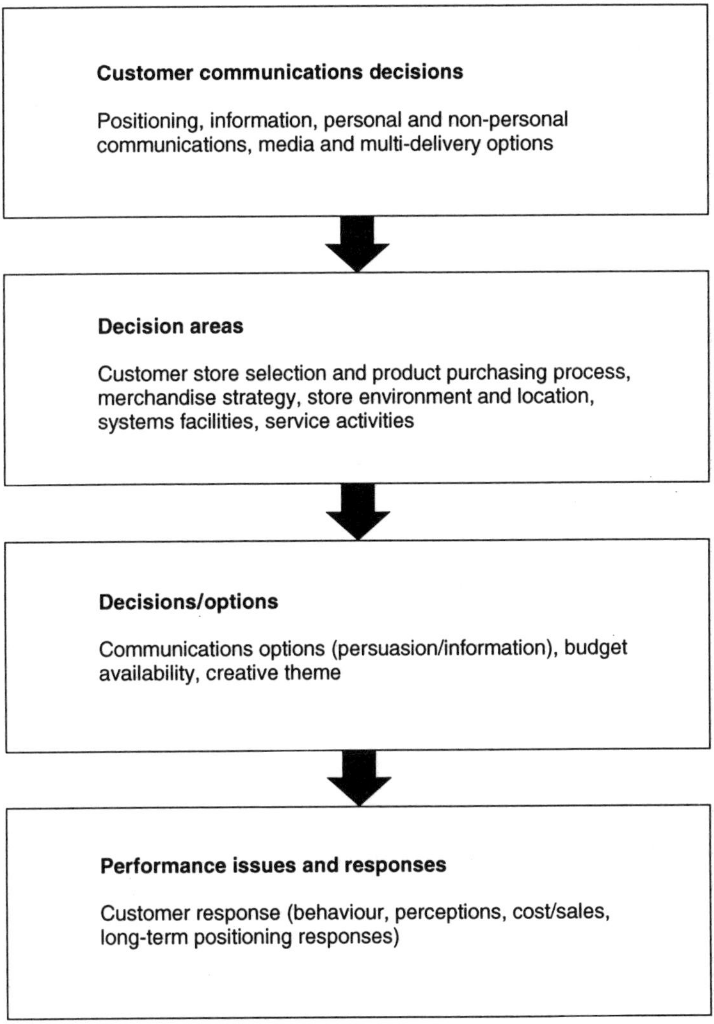

Decision Types

Customer communications decisions

Positioning, information, personal and non-personal communications, media and multi-delivery options

↓

Decision areas

Customer store selection and product purchasing process, merchandise strategy, store environment and location, systems facilities, service activities

↓

Decisions/options

Communications options (persuasion/information), budget availability, creative theme

↓

Performance issues and responses

Customer response (behaviour, perceptions, cost/sales, long-term positioning responses)

Figure 9.11 Strategic customer communications decisions

A situation such as this does have wider implications for productivity and profitability. Figure 9.12 identifies the issues that may be involved. The **decision areas** include store format, merchandise characteristics and customer services. Support decision areas include visual merchandising and information systems. The resultant **decision/options** detail the various options and considerations. **Performance issues** are resource input-based and **performance responses** are those identified in the earlier examples. Table 9.8 identifies issues, objectives decisions and

Decisions and Information

Table 9.7 Strategic communications decisions: developing customer loyalty and customer spend

Issue:	Increasing competitive activity within the segment requires an innovative use of IT to develop a customer data base for communicating with customers to promote both customer loyalty and sales.
Objectives:	To increase customer awareness of the company and its offer to existing and new customers To add convenience to customers' transactions To increase customer transactions To make selected offers to selected customers To build and maintain an accurate customer data base

Decision options (sales responses):	S1. Develop a store credit card.
	S2. Develop a loyalty scheme which identifies:
	    • customer purchasing behaviour;
	    • customer merchandise preferences;
	    • customers' responses to promotional offers;
	    • customers' cumulative expenditures.
	S3. Develop opportunity for catalogue sales.

Implications:	1. Credit cards are expensive to operate and typically have higher interest charges than bank cards. 2. A loyalty scheme will enable the company to profile promotions and stockholding to ensure an accurate response to customers' requirements, thereby maximising sales.
Decision options (gross margins):	G1. An effective data base will provide information which will enable the company to plan both sales and margin mix with suppliers and therefore increase gross margins. G2. An effective data base will enable the company to manage the 'sell through' more effectively. G3. Develop more effective merchandise augmentation strategy from sales history. G4. Identify non-price sensitive merchandise areas for direct marketing activities. G5. Use data base to sell slow-moving items through promotional offers. G6. Use data base to monitor core product range content. G7. Use data base to modify and structure assortment.
Implications:	Gross margins are likely to be more effectively managed thus improving the GM yield. However, it must be recognised that these benefits are accompanied with costs!
Decision options (operating margins):	The data base will identify the current sales and potential for merchandise items that are:

Table 9.7   Continued

	• limited in demand: specialist items with high margins; • difficult to stock: perishable, high value, easily damaged; • product-service items.
Implications:	1. The data base will therefore provide additional 'service' to customers. It enables the assortment to be expanded to include exclusive, slow-moving items. 2. A catalogue based on a data base will reduce stockholding and release space and staff instore. 3. Training costs will occur.
Decision options (trading assets):	A1. Investment in hardware and software is required. This can be varied: • the company can build its own data base; • the company may prefer to use an existing system developed by either a hardware or a software specialist company.
Implications:	The company-developed data base will meet exactly the information/communication requirements of the company. However, a more rapidly built system, at lower cost, is likely from a specialist company.
Overall implications:	There will be considerable benefits to be made available from an effective data base: • the 'offer' may be tuned with precision; • customer preferences can be tracked and a response developed; • overall, revenues and margins are likely to be improved, provided the full benefits of the data base are understood: this will require staff training.

options A decision/performance trace together with a margin spread asset base components analysis will amplify the issues.

SUMMARY

The examples we have given in this chapter demonstrate a process by which management may identify issues and options relating to productivity and profitability problems.

Clearly the decisions that confront managers are not usually exclusive, they involve a mix of merchandise and customer service issues or perhaps merchandise and store environment considerations. An example of such a problem is the attempt to increase customer traffic. The overall

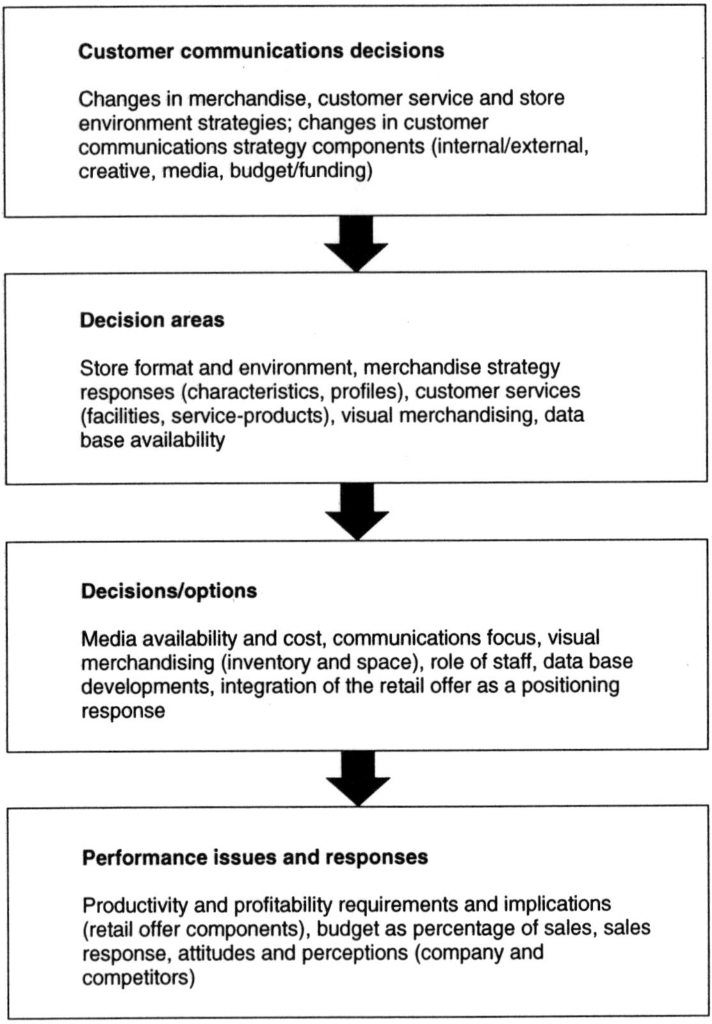

Customer communications decisions

Changes in merchandise, customer service and store environment strategies; changes in customer communications strategy components (internal/external, creative, media, budget/funding)

Decision areas

Store format and environment, merchandise strategy responses (characteristics, profiles), customer services (facilities, service-products), visual merchandising, data base availability

Decisions/options

Media availability and cost, communications focus, visual merchandising (inventory and space), role of staff, data base developments, integration of the retail offer as a positioning response

Performance issues and responses

Productivity and profitability requirements and implications (retail offer components), budget as percentage of sales, sales response, attitudes and perceptions (company and competitors)

Figure 9.12   Operational customer communications decisions

problem has several components and the 'solution' requires managers to consider a range of productivity and profitability problems. Having considered the individual issues gives management a broader perspective on all of the issues, and it follows they are able to develop an optimal solution to any problem. The case studies which follow (Chapters 10, 11, and 12) will amplify this point.

Decision Types

Table 9.8 Operation communications: a response to improve the perceptions of company prices

Issue:	Price competition by market entrants has resulted in customers' perceptions being unfavourable towards the company's pricing policy – sales volumes and market share have declined.
Objectives:	To improve the customers' perceptions of the customers' price offer To regain market share
Decision options (sales responses):	S1. Promote core product ranges at competitive prices. S2. Promote 'special offers' within the existing assortment: 'multi' buys, and so on. S3. Promote 'special offers' introduced for a price promotion exercise. S4. Increase the frequency of sales events. S5. Revise pricing policy, for example, a discount positioning versus selected offers.
Implications:	1. Stock levels may increase, particularly if 'special offers' are introduced. This may also be a problem for offers based upon regular merchandise unless effective control is exercised. 2. In-store availability is essential: poor control of stock levels will result in customer dissatisfaction.
Decision options (gross margins):	An increase in gross margins (and therefore the ability to lower prices) may be achieved by: G1. eliminating slow-moving ranges G2. eliminating slow-moving items within *all* merchandise ranges G3. rationalising suppliers G4. evaluating 'secondary' brands G5. increasing 'own brand' ranges (long term).
Implications:	1. Rationalisation of merchandise ranges and items may have an adverse effect on variety: customers may have 'trade-off' tolerances which set expectations of minimum levels of choice. 2. Rationalisation of suppliers may result in shortages unless some 'back up' supply measures are planned.
Decision options (operating margins):	A reduction of operating costs (which will enable the productivity increases to be used to lower prices may be achieved by: O1. reducing or rescheduling staff; O2. eliminating some in-store merchandising activities, for example, using packaging and pallets as selling fixtures for fast-moving and/or bulky items;

Table 9.8 Continued

	O3. reducing distribution delivery frequencies: this will require an increase in the branch stocks, space will be available after rationalising ranges offered;
	O4. an increase in 'price-led' advertising.
Implications:	1. In-store customer service will decrease as service intensity (total or part time-period) is decreased.
	2. Store presentation and ambience will be 'damaged' by using pallets and cut cases for presentation purposes.
	3. Both may have an adverse effect on customer perceptions *and* purchasing activities.
	4. Advertising would be justifiable to increase customer awareness and transactions.
Decision options (trading/branch assets):	In the short term it is neither possible nor desirable to make large changes to outlet numbers, size or design: the required response is to convince customers of price/quantity value – quickly. No major options exist.
Implications:	From the comments made above, none are likely.
Overall implications:	1. In an attempt at increasing productivity (in order to offer lower prices) care should be taken *not* to lower customer perceptions of key features of the offer, particularly those which have proven to offer competitive advantage.
	2. Long-term solutions (shifts in strategic positioning) should be avoided.

PART III

Applying the Productivity/Profitability Model: Three Case Studies

Introduction

In the three cases which comprise this final section of the book, the concepts developed in the two previous parts are explored.

The case in Chapter 10 is a situation in which a department store group, Doleys, having recently repositioned itself successfully, finals itself facing problems. The recession has had a serious affect on sales and the company seeks a solution which will improve its productivity and profitability without creating long-term problems for its positioning, which it considers it should maintain. The case considers change to Doley's offer which will improve productivity and profitability.

Chapter 11 explores a strategic case in which the conglomerate Kookaburra Holdings is looking to expand its activities. Kookaburra comprises a DIY activity, a consumer durables chain, a healthcare multiple operation and chain of variety merchandise stores. The case considers the options for expansion facing the business by examination an offshore acquisitin. Using the BCG model for establishing maximum sustainable growth rate, an offshore acquisition is evaluated. The evaluation considers the impact of the acquisition on the revenues, margins and cash flow profile of Kookaburra before and 'after' the acquisition.

In Chapter 12 there is a case study which applies both the operational and strategic topics discussed in the text. Floorwise Plc is a successful business in floor coverings. It is looking to exapnd its activities and the case study explores the issues and implications of a concession activity in a number of department stores.

The cases are hypothetical but are based on actual companies. The data presented and used was obtained from published sources.

10   Doleys Plc

INTRODUCTION

Doleys, a department store group, operates five outlets. It has a 'flagship' store in London and four smaller stores in the suburbs. Turnover from five stores in the late 1980s was in the region of £120m. The London store, with 150 000 square feet of sales area accounted for £40 m and the suburban stores average some £20 m each from approximately selling areas of 60 000 square feet. Since 1990 sales had not increased.

Doleys had evolved over time. It was in fact quite old, having been established in the early nineteenth century. For much of its trading history it has been associated with drapery merchandise. Originally it sold household linens and, as transportation developed in the early twentieth century it expanded its offer into ladieswear and associated products; a restaurant was added, and during the 1920s the assortment was expanded further to include service activities such as hairdressing.

With the boom period of the 1960s came further opportunities. The assortment expanded beyond its core range of ladieswear and menswear, into china and glass, and domestic appliances in the redeveloped basement areas. During the 1970s the four smaller suburban branches were opened.

THE NEED FOR CHANGES

The success of the 1970s and early 1980s began to decline, and by 1985 it became clear to Doleys' management that it had not kept abreast of the changes in the marketplace. There was an affluent market segment opportunity available, based on the C1/C2, 25–44 age group, but this segment was receiving considerable attention from multiple fashion groups as well as from fashion departments of department stores. The department stores, however, were finding the going difficult and the fashion multiples were becoming increasingly attractive to this segment. Doleys was at a greater disadvantage because traditionally their typical customer was an AB, possibly a C1, aged around 50–55. This customer was *not* particularly a frequent high-spend customer. There was little doubt concerning her loyalty, but such a customer profile was unlikely to have provided the level of sales necessary to maintain an acceptable profit.

Furthermore, the remainder of the business was not achieving acceptable levels of sales and profit performance. It became very clear that as a fully ranged department store Doleys could not achieve the volumes necessary in order to offer competitive pricing in areas such as durables and housewares, where specialist multiples were clearly price-leaders.

CHANGES IN THE MID-1980s

During 1985–86 it was decided to make fundamental changes to the trading policies of the company. A drastic review of the assortment was undertaken, following a decision to refocus the store on fashion. Many product groups were discontinued in what amounted to a major strategic repositioning programme.

An important issue in this decision was the noticeable change occurring in consumer attitudes and behaviour and the strong influence this exerted on consumer expectations. An 'expressive' revolution, which emerged in the 1960s, continued to have a powerful influence on attitudes and behaviour. Research in Doleys confirmed that customer profiles were dominated by professional and managerial groups, but a visual check suggested them to be predominantly C1 and C2. Clearly, the changes that had occurred had been *within group categories*, and the occupants had attitude and behaviour characteristics quite different from those of previous occupants.

PLANNING FOR A STRATEGIC REPOSITIONING

The conclusion reached was that the department stores' best response to these emerging segments was tighter segmentation based much more upon attitude and behaviour characteristics. The Doleys strategy was clear: once the segment had been identified the strategy was to seek to dominate the segment rather than the product category. This implied *specialisation* by combining product and trading themes, together with relevant services and service products, rather than an effort to offer the traditional department store product categories.

Competitors had realised the changes and were focusing their efforts towards potential customers sharing an attitude towards style and its interpretation rather than demographics and socio-economics. Clearly income levels were important as they determined the ability to purchase, but more important were the attitudes towards style, choice and store ambience.

The response of the variety chain stores was to adopt mass merchandiser strategies with positioning aimed at the C1/C2, 25–44 age group. The attraction of the segment was its size and the fact that at that time its occupants had attractive levels of disposable incomes.

The target customer profile described the strategy at the time:

> Those customers who share a similar attitude towards fashion and style. They (and/or their partners) will be in their thirties, forties and early fifties, working in professional and management occupations. It is in these groups where there exists an above average interest in fashion and style, a willingness to travel to buy clothes and, more importantly, the disposable income to allocate to these products. Doleys' target customers will be socially active with a range of interests outside their homes that requires them to be allocating larger than average amounts of their disposable income to clothing and accessory products.
>
> Doleys' target customers is a person interested and knowledgeable in fashion who expects the staff to be equally knowledgeable of customer needs and requirements.
>
> The Doleys proposition to that customer will be based upon repositioning the Company as their first choice for their fashion apparel needs.

The Doleys' business definition was derived as a means by which all stakeholders would understand the company's response to the opportunities offered in the marketplace:

> Doleys can no longer be considered as a department store in the traditional sense. It is becoming a specialist in ladies' and menswear and accessories, with an emphasis on fashion, style and service. It aims to appeal to the customer who appreciates good design, quality and service and is prepared to pay a little extra to be discerning and *different*. The intention is that it should become: 'A Fashion Gallery'.

With these in place, the retail offer was constructed to make an explicit statement in support of the offer. Merchandise strategy was an important element. Customers were now segmented on the basis of fashion attitudes and these were described in generic terms:

- **Traditional**
  — **conservative** (replacement purchasing);
  — **classic** (timeless and enduring styles);
- **Transitional** – a blend of traditional and contemporary styles;
- **Contemporary** – up-to-date (trend-conscious, self-assured, experimental);
  — **young contemporary** (fad orientated, impulsive) and
  — **innovators** (creates own 'image').

The merchandise mix represented company views on risk and a need to retain some contact with those existing customers who shared the fashion attitudes of the targeted, new, customer segment. The shifts can be shown as 'proportions' of the merchandise offers:

Ladieswear

Pre-1985   (%)

Conservative	25
Classic	50
Transitional	20
Young contemporary	5

Post-1985

Classic	20
Transitional	45
Young contemporary	20
Innovators	15

In addition to the apparel merchandise, the assortment included fragrances and fashion accessories.

Customer service was reviewed to ensure that it too supported the new direction now asserted by the positioning statement. An advisory service (or range of services) was introduced. A shopping advisory activity had been successful for a number of years. Based mainly on personal contact, this was expanded to include: a **fashion adviser**, a **wardrobe service** (which offered the 'executive woman' an advisory service in terms of individual advice on appropriate apparel and on new products (as and when they arrived) known to be within the customer's range of appeal and price), an **entertainment wardrobe service**, and a

special occasions wardrobe service (dress *and* gifts for weddings, wedding anniversaries and important birthdays). Staff training was devised to emphasise the need to build strong links with customers as part of the strategy to make Doleys the company for their 'first choice for their fashion apparel needs'.

The *store environment* required considerable redevelopment. The space released by the electrical appliances, the restaurant and housewares was taken up with an expanded menswear activity. Furthermore, customer movement around the store needed to offer more convenience. The 'environment' became: lower ground floor, **casual wear and activities**, the ground floor housed fashion accessories and fragrances; the first floor offered a 'new' fashion area of **day/businesswear** merchandise consisting of comprehensive fashion ranges of separates, co-ordinated shirts and skirts, trousers, suits and jackets, knitwear and dresses, all within a carefully planned range of price points. The second floor offered a designer-based collection of **Formalwear** (furs, knitwear and British collections. Weddings had always made a significant contribution to Doleys profits, and were located for planned purchases on the third floor, together with customer services and accounts.

Doleys approached the end of the 1980s with a successful record. The return on capital employed doubled; sales increased by 50 per cent and gross margin targets were achieved. An interesting performance issue was the stock turn, which achieved a 30 per cent increase.

PROBLEMS IN THE FORESEEABLE FUTURE

By the end of the 1980s Doleys became concerned that the impending recession was likely to be long and deep. As the 1980s became the early 1990s their fears were confirmed. Their target customer group was among the hardest hit of consumers: typically, they had high mortgages and credit card balances, and therefore, high interest payments. The customer group was researched in order that changes in their expectations could be identified. The results of this research are shown as Table 10.1, where they are compared with results of previous years. Some significant changes occurred over the six-year period.

Store environment topics showed no major changes at all. Ambience decreased as an issue, while the need for informative displays remained important but the decline in the importance of 'space' confirmed the conclusions concerning ambience. Customer communications showed some interesting issues. In-store communications, particularly those that

Table 10.1 Customer preferences survey, 1988–93 comparisons (1988 = 100)

	1988	1989	1990	1991	1992	1993
Merchandise issues						
Choice	100	110	110	105	95	90
Availability	100	105	105	100	100	95
Quality	100	105	110	115	115	120
Price	100	100	110	115	120	125
Coordination	100	100	100	100	105	105
Exclusivity	100	110	105	100	95	90
Style	100	110	110	115	115	115
Customer service						
Helpful staff	100	105	105	100	100	100
Knowledgeable staff	100	105	100	110	110	105
Availability of staff	100	105	105	100	100	100
Facilities, for example:						
cloakrooms	100	100	100	100	100	100
crèche	100	105	105	100	95	90
Services, for example:						
wardrobe	100	110	105	100	95	90
garment care	100	110	110	115	115	115
credit	100	105	105	110	110	110
financial	100	110	105	100	95	90
Store format and environment						
Located near home, for example, 20–30 minute travel time	100	110	100	100	100	100
Adjacent parking at reasonable cost	100	110	100	100	100	100
Uncluttered	100	110	105	100	90	90
Informative displays	100	110	110	110	110	110
Exciting ambience	100	110	110	100	95	90
Logic in layout	100	110	110	100	100	100
Easy to move around	100	110	100	95	90	85
Customer communications						
In-store communications:						
well signed	100	110	115	110	110	110
advice on product uses	100	110	115	120	120	120
advice on product care	100	110	120	125	125	130
External communications:						
frequent informative mailings	100	100	100	95	95	95
informative advertising	100	100	95	95	95	90
exciting advertising	100	100	95	90	90	85

Merchandise preferences have clearly changed. The obvious change is that concerning price: it has become an issue within the customers' choice set, with choice, exclusivity and availability assuming less importance. It is significant that quality became increasingly important, as did co-ordination. However, style remained a strong preference.

Customer service also showed changes in customer preferences. Although these did not show major changes, there was evidence to suggest that the customers valued certain aspects of service more than others. Staff characteristics showed no major changes but peripheral services such as wardrobe, financial services and crèche facilities had decreased in importance significantly.

Store enviroment topics showed no major changes at all. Ambience decreased as an issue, while the need for informative displays remained important, but the decline in the importance of 'space' confirmed the conclusions concerning ambience. Customer communications showed some interesting issue. In-store communications, particularly those that could be seen to add value to the merchandise by extending its use and life span, could be seen as being important. External communications decreased significantly, particularly those elements that may be considered to be persuasive.

could be seen to add value to the merchandise by extending its use and life span could be seen as being important. External communications decreased significantly, particularly those elements that may be considered to be persuasive.

SOME ISSUES FOR CONCERN

Doleys faced a number of problems. The research for merchandise preferences suggested a move towards quality at a price with style remaining an important issue. The research also suggested there to be trade-off possibilities. For example, it appeared that the customer would be prepared to accept a price/quality combination that maintained the 'style' profile Doleys had generated but would accept less choice and exclusivity and would be prepared for less availability.

The company response to the customer service research findings (when considered in conjunction with the merchandise issues) was one of no surprise. The customer responses reinforced the view that they (the customers) were responding to the changed economic circumstances. They had become selective and were rejecting the 'peripherals' or trimmings.

Much the same conclusion was reached for the results on store format and environment. The customer saw ambience and excitement as unimportant when faced with a decrease in real spending power. Information remained important but in-store aesthetics had become relatively unimportant.

The information preferences were reflected in the communications research. Here it was very clear that customers' concerns were directed towards budget consolidation rather than unnecessary expenditure.

Before taking steps to adjust the offer, further research was undertaken. Over time companies may choose to use customer perceptions to indicate attribute comparisons between themselves and competitors. Table 10.2(a) and 10.2(b) shows a series of tracking studies.

Some interesting comparisons emerged from the studies. Doleys considered Allots as their primary competitor, with Bellnots comparable in most of the merchandise areas. Crane was not seen as a major competitor. However, all of the companies included in the tracking studies were competitive in that they were all in the catchment areas serviced by Doleys.

The findings suggested to Doleys' management that Allots had detected the changes in consumer preferences and were already responding.

Table 10.2 Tracking study: six-monthly reporting of customer perceptions of competitive performance, October 1993 and April 1994

	Better than			Inferior	
	Excellent	Superior	No difference	Poor	Very poor
(a) October 1993					
Merchandise issues					
Choice	D	A	B	C	
Availability		D	AB	C	
Quality	A	B	CD		
Price/Value			ABD	C	
Co-ordination	A	B	D		C
Exclusivity		AD	B		C
Style	A	D	B_	C	
Customer service issues					
Staff helpfulness		AB	D	C	
Staff knowledge	A	D	B	C	
Staff availability		A	BD	C	
Facilities					
cloakrooms		AD	BC		
crèche		A only			
restaurant		A	B		C
Services					
wardrobe	A	D	B	C	
garment care	A	B	D	C	
credit			ABCD		
financial services	A	BD			C
Store format and environment					
Convenient to get to		AD	B	C	
Easy to park, inexpensive	D	A	B	C	
Uncluttered store	DA		B	C	
Informative displays	A	D	B		C
Excitement	AD		B	C	
Logical layout	A	D	B	C	
Easy to move around	AD	B	C		
Customer communications					
Clear store signing	AD		B	C	
Ideas for product use	A	DB		C	
Instructions for produce care		AD	B	C	
Frequent contact	DA		B		C
Informative mailings	A		D		
Exciting advertising		AD	B	C	
(b) April 1994					
Merchandise issues					
Choice		D	ABC		
Availability	D	A	BC		
Quality	A	D	B	C	

Table 10.2 Continued

	Better than			Inferior	
	Excellent	Superior	No difference	Poor	Very poor
Price/Value		A	BD		C
Co-ordination		AD	B		C
Exclusivity		D	AB		C
Style	A	D	B	C	
Customer service issues					
Staff helpfulness			AD	BC	
Staff knowledge	A		BD	C	
Staff availability			ABD		C
Facilities					
cloakrooms		ABD	C		
crèche			A		
restaurant			AB		C
Services					
wardrobe	D	A	B		C
garment care		AD	B	C	
credit			ABCD		
financial services	A	D	B		C
Store format and environment					
Convenient to get to		AD	B	C	
Easy to park, inexpensive			ADB	C	
Uncluttered store	D		A	BC	
Informative displays			AD	B	C
Excitement	D	A	B	C	
Logical layout		AD	B		C
Easy to move around	D		ABC		
Customer communications					
Clear store signing	A	D	B	C	
Ideas for product use	A		DB	C	
Instructions for produce care	A	D	B	C	
Frequent contact	D		AB		C
Informative mailings	D		AB		C
Exciting advertising	D		AB	C	

A = Allots
B = Bellnots
C = Crane
D = Doleys

The responses to merchandise base questions suggested that choice (range) had been reduced, as had availability (neither being seen as currently of major importance). It will be recalled that quality was important, and here Allots have again sensed the market need. Price, again important, was favourable to Allots. The quality and price data

Three Case Studies

Table 10.3 Identifying operational response options to changes in the competitive environment

Issue:	Consumer buying responses and attitude surveys suggest that the influence of the recession has resulted in preferences that may prevail for some two or three years. The overall positioning of Doleys has been successful, but short-term adjustments are required if sales and margins are to be increased.
Objectives:	To increase sales (in real terms) from £120 m for the next two financial years by 5 per cent per year.
	To increase gross margins from 42.5 per cent to 47.5 per cent
	To improve operating margins from 4.5 percent to 6.0 per cent.
	These increases will require productivity and profitability increases for space, staff and stockholding.
Decision options (sales revenues):	Sales increases are likely to increase by selective promotional activities:
	S1. price reductions
	• overall price reductions to increase volume
	• selected price reductions; ongoing or 'sales; loss leaders; related purchases
	S2. an increase in advertising and promotional spend:
	• on selected ranges;
	• in selected underperforming stores;
	S3. identifying core product ranges and items and increasing promotional activities on a joint venture basis with suppliers, thereby enhancing sales and margins;
	S4. reducing choice (and therefore ranges offered) – this would offer the opportunity for reducing costs in a number of areas, which could be passed on to customers as lower prices;
	S5. reducing the current number of seasons in the offer (day/businesswear, casual wear formal/evening wear).
	S6. reducing the current level of merchandise co-ordination/themes in merchandise groups not sensitive to display, specifically in core product items;
	S7. Reviewing allocation of space between sales and service areas: within sales areas considering the reduction of space allocated to visual merchandising. An increase in merchandise density, particularly of core merchandise, will lower distribution costs (and therefore operating costs);
	S8. Increasing the emphasis of promotional activities and advertising expenditure towards 'persuasion' and reducing the level of spend on information; maintaining level of advertising expenditure;
	S9. Reducing service intensity in merchandise areas where sales assistant activity is less important;

Table 10.3 *Continued*

	S10. Increasing stock cover and selling activity in strongest departments (that is, day/businesswear and casualwear).
Implications	
	1. Price reductions may be matched by competitors and would only result in temporary increases of sales (which may become decreases over time) together with lower overall gross margins.
	2. Price reductions may result in an inappropriate positioning response by the customer.
	3. An increase in advertising expenditure may encourage competitors to do likewise.
	4. Adjustments to core product merchandise may result in worthwhile increases in sales as customers currently appear to be restricting purchasing activities to essential items. Furthermore, a joint venture with suppliers would ensure that costs would be shared and possibly margins enhanced.
	5. Reductions in range choice and the number of seasons would result in lower stocks and therefore costs: margins may also improve, particularly if suppliers are also rationalised.
Decision options (gross margins):	
	G1. Gross margins could be increased by: • reducing duplication of suppliers (however, caution is necessary where suppliers do not have strong service records); • reducing sales activity in high risk items and those where competition is fierce, such as activities (sportswear); • reducing overall mark-downs by focusing on more 'durable' styling such as 'classic' rather than 'high fashion'.
	G2. Review sales performance/markdowns of branches to identify performance differences by location.
Implications:	
	1. A reduction of the supplier base may expose the business to stockouts.
	2. Moving away from activity merchandise may disappoint some customers and result in some lost sales.
	3. The shift away from high fashion to more classic styling will reduce overall appeal to customers, however, this would appear to be justified by research findings.
Decision options (operating margins):	
	O1. Operating margins may be increased by reviewing staff requirements by: • department; • time of week (and day).

Table 10.3 *Continued*

	O2.	The reduction of service activities will release space which, if allocated appropriately, may be used to increase merchandise density of core product items and, therefore, availability. This should lead to a reduction of distribution service costs.
	O3.	An additional reduction in distribution costs may be obtained by negotiating direct deliveries of volume selling items with relevant suppliers.
Implications:		
	1.	An increase in the return on branch assets will be achieved only if planned sales increases are realistic.
	2.	The planned increases in stockturns and the reduction of the number of seasons will result in lower working capital requirements.
Overall implications:		
	1.	By remaining with the merchandise groups currently sold the positioning shift will be operational rather than strategic.
	2.	The existing customer base should be encouraged to increase spending as the changes made respond to their preferences.
	3.	Additional customers may be attracted by the modified offer.
	4.	By offering lower prices in core product merchandise areas total revenue (and operating profits) will be increased.

suggested to Doleys that Allots was strengthening their its position within the segment.

An interesting finding concerning visual merchandising and merchandise density shows no clear superiority for Allots over Doleys and the data for store environment (uncluttered store and ease of movement) suggested that Allots had increased merchandise density, presumably to decrease distribution costs.

Changes in customer perceptions of service features were also interesting, again some retrenchment was in evidence. There were areas where Allots previous 'apparent' strengths had declined. Doleys' management were convinced that this was as a result of a deliberate move by Allots to reduce costs.

A similar conclusion was drawn concerning customer communications. Here frequency had clearly been reduced and content changed to reflect the customer mood.

Clearly there were some issues facing the Doleys executive and it met to consider how best to handle theses. They first identified the issues and set themselves some clear objectives. Following from this there were a range of options to be considered together with the implications of the implementation of the alternatives. The impact on margins and the overall performance responses were evaluated.

The Doleys management detailed the options they considered available to them. These appear as Table 10.3.

Following this exercise, a decisions options trace was constructed (Figure 10.1) which identified performance areas of the business which would be influenced by the options identified and discussed. The other information required was a quantitative summary of the options considered, together with a projection of costs. These items are shown as Tables 10.4 and 10.5.

The planned sales and profit performance increases accompanying the merchandise and operations changes are shown in Figure 10.2.

Table 10.4 Performance review and revised objectives: current period + 2 years

Current period		+2 Years
Sales	£120 m	£132 m (increase 5% p.a.)
Operating profit	£5.4 m (4.5% sales)	£7.9 m (6.0% sales)
Gross margin (average)	42.5% sales	47.5% sales
Space (total: all stores)	400,000 sq. ft	400,000 sq. ft
	350,000 merchandise	375,000 merchandise
	50,000 services	25,000 services
Sales (sq. ft)	£342	£330
Merchandise density (sq. ft)	£60	£50⇒£55
Stockholding	£24 m	£20 m
Stockturn	5×	6.5×
Staff costs	£15 m (12.5% sales)	£14.5 m (11.0 sales)
Staff nos.	800 employees	700 employees
	(750 sales, 50 service)	(670 sales, 30 service)
Staff productivity	£150,000 FTE	£187,500 FTE

Merchandise and services offer

	Current			Planned		
Product group	Seasons	Space (%)	Sales (%)	Seasons	Space (%)	Sales (%)
Day/businesswear	6	30	30	5	40	40
Casualwear	8	35	35	6	40	40
Formalwear	6	10	15	4	7	10
Activities (2)	2	12	10	2	6	5
Wedding		1	3	1	1	1
Service		12	7		6	4
		100	100		100	100

256

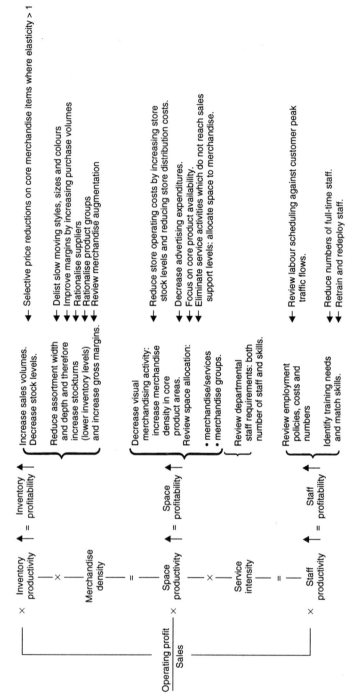

Figure 10.1 Mapping the available options

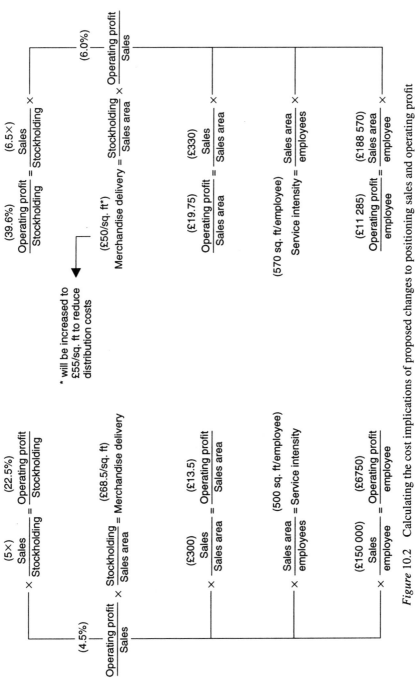

Figure 10.2 Calculating the cost implications of proposed changes to positioning sales and operating profit

Table 10.5 Current and planned performance for key activities

	Current (£m)	Current (%)	Planned (£m)	Planned (%)
Sales	120	100	132	100
COGS	66	55	69.3	52.5
Gross profit	54		62.7	
Gross margin		45		47.5
Wages/salaries	15	12.5	14.5	11
Occupancy (rent and utilities)	18	15	19.8	15
Advertising/marketing (including visual merchandising)	6	5	5.4	4
Distribution	6	5	4.6	3.5
Depreciation	3.6	3	3.3	2.5
Overhead	12	10	13.2	10
Operating profit	5.4		7.9	
Operating margin		4.5		6.0

11 Kookaburra Holdings Plc

INTRODUCTION

Kookaburra Holdings is a retail conglomerate. Sales revenues for 1993 were in the region of £3550 m, with an overall operating profit of £210 m. Kookaburra's interest are essentially in retailing consumer products across a diverse merchandise range of home improvement, consumer durables, healthcare, automotive, home entertainment, office equipment and a variety of mix merchandise offer. In addition to the retailing activities there are support companies in retail finance (a store credit card) and property operations.

The company had weathered the recession of the late 1980s and early 1990s and shown growth in productivity and profitability. The performance of the group and component companies is shown as Table 11.1. Table 11.2 shows the growth rates of the component companies for the years 1989–93, together with year-on-year growth (losses).

A REVIEW OF THE COMPONENT COMPANIES

Table 11.2 suggests that the Variety Merchandise offer and the Home Improvement businesses were dominant in the fortunes of Kookaburra Holdings. Together these companies account for 65 per cent of revenues and 75 per cent of profit as at year end 1993.

Home Improvements is in a fiercely competitive market, with at least one competitor of equivalent size and three other companies who are smaller but nevertheless significant in the marketplace. Home Improvements had a market share of some 14–15 per cent in 1993.

Home Improvements operate some 280 stores and has differentiated the offer over recent years in order to provide an improved range to trade customers, serious DIY customers and those undertaking occasional home maintenance projects.

The total sales area is approximately 11 m sq. ft, with a sales density of £95 per sq. ft and operating profit of £8 per sq. ft. Sales increases in department stores (trade and serious DIY customers) increased more

Table 11.1 Kookaburra Holdings: contribution to revenue and profit

	1989		1990		1991		1992		1993	
	Revenue (£m)	Operating profit (£m) (%)	Revenue (£m)	Operating profit (£m) (%)	Revenue (£m)	Operating profit (£m) (%)	Revenue (£m)	Operating profit (£m) (%)	Revenue (£m)	Operating profit (£m) (%)
Kookaburra Holdings	2700	210 7.8	3000	235 7.8	3250	240 7.3	3390	220 6.4	3550	210 5.9
Home Improvement	780	76 9.8	835	87 10.4	905	96 10.6	1030	90 8.8	1050	81 7.7
Consumer Durables	485	26 5.2	520	18 3.5	500	7.5 1.5	465	9 2.0	495	18 3.5
Healthcare	375	22 5.8	450	30 6.6	520	35 6.7	560	35 6.2	590	35 5.9
Variety Merchandise	965	50 5.2	1042	55 5.3	1120	63 5.6	1165	72 6.2	1230	78 6.3
Retail Property					120	54 45	90	40 44	95	8.0 8.5
Other:	55	(21)	60	(15)	75	(15)	88	(25)	90	(10)
Automotive										
Home Entertainment										
Office Equipment										
Retail Finance										

Table 11.2 Growth of revenues profits

	1993 % of total revenue or profit	Growth at 1989 prices (and year-on-year)								
		1989	1990		1991		1992		1993	
Kookaburra Holdings										
Revenue	100	100	111	(11)	120	(8.3)	125	(4.3)	131	(4.7)
Profit	100	100	112	(12)	114	(2.1)	105	((8.3))	100	((4.7))
Home Improvement										
Revenue	30	100	107	(7)	116	(8.4)	132	(13.8)	134	(1.9)
Profit	38	100	114	(14)	126	(10.3)	118	((6.2))	106	(10)
Consumer Durables										
Revenue	14	100	107	(7)	103	((3.8))	96	(7)	102	(6.5)
Profit	8	100	69	((30))	28	((58))	34	(20)	69	(100)
Healthcare										
Revenue	17	100	120	(20)	139	(15.5)	149	(7.7)	157	(5.4)
Profit	17	100	136	(36)	159	(14)	159	(0)	159	(0)
Variety Merchandise										
Revenue	35	100	108	(8)	116	(7.5)	121	(4.0)	127	(5.6)
Profit	37	100	110	(10)	126	(14.5)	144	(14)	156	(8.3)
Other Retail										
Revenue	2	100	109	(9)	132	(1.5)	160	(20)	165	(3.5)
Profit	4	—	—	—	—	—	—	—	—	—
Property										
Revenue	2	—	—	—	100	—	73	(25)	79	(7)
Profit	0	—	—	—	—	—	—	—	—	—

rapidly than in the superstores. Branded 'Depot' they were seen as a growth opportunity for the future. 'Superstores' the other brand, offering home maintenance and home improvement products, experienced a much lower rate of growth.

An emphasis on customer services provided a range of practical help from experts (carpenters, plumbers, electricians and so on) based upon POS advice centres and by holding demonstration sessions. Trade customers receive similar service. An installation service is offered for major product installation tasks. Price is a major promotional issue in the sector. Home Improvements offers a price/value offer across the range of most frequently purchased items.

Considerable investment has been made in information systems and logistics. The introduction of store-based systems will increase flexibility and effectiveness at store level more than did the previous, centrally-controlled systems used hitherto. A review of distribution facilities has resulted in the development of facilities located to support the stores by improving productivity and, concurrently, reducing supply chain costs.

Consumer Durables has experienced difficulties in the market, which itself declined. Both revenues and profits declined during 1991/92, showing a move back towards some growth by 1993. Sales in 1993 were £495 m from 226 stores and a total selling area of 1.15 m sq. ft. Sales density was £431 per sq. ft with operating profit at £16 per sq. ft.

The performance of level was influenced by two issues. One was the deep recession of 1990–3 and the other may well be that many of its locations were too small and in off-centre locations. Considerable investment has taken place to relocate into larger stores. An example of the 'new look' stores profile is the size of 17 000 sq. ft with an expanded merchandise range including more than 100 televisions, around 60 VCRs, almost 100 each of refrigerators and cookers, and almost 50 microwaves. The range has been expanded to include an extensive range of home entertainment merchandise.

Customer service has also been enhanced. Staff have been trained to become 'specialists' in specific product groups. Product availability data is accessed from a real time data base. Expenditure on retail systems is planned at a total of £14 m. The benefits will provide instant credit checking in-store, shorten average transaction times and improve stock availability. After-sales services are being rationalised from twenty-six locations down to five large and efficient facilities strategically located across the UK.

Healthcare had not produced exciting results during the 1990/93 period. This has resulted in a review of merchandise strategy and the result is a focus towards the fast growing personal care sector, away from the highly competitive household and grocery products market: development of own-brand merchandise will also contribute towards improved performance. Store environment changes are also planned.

The 1993 sales and operating profit of £590 m and £35 m respectively resulted in sales density of £304 per sq. ft (from some 1.95 m sq. ft) and an operating profit of £18 per sq. ft from 675 stores. Employee productivity was £100 700 sales per employee from some 14 000 employees. An expansion of EPOS into all stores by 1994 was forecast to increase productivity (by eliminating manual item-pricing and recording) and improve buying and inventory management.

Variety Merchandise, like Home Improvements, is a major profit and cash contributor to Kookaburra Holdings. Table 11.2 shows a situation whereby growth of sales and profits has expanded but year-on-year increases show that though growth continues, there is evidence of a decline in the rate of growth.

Sales at £1230 m produced a sales density of £201 and an operating profit of £13 m. Employee productivity and profitability were £72 000 per FTE employee and £2820 respectively. These performances are expected to show improvement when the EPOS installation is completed. In addition to investment in systems, considerable capital has been allocated to refurbishing existing stores, following the success of a test location.

The merchandise assortment has undergone development during the 1990–3 period. Ranges have been adjusted to meet customer expectations for price and value combinations. Improvements in quality choice and exclusivity had begun to meet with responses from the customer.

COMMENT: 1989–93

From the data presented in Tables 11.1 and 11.2 the overall performance of Kookaburra suggested that, in the longer term, if the growth of profit and sales was to return to the 1990 levels, dependence upon the UK market was unlikely to achieve this on its own. An off-shore merger or acquisition may be what is required.

The investment made by Kookaburra had largely been on improving productivity within the component companies (see earlier review) and on (currently) smaller ventures which would take time to come 'on stream' as major contributors. Furthermore, an analysis of shareholding suggests that with over 80 per cent of the ordinary share capital held by banks and nominee companies (some 25 per cent of total holders) the company should be concerned with maintaining a rate of growth that would increase the value of the share price. The average values of share price over the period 1989–93 were:

1989	1990	1991	1992	1993
268p	301 (12%)	335 (11%)	501 (49%)	503 (0.4%)

and dividends (per share) were:

1989	1990	1991	1992	1993
10.5p	11.5p (8.7%)	12.2p (6.0%)	13.0p (6.5%)	13.7p (5.4%)

This suggests that the existing business was unlikely to provide the level of growth that would generate the performance levels of the 1989–91 period. The overall profit performance of Kookaburra was showing no signs of strong growth. The increases in profitability from the constituent companies was largely due to productivity increases rather than from sales. An analysis of the components of 'maximum sustainable growth' (see Chapter 2) in Figure 11.1 suggests that key areas for expanding the growth rate are margin spread management, asset base management and financial policy, together with the judicial use of gearing. The sustainable growth rates for 1990–3 are calculated for Kookaburra. These are shown as Table 11.3.

The data suggests a decline in the pretax return on sales over the period which has been subsidised by a constant improvement in asset utilisation. This factor has been helped by an increased rate of retention of earnings but the decline in gearing ratio has not assisted in increasing the growth rate.

'HYPOTHESIS 1994'

If the company was to expand at a more exciting rate it was clearly necessary to look outside the business (and the UK) for a growth opportunity. One opportunity was examined and the potential year ending results looked attractive.

A merger/acquisition opportunity existed off-shore. The company in question could add considerably to Kookaburras' revenue, profits and

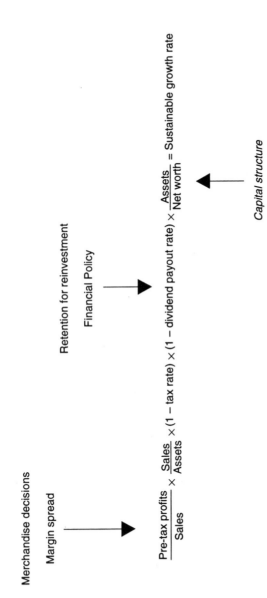

Figure 11.1 The components of the maximum sustainable growth rate

Table 11.3 Calculation of Kookaburra maximum sustainable growth rates, 1990–3

1990

$$\frac{200}{3000} \times \frac{3000}{1215} \times (1-0.33) \times \left(1-\frac{51.75}{138}\right) \times \frac{1215}{960} = 8.63\%$$

0.067   2.47   0.66   0.625   1.265

1991

$$\frac{167.5}{3250} \times \frac{3250}{1205} \times (1-0.33) \times \left(1-\frac{58.125}{102.5}\right) \times \frac{1205}{975} = 4.9\%$$

0.052   2.7   0.66   0.433   1.236

1992

$$\frac{195.5}{3390} \times \frac{3390}{1200} \times (1-0.33) \times \left(1-\frac{65.0}{134}\right) \times \frac{1200}{1085} = 6.05\%$$

0.057   2.83   0.66   0.515   1.106

1993

$$\frac{205}{3550} \times \frac{3550}{1265} \times (1-0.33) \times \left(1-\frac{69.525}{148}\right) \times \frac{1265}{1160} = 6.2\%$$

0.058   2.81   0.66   0.53   1.09

growth rate. The company, a market leader, operated some 135 stores selling electrical consumer products. It had managed to achieve an operating margin in excess of 10 per cent (compared with the 3.5 per cent of Consumer Durables). Apart from immediate benefits to revenues and profits, the long-term potential of increased gross margins from rationalised sources of supply was attractive.

A potential scenario was offered for **Electrical Durables** based upon projected twelve-month performance figures:

	(£)
Sales	1050m
Operating profit	120m
Stores	135
Employees	8 600 number
Sales per FTE	122 000
Total sales area (sq. ft)	1.73m
Sales per sq. ft	607
Operating profit per FTE	14 000
Operating profit per sq. ft	70.00

Clearly the performance of Electrical Durables was superior to that of any of the Kookaburra companies. Furthermore considerable other benefits were likely to develop from their expertise in merchandise selection and management and in managing a wide range of customer services.

A calculation of the growth rate ratio suggested the following:

$$\frac{360}{4840} = \frac{\text{Pre-tax profit}}{\text{Sales}}$$

$$\frac{4840}{1450} = \frac{\text{Sales}}{\text{Assets}} \quad \text{(Assets adjusted to include effect of the acquisition)}$$

$$(1 - \text{tax rate}) = \text{corporation tax rate at 33 per cent}$$

$$\left(1 - \frac{100}{2350}\right) = \text{retentions, adjusted for post-acquisition}$$

$$\frac{1450}{1090} = \text{revised gearing}$$

Thus gives us:

$$\frac{360}{4840} \times \frac{4840}{1450} \times 0.66 \times \left(1 - \frac{100}{2350}\right) \times \frac{1450}{1090} = 20.8\%$$

$$0.074 \times 3.34 \times 0.66 \times 0.96 \times 1.33 = 20.8\%$$

Clearly the increase in growth rate is brought about by the enhanced margins, improved asset utilisation and increased use of gearing.

The Kookaburra 'portfolio' for 1994 potentially would take the following format, projected on 1992/93 growth.

	Revenue (£ m)	(%)	Operating profit (£ m)	(%)
Kookaburra Holdings	4770	100	380	100
Home Improvement	1070	22	89	23
Consumer Durables	527	11	25	7
Healthcare	622	13	45	*11
Variety Merchandise	1300	27	84	22
Electrical Durables	1050	22	120	32

Retail Property	100	*2	10	*3
Other	100	*2	5	*1

*Estimate

Table 11.4 displays the 1993 balance sheet, together with the proforma balance sheet for 1994. Of particular interest are the growth in fixed assets, stocks and debtors which would be expected subsequent to a merger/acquisition. The long-term debt has also increased significantly by a factor in excess of 3.5. For many businesses this could be alarming. However, if we return to the calculation for the sustainable growth rate, we can see a projected net earnings to sales ratio of 7.4 per cent, considerably larger than those of previous years (1993/94) – an increase of 27.5 per cent. This increase in margin spread would be sufficiently large to cover interest payments *and* reduce the outstanding debt over a period

Table 11.4 Kookaburra Plc balance sheet 1993 and 1994 proforma (£m)

	1993	1994
Fixed Assets		
Tangible assets	1000	1250
Investments	30	45
	1030	1295
Current Assets		
Stocks	570	730
Debtors	250	400
Investments	155	150
Cash	220	280
	1195	1560
Creditors		
Amounts due *within* one year	(1000)	(1300)
Net current assets	195	260
Total assets less current liabilities	1225	1555
Creditors		
Amounts falling due *after* one year	(130)	(470)
Provisions for liabilities and charges	(1)	(1)
	1094	1084
Capital and reserves		
Called-up share capital	125	170
Share premium account	150	190
Reserves	106	115
Profit and Loss account	713	609
Equity shareholders funds	1094	1084

of a year or so. The proposed venture with Electrical Durables would appear to be worthwhile financially. The marketing benefits are also likely to be considerable.

CONCLUSIONS

Though this case study is hypothetical there are a number of companies for which the argument could obtain. It suggests that both strategic productivity and profitability can benefit from growth by merger or acquisition if the target identified can add synergy to the overall business. In this case study it would be worth while to extend the hypothesis to consider the potential improvements to overall margins in the durables activities due to changes in selling methods, as well as buying economies of scale.

With more data (stock levels, cash flows) it would be possible to pursue the growth/gain matrix discussed in Chapter 2. Nevertheless, even without these data a very strong message emerges: the **sustainable growth rate** can be used as a benchmark for evaluating how realistic the **future** growth plans of a company may be, as well as for investigating the attractiveness of acquisitions that may **enhance** the growth of the business.

12 Floorwise Plc

INTRODUCTION

Floorwise is a medium-sized carpet and floor coverings retailer. It operates some 150 outlets throughout England, Wales and Scotland. Currently, turnover is in the region of £120 m with a pre-tax profit of £14.4 m. The company claims a 10 per cent market share. It has been opening new outlets at a rate between 25 and 30 per year and sees a potential for a total of 250. This would increase market share to 20 per cent. Like-for-like sales show a growth rate of 15 per cent: the overall growth rate for sales was 40 per cent and profit 75 per cent. Gross margins have also shown increases and are currently 42.5 per cent (a 0.75 per cent increase for 1993/94); operating margin has increased by almost 30 per cent over the year and is currently 12.0 per cent. Average turnover per sq. ft is also increasing and is now £100 per sq. ft. Stores are operating from an average selling area of 10000 sq. ft. Stock holding at £11 m gives a stockturn of 10.9: in 1993 it was a little over 11. This very small decrease is seen as an achievement by the company, when the

Table 12.1 Floorwise Plc profit and loss account 1993/94

		(£000)		(%)
Sales revenue		120 000		100.0
Cost of goods sold		69 000		57.5
Gross profit		51 000		42.5
Operating expenses		39 600		33.0
Wages and salaries	14 400		12.0	
Occupancy	15 600		13.0	
Promotion, advertising, display	2 400		2.0	
Distribution	4 200		3.5	
Operating profit		14 400		12.0
Depreciation		3 000		2.5
Interest		600		
Profit before tax		10 800		5.0
Taxation		7 100		
Profit for 1994		3 700		
Dividends (50% payout ratio)		1 850		
Profit retained (transfer to reserves)		1 850		

Table 12.2 Floorwise Plc balance sheet data: 1989/90–1993/94

£000

	1989/90	1990/91	1991/92	1992/93	1993/94
Fixed Assets					
After depreciation	9 000	11 000	12 000	13 500	14 500
Current Assets					
Stocks	9 500	10 000	10 500	10 500	11 000
Debtors	2 300	2 800	2 700	2 750	3 000
Cash	8 500	9 000	9 750	10 000	14 000
Current Liabilities					
Trade creditors	18 000	20 000	21 000	22 000	25 000
Provisions	160	180	200	225	225
Net Current Assets	2 140	1 620	1 750	1 025	2 775
Total assets less current liabilities	11 140	12 620	13 750	14 525	17 275
Creditors: due after more than one year	18	20	22	23	25
Net Assets	*11 122*	*12 600*	*13 728*	*14 502*	*17 250*
Capital and Reserves					
Ordinary share capital	7 000	7 000	7 500	9 500	9 500
Share premium a/c	400	450	450	500	500
Reserves	3 722	5 150	5 778	4 502	7 250
Ordinary Shareholders Funds	11 122	12 600	13 728	14 502	**17 250**

increase in the number of stores is considered – more than over 30 stores were opened during the year.

Financially, the business is strong (see Tables 12.1 and 12.2 for profit and loss and balance sheet details) and cash flow is very positive, increasing by £5.5 m during the trading year 1993/94 to a total of £13.5 m. Of the fixed assets valued at £14 500 m, £4500 were leases on property and £8250 fixtures and fittings, with £1750 m in plant and machinery. As the financial management had established a depreciation policy which had depreciated fixtures and fittings rapidly, Floorwise thus achieved an asset productivity (turnover) of 8.3 times and a total (net) assets turnover of 7.0.

Floorwise' merchandise strategy is to provide a very wide range of roll-stock carpets and vinyl floor coverings which may be taken away with the customer or delivered and fitted. An expensive (Aristocrat) range is offered to customers but this is held in four warehouse locations and is delivered to order.

Customer service is essentially a delivery and fitting service. Both delivery and fitting are free for orders of £500. Sales staff average 7 per store (full-time equivalents) all of whom are sales *and* service staff.

Store environment comprises displays of carpets usually ordered for delivery on stand alone units or carousels and wall panel displays of medium-priced, slower moving carpets.

Customer communications is principally newspaper advertising using price as a promotional theme together with variety. On average customers have a choice from approximately 3000 stock items.

The UK market in 1994 began to show some recovery but growth was well below the levels experienced in the mid and late 1980s. Floorwise have managed to increase sales growth at a rate faster than that of the market by expanding marketshare. This has been achieved by very effective merchandise and operations management as the asset circulation figures, and in particular stock turn and employee productivity and profitability, demonstrate.

The primary performance characteristics of the business are shown in Table 12.3. The operational and strategic productivity and profitability performance profiles of Floorwise Plc are shown as Tables 12.4 and 12.5.

Floorwise has some very interesting performance figures. The lack of debt and low level of fixed assets represented as property (freeholds) gives some startling returns, quite different from those of a more conventionally geared business. A closer look at the merchandise strategy identifies some additional interesting data.

Floorwise Plc

Table 12.3 Floorwise Plc: primary performance characteristics

- Sales year ending 1994 £120 m
- Stores 150, average size 10 000 sq. ft
- Sales per square foot (from sales area) is £89 sq. ft; approximately 10 per cent of store space is utilised for customer service and storage activities.
- Sales per full-time employee is £100 000 (total staff 1200)
- Sales per employee (1050 store staff) is approximately £114 000
- Stockholding is £11 m
- Stock turn for the company is 10.9×

	(%)		(£m)
• Gross margin averages	42.5		51
• Operating margin is	12.0		14.4
• Wages and salaries	12.0	sales	14.4
• Occupancy	13.0	sales	15.6
• Promotion, advertising, etc.	2.0	sales	2.4
• Distribution	3.5	sales	4.2
• Depreciation	2.5	sales	3.0
• Interest	0.5	sales	0.6
• Profit AI and BT	9.0	sales	10.8
• Tax			7.1
• Profit AT			3.7

- Branch fixed assets (1994) (Stock + F&F: £99000 per store)
- Average sales per store £800 000 per year
- Stockturn 18X (stockholding in store £44,000)
- Stockholding per store £44,000 (Sales are 60 per cent take away, 40 per cent for delivery and fitting; stock figure therefore includes both display merchandise *and* sales merchandise.)
- Merchandise density is £4.89 per selling sq. ft (per store)
- Space productivity £89
- Space profitability £10.60 (operating profit/space)
- Service intensity 1286 sq. ft per employee
- Operating profit per employee total £12 000; store employee £13 714
- Operating profit per store (average) £96 000

FLOORWISE MERCHANDISE STRATEGY

The Floorwise product range has a large spread of over 2000 choices. A 'basic offer' ranges from £3.99 to £5.99 comprises eight colours in two carpet types. The 'basic plus' range starts at £6.99 and goes up to £11.99, has thirty colours and patterns in five carpet types. The 'intermediate range' starts at £12.99 and has a top price of £18.99. The range has forty colours and patterns in six carpet finishes. The 'premium' range starts at £19.99, with a top price of £29.99, there are thirty colours and eight carpet types. Finally the 'aristocrat' range is priced between £30.99 and a top price of £35.99, it offers forty colours in six carpet types. Stocks are not held in branches: customer orders are serviced with a

Table 12.4 Branch assets: Operational productivity and profitability for Floorwise Plc

Branch assets productivity and profitability

$$\frac{(8.1X)}{\pounds 800\,000} \times = \frac{(97\%)}{\pounds 96\,000} \quad \text{(Note: Branch assets are partial stock + F\&F)}$$

Stockturn   Operating return on stockholding

$$\frac{(18.2X)}{\pounds 800\,000} \times = \frac{(218\%)}{\pounds 96\,000} \quad \text{(Partial stock at branch)}$$

$$\frac{(12\%)}{\pounds 96\,000} \times \frac{(\pounds 4.89)}{\pounds 44,000} =$$
$$\frac{}{\pounds 800\,000} \quad \frac{}{9000 \text{ sq.ft}}$$

Operating return on sales   Sales density   Operating profit/space (sq.ft)

$$\frac{(\pounds 889)}{\pounds 800\,000} \times = \frac{(\pounds 10.67)}{\pounds 96\,000}$$
$$\frac{}{9000 \text{ sq.ft}} \quad \frac{}{9000 \text{ sq.ft}}$$

$$\times \frac{(1286)}{\dfrac{9000 \text{ sq.ft}}{7}} = \text{Service intensity}$$

Staff productivity and profitability (per FTE)

$$\times \frac{(\pounds 114{,}286)}{\dfrac{\pounds 800\,000}{7}} = \frac{(\pounds 13{,}714)}{\dfrac{\pounds 96\,000}{7}}$$

measuring and fitting service, which with underlay, is free of charge. Table 12.6 has details of sales and gross margins.

Table 12.6 indicates very clearly where the major contribution in terms of sales and gross margin is generated. The 'basic plus' and 'intermediate' ranges generate 65 per cent of sales. Margins of premium and aristocrat price ranges are attractive but volumes of both are low, and if they are to be exploited management requires to identify possible strategies whereby this can be achieved. At the same time there is a strong argument for expanding further the sales of 'basic plus' and the 'intermediate' ranges, because if their sales volumes were expanded this

Table 12.5 Strategic profitability and productivity for Floorwise Plc (£ 000)

Net asset profitability and productivity			
(62.6%) (83.5%)	(6.96X)		
£10 800 / £17 250 = £14 400 / £17 250	£120 000 / £17 250	×	
Fixed asset profitability and productivity			
(74.5%) (99.3%)	(8.28X)		
£10 800 / £14 500 = £14 400 / £14 500	£120 000 / £14 500	×	
Net current asset profitability and productivity			
(389%) (519%)	(43.2X)	(9%) (12%)	Net return (BT) on sales Operating return on sales
£10 800 / £2775 = £14 400 / £2775	£120 000 / £2775	× £10 800 / £120 000 £14 400 / £120 000	
Return on capital employed			
(62.6%) (83.5%)	(6.96X)		
£10 800 / £17 250 = £14 400 / £17 250	£120 000 / £17 250	×	

would provide Floorwise with the leverage it requires to put pressure on suppliers to increase margins and service.

THE OPTIONS

Expanding the existing format

The company has researched a number of market opportunities. One is to continue the business as it is. It is expected that the existing format could continue to be expanded to its potential of 250 outlets. This might add a further £100 m to the turnover and, as a consequence, might increase market share to some 15 to 18 per cent. A more significant issue is the

Table 12.6 Product mix details, price levels, range profile, margins and sales

Range	Price levels (per sq.ft)	Finishes/types	Colours	SKUs	Realised gross margins	Proportion of sales	Weighted margins
Basic	£3.99 £5.99	4	8	32	32.5	10	3.25
Basic plus	£6.99 £11.99	6	30	180	38	30	11.4
Intermediate	£12.99 £18.99	10	50	500	46	35	16.1
Premium	£19.99 £29.99	10	60	600	45	15	6.75
Aristocrat	£30.99 £35.99	12	60	720	50	5	2.5
Carpet Tiles	£5.99 £10.99	6	9	48	50	50	2.125
				2080		100	42.5

Floorwise Plc

impact that it would have on gross and operating margins. Assuming that sales of 'basic plus' and 'intermediate' ranges maintained much the same proportion of total sales, the growth of both margins would probably be greater than the rate of increase of sales, thereby increasing the overall

Table 12.7 Floorwise Plc: concessions primary performance characteristics

- Sales year 1994/95: £50 m
- Stores: 50, average size of concession area 15 000 sq. ft (displayed with furniture, etc).
- Employees per store: 15
- Stockholding per store: £51 750 display stock
- Stockholding in distribution warehouses will be increased and there will be a marginal increase in store stock levels of £3.75 m, but this may be capitalised as fixtures and fittings and depreciated rapidly due to wear and tear. Additional stock increases will occur in order to expand choice. This may be used to extend the offer in existing Floorwise stores. Anticipated stock increase for sales is £6.5 m. Stock turn anticipated to be 7.5× (this reflects a large increase in choice).

	% sales	£ m
Gross margin (planned)	50.0	25.0
Operating margin	20.0	10.0
Wages and salaries	15.0	7.5
Occupancy	7.5	3.75
Promotion, etc.	3.0	1.5
Distribution	4.5	2.25
Depreciation	3.5	1.75
Interest	2.5	1.25

- Branch fixed assets £51 750 + £55 000 (F+F)
- Average sales per store £1 m
- Stockturn 19.3X for concession (display merchandise)
- Stockturn Floorwise (£6.5 m + £11 m) 9.71×
- Stockturn for premium and aristocrat (£6.5 + £2.2 m (20% of £11 m)) 19.5×
- Merchandise density £3.83/ selling sq. ft
- Space productivity £74.1
- Space profitability £14.81
- Service intensity 900 sq. ft per employee
- Sales per employee £66 700
- Operating profit per employee £13 333
- Operating profit per store £200 000

Assuming concessions in place in 1994:
- Total sales: £170 m
- Total operating profit: £24.4 m (£14.4 m + £10.0 m)
- Profit (AID): £17.8 m (£10.8 m + £7.0 m)
- Fixed assets: £15.75 m (£14.5 m + £1.25 m)
- Net current assets: £1.525m (assumes stock increase of £6.5 m funded by £2 m from each and £5.75 on trade creditors)
- Equity: no change
- Capital employed: no change

profitability of the business. The logic behind this is quite clear: the existing format would require little in terms of increases in fixed costs; this fact, together with the improved buying margins and the impact on cash flow, should be powerful factors in influencing managements decision to expand the chain to its potential 250 outlets.

Floorwise concessions

Another option for Floorwise is to expand the 'premium' and 'aristocrat' ranges. Consumer research suggests an opportunity to do so in concession situations within department stores and specialist furniture outlets.

The research suggests a number of expectations:

- wide choice of styles, finishes and colours;
- measuring and fitting services together with carpet type and colour advice;

Table 12.8: Operational productivity and profitability (concessions only)

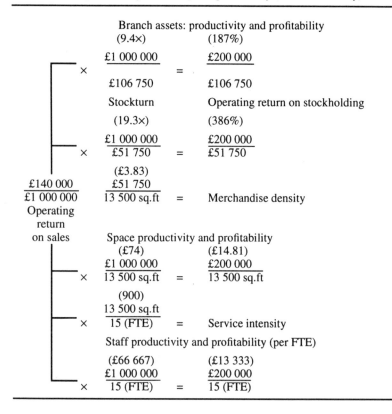

Floorwise Plc

- 'situation' displays – that is, carpets with furniture/room settings. Colour choices and so on to be extensively displayed;
- transactions could be large: research suggests that average transactions typically involve three or more rooms in contrast to the 'one room at a time' pattern of sales in established outlets.

Further investigation identified approximately fifty outlets with the potential for Floorwise to develop 'premium' and 'aristocrat' sales. Table 12.7 identifies the characteristics of this opportunity. We calculate the operating and strategic productivity and profitability implications in Tables 12.8 and 12.9. The 'case' is simplified by assuming that the concession offer is added to the 1994 performance. Clearly it would take time to put in place, meanwhile 25–30 additional existing format stores would be opened. However, as the results show given cost structures

Table 12.9 Strategic productivity and profitability including concessions

Net asset profitability and productivity

(103%)
(141%)   (9.9×)
£17 800
£24 400   £170 000
────── = ────── ×
£17 250   £17 250

Fixed asset profitability and productivity

(113%)
(155%)   (10.8×)
£17 800
£24 400   £170 000
────── = ────── ×
£15 750   £15 750

Net current asset profitability and productivity

(1167%)   (10.5%)   Net return on sales
(1600%)   (111.5×)   (14.35%)   Operating return on sales
£17 800   £17 800
£24 400   £170 000   £24 400
────── = ────── × ──────
£1525   £1525   £170 000

Return on capital employed

(103%)
(141%)   (9.9×)
£17 800
£24 400   £170 000
────── = ────── ×
£17 250   £17 250

(which are not unrealistic) there is an opportunity for Floorwise to increase both productivity and profitability in the short and long term.

CONCLUSION

This case suggests that the models produced during the progress through this text offer useful tools for the analysis of retailing opportunities. In this particular case example, we examined the situation which, while intuition might have suggested it to be worthwhile, was nevertheless proven to be so by conducting a vigorous analysis of the situation. Other examples of potential situations, or opportunities, are easily thought through and these could be examined using the model 'disk' available.

References

Ansoff, I. (1965) *Corporate Strategy* (McGraw-Hill).
Bates, A. D. (1990) 'The Troubled Future of Retailing', *Business Horizons* (August).
—— (1990) 'Pricing for Profit', *Arthur Andersen Retailing Issues Letter* (vol. 2).
Bahivi, S. and Martin, H. W. (1970) 'Productivity Costing and Management', *Management International Review*, 10(1), 55–77.
Cooper, R. (1987) 'Does Your Company Need a New Cost System?', *Journal of Cost Management* (Spring).
Dalrymple, D. J. (1966) 'Merchandising Decision Models for Department Stores', Bureau of Economics and Business Research, Graduate School of Business Administration, Michigan State University, 1989.
Davidson, R. W. and A. F. Doody (1966) *Retail Management*, (Ronald Press), 3rd edn.
Davies, H. (1991) *Managerial Economics* (London: Pitman).
Doody, A. F. and B. C. McCammon (1969) 'High Yield Management in the Department Store Field', Parts I and II, *Department Store Management*, Feb. and Apr.
Eilon, S. and B. Gold (1973) *Applied Productivity Analysis for Industry*.
Fitzgerald, L. R. Johnston, S. Brignall, R. Silvestro and C. Voss (1991) *Performance Measurement in Service Business* (London: The Chartered Institute of Management Accountants).
Fox, A. F. and R. J. Limmack (1989) *Managerial Finance* (London: Cassell).
Holmes, G. and A. Sugden (1993) *Interpreting Company Reports and Accounts* (London: Woodhead-Faulkner).
Horngren, C. T. (1965) *Accounting for Management Control* (Englewood-Cliffs, NJ: Prentice-Hall).
Knee, D and D. Walters (1985) *Strategy in Retailing* (Philip Allan).
Livingstone, J. L. and D. J. Tigert (1987) 'Financial Analysis of Business Strategy' Babson College Working Paper.
Lusch (1980) 'Gross margin Return on Inventory, Staff and Space', *Retail Control*, April.
Lusch, R., K. Coy, J. M. Kenderine and B. C. McCammon, Jr. (1992) *Wholesaling in Transition*, in L. Stern and A. I. El-Anseny, *Marketing Channels*, 4th edn (Englewood Cliffs, NJ: Prentice-Hall).
McCammon, B. C. (1970) ' Perspectives for Distribution Programmming', in L. P. Bucklin (ed.), *Vertical Marketing Systems* (New York: Scott, Foresman).
Moose, S. A. and Zakon, A. J. (1972) 'Frontier Curve Analysis: As a Resource Allocation Guide', *Journal of Business Policy*, Spring, 63–70.
Porter, M. (1980) *Competitive Strategy* (New York Press).
Robinson, G. (1986) *Strategic Management Techniques* (Durban: Butterworths).
Risk, J. M. S. (1965) 'Productivity Yardstions', *Management Accounting* (UK), 43 Yardsticks (11), 381–91.
Sweeny, D. J. (1973) 'Improving the Profitability of Retail Merchandise Decisions' *Journal of Marketing*, 37, Jan.
Walters, D. (1988) *Strategic Retailing Management* (Englewood Cliffs, N. J.: Prentice-Hall).
Walters D. and D. White (1989) *Retail Marketing Management* (London: Macmillan).
Walters, D. (1994) *Retailing Management: Analysis Planning and Control* (London: Macmillan).
Zakon, A. J. (1971) *Growth and Financial Strategies: A Special Commentary* (The Boston Consulting Group).

Index

AB 243
AC Nielsen 5
access 89, 91
Acorn 22
activity centres 204
activity costs 204
Adams 29, 30
Ahold (Holland) 38
Aldi 26, 38, 234
All Kauf (Germany) 38
Allots 249, 251, 254
alternative values 197
ambience/aesthetics 89, 139
AMS *see* Associated Marketing Services
Ansoff, I. 11, 14, 41
Argos Plc 36, 37, 38, 169–71, 173, 179
Argyll *see* Safeway
Asda 20, 21, 23, 37, 38
asset
 base management 54–6, 120–33, 163, 186, 187, 188; fixed assets 123–8; and margin spread management 105; net current assets 128–32; performance factors 132; productivity characteristics 120–3
 productivity characteristics 120–3; asset performance influences 121; fixed capital intensity 120–1; fixed capital utilisation 121–2; investment intensity 122; working capital intensity 122–3;
 return on 104, 105
 see also fixed; net; net current; trading
Associated Marketing Services 38
auditing customer expectations and responses 188

B & Q 232
Bahivi, S. 66
Bates, A. D. 103
BCG *see* Boston Consulting Group matrix
Bellnots 249
Benetton 35–6, 37

BhS 28, 99, 116
Blazer 28
Boots 34–5, 38, 112
 Health and Beauty 35
 Opticians and Photographic Processing 35, 45
 Boston Consulting Group matrix 43, 44, 45, 48, 58, 78, 242
branding decisions 113–14, 129
Brazil 30
British Shoe 9, 29
BSC 33
Budgen 25–6, 37, 38
Burton 4, 32–3, 37
 asset base 125
 cash flow 43
 decisions and information 227
 margin spread 116
 strategic resource allocation and rationalisation 20
buying and merchandising effectiveness 113–15

C1/C2 243, 244, 245
CAD *see* computer-aided design
capital
 fixed 120–2
 return on 71, 165, 195, 218
 structure 56, 86
 cash 130–1
 cash flow 41–78, 98
 assortment/business profile, hypothetical 54
 business performance components 70
 corporate expectations 77
 discounted 195
 financial ratios 66
 management 156–9
 operational 148
 performance measures 71–7
 productivity costing approach 66
 transfer pricing 66
 value-added 66–71
Casino (France) 38
casual wear and activities 247
catchment penetration 95

282

Index

Catteau 22
Champion Sport 33
China 11, 30
Circle K(9) 26
COGS *see* core product gross margins
Comet 29
communications
    decisions 89, 231–7; operational 232–3, 234–7, 238, 239–40; strategic 231, 233–4, 235, 236–7
    see also customer
company prices 239–40
competition
    competitive environment 206–8, 213–16
    competitiveness components 94
    competitor performance measures 194
    competitors' customers 108
    and differentiation 114
computer-aided design 127
concessions 109
Conran, T. 231
consumer durables 262
control *see* planning and control
Cooper, R. 71
core product gross margins 190
corporate performance 77, 138–40, 141, 142, 144, 188
cost *see* price
Country Casuals 48, 88
Crane 249
credit 131, 132
critical success factors (CSFs) 81
Curry's 30, 31
customer
    access 116
    communications 179, 201, 235, 238, 248, 250, 251
    credit 132
    expectations 134–8, 135, 188, 198
    loyalty 236–7
    perceptions 95, 174, 250–1
    preferences 248
    sales responses 174
    spend 236–7
    see also customer service
customer service 126–7, 246, 248
    decisions 212, 217–26; operational 221–6; strategic 217–21
    issues 250, 251
    -led positioning 200
    objectives 179

Dalrymple, D. J. 149, 161
Dansk Supermarketed (Denmark) 38
Darty 20, 29, 40
Davidson, R. W. 13
Davies, H. 68, 81
day/business wear 247
DCF *see* discounted cash flow
Debenham 32
debt, use of 51–2
debtors 130
decisions
    areas 79–100; facilitating 83–7; framework 80–3; operational 98–9, 209, 212, 222, 230, 238; performance determination areas 92–8; performance facilitating factors 87–92; performance-related 82; strategic 98–9, 201, 203, 204, 205, 218, 221, 226, 235
    and information requirements 177–97; asset base 186, 187; auditing customer expectations and corporate performance responses 188; competitor performance measures 194; decision support approach 182–7; margin spread 186, 187; objectives establishment 179–82; operational 185, 187, 189; productivity/profitability, operational 192; productivity/profitability, performance approach of 178; productivity/profitability, planning and control of 188–90; productivity/profitability, strategic 191; strategic 184, 186, 189, 196, 197; structuring information 193; support system 190–5
    options: operational 185, 212–15, 223–6, 228–39, 235–40 *passim*, 252–4; strategic 184, 203–8 *passim*, 218–21, 232–3
    support 182–7, 190–5
    topics 201, 204, 209, 230
    types *see* planning and control
    see also communication decisions; merchandise; strategic
delivery
    effectiveness 125
    speed flexibility 92
    systems, new 18, 110

284 Index

Denmark 38
developments 3–40
  food retailing 21–7
  generic financial model of the firm 8
  management implications 36–40
  mixed and non-food retailing 27–36
  retailing decisions, recent 21
  strategic decision making 37
  strategic view of retailing 7–11
  'strategy model' 11–21
differentiation and competition 114
Direct Insurance 112
direct product productivity 35
discounted cash flow 195
distribution 116, 127–8
diversification 18–19
dividend policy 52
Dixons 29, 30–1, 37
Doleys Plc 242, 243–58
  available options, mapping of 256
  changes 243–4
  cost implications 257
  current and planned performance for key activities 258
  customer perceptions of competitive performance 250–1
  customer preferences survey 248
  future problems 247–9
  issues for concern 249–58
  operational response options 252–4
  performance review and revised objectives 255
  strategic repositioning 244–7
Doody, A. F. 13, 161
Dorothy Perkins 32
DPP *see* direct product productivity
Dunn 5
durables 262, 266–7

Eastern Europe 115, 130
economic change 3
EFTPOS *see* electronic funds transfer at point of sale
Eilon, S. 64, 65, 66, 69, 78
electrical durables 266–7
electronic funds transfer at point of sale 5
electronic point of sale 5, 31
  asset base 127
  Boots 34–5
  Kookaburra Holdings Plc 263
  margin spread 116
  modelling performance options 147

  operational resource allocation and rationalisation 19
  performance facilitating factors 92
entertainment wardrobe service 246
entry barriers 108
environment *see* store
environment-led positioning 202
EPOS *see* electronic point of sale
EPS 34
equity *see* external
ERA *see* European Retail Alliance
Europe 4, 11, 29, 38
  Eastern 115, 130
European Retail Alliance 20, 26, 38
European Single Market 18
extended supply chain 131–2
external equity funding 52–64
  asset management 54–6
  margin management 56–64

facilities 136–7, 138
Far East 6, 11, 27, 130
fashion adviser 246
financial
  management 56
  performance 95–8
  productivity 96
  ratios 66
  resources and structure 83–7
financing *see* funding
Finland 38
Fitzgerald, L. R. 79–80, 87, 89, 92, 99
fixed assets 123–8
  distribution facilities 127–8
  fixtures 126–7
  and net current assets 124
  property 123–6
  systems 127
fixed capital 120–2
fixtures 126–7
flexibility 91–2
Floorwise Plc 242, 270–80
  balance sheet data 271
  branch assets 274, 278
  concessions 277, 278–80
  existing format, expansion of 275, 277–8
  merchandise strategy 273–5
  net asset 279
  primary performance characteristics 273

product mix details, price levels, range profile margins and sales   276
profit and loss account   270
strategic productivity and profitability   275
Food Giant   25
food retailing   21–7
   Argyll/Safeway   26–7
   Asda   21
   Budgen   25–6
   Gateway   25
   KwikSave   23–4
   Sainsbury   24–5
   Tesco Plc   22–3
formalwear   247
format
   new   18, 87
   store   202, 248, 250, 251
Foster   30, 43, 116
Fox, A. F.   122
France   38
Freeman   29
frontier curve analsyis   58
funding   125–6, 196
   see also external

Gateway   25, 37
gearing   96
General Agreement on Tariffs and Trade (GATT)   10
Germany   26, 38
GM   see gross margins
GMROI   see gross margins return on inventory investment
Gold, B.   64, 66–8, 75
gross margins   206–7, 214–15, 220, 224, 228, 232, 236, 239, 253
   core product   190
   return on inventory investment   162–3, 164
growth   61, 96, 269
   see also sustainable

Habitat   9, 99, 231
Hamleys   113
Harrods   114
Harvey Nichols   20
Heals   231
healthcare   35, 263
Hepworth   4
Holmes, G.   72
home improvements   259, 262, 263
Homebase   232

Hong Kong   11
Hornes   30, 43, 116
Horngren, C. T.   66

ICA (Sweden)   38
IKEA   9, 99, 232
improving productivity and profitability   172
in-store information   223–5
industry structure model   14
information   89, 136, 138
   in-store   223–5
   technology   26, 28, 231, 233, 236
   see also decisions
innovation   87–8
input measurement   65
inventory   128–30
   holding costs   116
investment
   decisions   86–7
   intensity   117, 122
   return on   43
   see also net margin; operating margin
IT   see information technology

Japan   11, 27
John Lewis Partnership   9, 48, 88, 92

Kesko (Finland)   38
Kingfisher   20, 29, 37, 40
Knee, D.   11, 12
Kookaburra Holdings Plc   242, 259–69
   balance sheet   268
   component companies' review   259–63
   contribution to revenue and profit   260
   growth of revenues profits   261
   maximum sustainable growth rate   265, 266
   1989–93   263–4
   1994 hypothesis   264, 265–9
KwikSave   23–4, 37, 38, 234

labour   116, 127
Lands End   179
Laura Ashley   5, 48
Limited   4
Limmack, R. J.   122
liquidity   96
Littlewoods   31, 37, 179
Livingstone, J. L.   103
Lo Cost   26

location effectiveness 123, 125
Londis 26
London Electricity 30
Lusch, R. K. 106, 149

Magnet 231
Malaysia 11
management
  implications 36–40
  information service 10
  managerial control system 67
  managerial purposes 65
  merchandise 127
  see also asset base; margin spread
margin spread management 56–64, 85, 101–19, 186, 187, 188, 211
  and asset management 105
  components 102, 117
  costs 104–6
  facilitating/determining factors 118
  operational sales volume increase 108–13
  performance improvement 106–8
  productivity and profitability improvement 113–17
marketing
  and buying decisions 83
  development 109–10
  penetration 108
Marks & Spencer 4, 27–8, 37, 39
  cash flow 45, 48
  decisions and information requirements 179
  margin spread 112, 114
  performance facilitating factors 88
  strategic retailing 9
Martin, H. W. 66
maximum sustainable growth rate 265, 266
Mercandona (Spain) 38
merchandise
  assortment 128–9, 136, 137
  augmentations 109, 136
  availability 137
  costs 161, 162, 164
  decisions 201–17; competitive environment 206–8, 213–16; operational 209–17; store format and environment-led positioning 202; strategic 201–9
  development 109
  effectiveness 113–15
  focus 128

  issues 248, 250–1
  -led positioning 199
  management 127
  mix 47, 48, 113
  objectives 179
  offer, characteristics of 111
  quality 137
  and range extensions 109
  strategy 273–5
  see also visual merchandising
'Metro' format stores 22
MFI 20, 33, 231
Migross (Switzerland) 38
Millets 29
MIS 10
MIS *see* management information service
Miss Selfridge 29
mixed and non-food retailing 27–36
  Argos 36
  Benetton 35–6
  Boots 34–5
  Burton 32–3
  Dixons 30–1
  Kingfisher 29
  Littlewoods 31
  Marks & Spencer 27–8
  MFI 33
  Next 33–4
  Sears 29–30
  Storehouse 28
  Tie Rack 31
modelling performance options 134–60
  cash flow management 156–9
  corporate performance expectations and resource allocation 138–40, 141, 142, 144
  customer expectations 134–8
  operational decisions and actions 153–6, 157
  operational performance 144–5
  performance measurement model 149–51
  profitability and operational cash flow 148
  strategic decisions and actions 151–3, 154
  strategic performance 140–4
  time perspectives: operational and strategic trade-off choices 145–8
  see also strategic
Moose, S. A. 68

Mothercare 10, 28, 39, 43, 99, 116
'multibuys' 22, 108

net assets (NA) 165
net current assets (NCA) 124, 128–32, 165
  cash 130–1
  creditors 131
  debtors 130
  inventory 128–30
  overdrafts 131–2
net margin return on investment 164
net return on sales 171
Netherlands 38
Netto 26, 38, 234
Next 33–4, 37, 39, 125
  Directory 34, 110
NMROI *see* net margin return on investment
non-food retailing *see* mixed and non-food retailing
North America 4

Olympus Sports 29, 30
OMROI *see* operating margin return on investment
operating
  decisions 83, 85
  hours 125
  margin return on investment 163, 164, 166, 171
  margins 95; operational 215, 224–5, 232–3, 239–40, 253–4; strategic 207, 219, 228–9, 236–7
  profit 73, 77
  return on sales 171
  sales volume, increase in 56
  trade-off choices 145–8
operational
  cash flow 148
  decision topics 170
  decisions and actions 98–9, 153–6, 157, 185, 187, 189, 815
  effectiveness 115–17
  gearing 85
  performance 144–5, 168
  productivity and profitability 56, 192
  purposes 65
  rationalisation 116
  repositioning 111
  resource allocation and rationalisation 99
  response options 252–4
  sales volume increase 108–13; market development 109–10; market penetration 108; merchandise development 109; operational repositioning 111; specialisation/focus 112; strategic repositioning 112–13
  see also decisions
optimal profitability 106
outlet
  base expansion 110
  concentration, increasing 109–10
output, measurement of 65
overdrafts 131–2

Pacific Rim countries 11
Past Times 39, 112
payment terms 131
PC World 31
Penny Market 26
performance 183, 184, 185, 216
  determination areas 92–8; competitiveness components 94; financial performance 95–8; facilitating factors 87–92; flexibility 91–2; innovation 87–8; quality of service 89–91
  issues and responses 183; operational 185, 212, 222, 223, 230, 238; strategic 184, 203, 205, 218, 226, 235
  measures 71–7, 149–51; operating profit 73; strategic profit 73–7
  operational 144–5, 168
  options 212
  responses 223, 235
  see also corporate; modelling
planning and control 161–74, 188–90
  Argos Plc 169–71, 173
  decision types 198–242; communications 231–7; customer communications 201; customer service 217–26; customer-service-led positioning 200; merchandise 199, 201–17; positioning: co-ordinated response to customer expectations 198; store environment 226–31
  gross margin return on investment 162, 164
  margin spread performance increase 173

planning and control – *continued*
  operational 168, 170
  overall approach 167–9
  productivity and profitability improvement 172
  strategic 164, 165–6, 168, 169
  visual approach 162–6
planning gap 41–64
  Boston Consulting Group growth/share matrix 44, 50
  for cash flow projection 57
  closure 63
  debt, use of 51–2
  dividend policy 52
  external equity funding 52–64
  frontier curves 59, 60, 62
  market segment characteristics 49
  maximum sustainable growth rate 50, 55
  merchandise (format) mix 47, 48
  operational decisions 42
  product life cycle, ideal 46
  rate of return 51
  strategic decisions 42
  target growth rates for business 61
planning purposes 65
point of sale (POS) 126, 223, 262
  see also electronic
Porter, M. 14
positioning 81, 183
Presto 26
price
  adjustments 108, 113
  company 239–40
  effectiveness 102
  transfer pricing 66
Principles 32
productivity costing approach 66
productivity and profitability
  improvement 113–17
  operational 56, 192
  strategic 275, 291
productivity–performance–profitability model 80, 178
products 35, 46, 87–8
profit 96, 148
  decision retention 85–6
  operating 73, 77
  optimal 106
  paths 106
  strategic 73–7, 101, 134, 135, 161
  see also productivity and profitability
property 123–6

quick response facility 127

R&D *see* research and development
Racing Green 39, 179
rate of return 51
Reebok 30
replenishment frequency and reliability 127
research and development 10, 44
resource
  allocation 16, 19–20, 99, 138–40, 141, 142, 144, 146
  inputs 77
responsiveness 89
return
  on assets 104, 105
  on capital employed 71, 165, 195, 218
  on investment 43; *see also* gross margin; net margin; operating margin
  on sales 171
  to shareholders 174, 218
REWE 26
Richards Shops 9, 29, 30, 43, 99, 116
Risk, J. M. S. 66, 69
ROA *see* return on assets
Robinson, G. 51, 58, 60
ROCE *see* return on capital employed
ROE *see* return to shareholders
ROI *see* return on investment

Safeway/Argyll 20, 21, 23, 26–7, 37, 38, 39
Sainsbury 4, 21, 23, 24–5, 35, 37, 38
  margin spread 114
  performance facilitating factors 88
sales
  format 123
  mix objectives 95
  net return 171
  responses 223–4, 228, 232, 236, 239
  revenues 206, 213–14, 219, 252–3
  seasonal patterns 130
  value 121
  volumes 56, 95; *see also* operational
  see also point of sale
SCP *see* structure–conduct–performance
Sears 29–30
  asset base 125
  cash flow 43
  decisions and information 227
  margin spread 116

operational decisions   99
strategic resource allocation and rationalisation   20
strategic retailing   9, 99
Selfridges   9, 29, 30
service
  attributes superiority   88
  augmentation   109, 136–7, 138
  density   116–17, 137, 138
  existing, improving attributes of 88
  facilities   219–21
  format   123
  intensity   116, 137, 138
  issues   129–30
  new   87–8
  quality   89–91
  see also customer
shareholders   174, 218
Shoe Express   30
Silo   30
Singapore   11
Single Market   20
SKU   see stock-keeping units
social change   3
Somerfield   25
sourcing issues   130
South America   11
space utilisation   115
Spain   38
special occasions wardrobe service   247
specialisation   112, 244
specification flexibility   91–2
speculative transactions   130
staff   89
Staples   29
stock allocation and levels   127
stock-keeping units   217
store
  ambience   137
  environment   111, 179, 226–31, 247, 248, 250, 251
  format   202, 248, 250, 251
  operating margins   95
  operations activities   95
  sales volumes   95
Storehouse   28, 29, 37
  margin spread   116
  operational decisions   99
  strategic resource allocation and rationalisation   20
  strategic retailing   9, 99

strategic
  decision   98–9, 184, 189, 197; and actions   151–3, 154; influences 186; making   196; topics 169
  performance model   140–4, 164, 165–6, 168
  productivity and profitability   275, 291
  profit   73–7, 101, 134, 135, 161
  purposes   65
  rationalisation   116
  repositioning   112–13, 244–7
  resource allocation and rationalisation 99
  trade-off choices   145–8
  view of retailing   7–11
  see also decisions; strategy model
strategy model   11–21
  competitive advantage   14
  consolidation and productivity   11, 15
  differentiation   13–15
  diversification   13, 18–19
  growth   11, 13, 17; new format   18
  market development   17
  operational repositioning   15, 17
  operational resource allocation and rationalisation   16, 19
  planning gap   12
  repositioning   11
  strategic repositioning   17–18
  strategic resource allocation and rationalisation   16, 19–20
Strong, L.   30
structure–conduct–performance   68–9, 71, 78, 80, 99, 120
Sugden, A.   72
supply/suppliers   114–15, 127, 131–2
sustainable growth rate   269
  maximum   265, 266
Sweden   38
Sweeny, D. J.   161
Switzerland   38

technological change   3
Tesco Plc   21, 22–3, 37, 38, 39, 108
Texas   232
Thatcher, M.   7
The Gap   4
Tie Rack   31, 37, 38
Tigert, D. J.   103

time perspectives: operational and strategic trade-off choices 145–8
Top Man 32
Top Shop 32
trade-off choices 145–8
trading assets 208, 220–1, 229, 237
trading/branch assets 215–16, 225, 233, 240
transactions 108, 126, 130
transfer pricing 66

value-added 66–71
Variety Merchandise 259, 263

visual merchandising 111, 115, 126, 136, 137
volume flexibility 92

Wallis 29
Walters, D. 11, 12, 43, 161, 167, 204, 227
wardrobe service 246
Warehouse 29
White, D. 161, 167
Woolworth 48
working capital 86, 122–3

Zakon, A. J. 52–3, 68